NO LONGER A BYSTANDER

A Radical New Way To Look At Our Christianity, Our Culture, Our Future, And Our Legacy

Bill Hull

⊛ BONHOEFFERpress

Long Beach, California

Bonhoeffer Press
The Bonhoeffer Project
329 Termino Ave.
Long Beach, CA United States 90814
TheBonhoefferProject.com
Edited by Kimberly L. Pennington, Ph.D

Library of Congress Control Number: 2021919018

ISBN-13: 978-1-956723-00-7
Ebook ISBN: 978-1-956723-01-4

1 2 3 4 5—25 24 23 22 21
Printed in the United States of America

NO LONGER A BYSTANDER

Dedication

I picture a single light coming from a remote house on the Hebridean Island of Jura as a Middle-aged man who looked like an old man, a cigarette hanging out of his mouth, typing for all he was worth, was in a race with time to finish his prophetic masterpiece. He had little strength left in his body, stopping now and then to cough up blood, but he kept at it because the society had to be warned of the dystopia he feared would come to rest on Western Civilization. George Orwell was right. The dystopia that was 1984 has now come to take residence in the hearts and minds of the citizens of the United States. It is to this Mid-20th century "crank" that I dedicate this book, for he had the gumption to speak up.

Table of Contents

INTRODUCTION 1

PHILOSOPHICAL FOUNDATIONS 11
   Defining Reality 12
   What Will Win, Civilization or Anarchy? 18
   Soft Totalitarianism.. 22
   Misunderstanding the Kingdom of
   God is Normal.. 27
   Would You Like It in Heaven? 34
   Evil.. 38

PROGRESSION OF DECLINE 45
   The Intoxicated Mind... 46
   The Spiral of Silence 52
   The Wasting of the Evangelical Mind.......................... 60
   Whose Mind is Wasted Now,
   Evangelical or Secular?.. 68
   Hath God Said? 76
   Order and Chaos... 83
   How We Got What We Have 91
   The Church's Secular Affair....................................... 97
   Justification of Sin, Not the Sinner 104
   Roll Over Beethoven 110

COURSE CORRECTION...115
   "What Have I Done?".. 116
   Replacement Culture 122
   Convincing the Contemporary Mind
   That Redemption is Needed..................................... 128

The Argument for Redemption 134
What Kind of Disciples Do We Need? 142
Politics are Sport..................................... 149
The Disciple Making Preacher 156
Deconstructing the Empire of Lies............... 165
Calling Out The Idols............................... 174
Calling Out The Idols Part 2 180
Calling Out Still More Idols........................ 185
Your Best Argument with God..................... 190
Don't Shut Up - Show Up 196
The Reckoning 203
The Medium is the Message 214

APPLICATION 219
Work Matters: Exploring the
Integration of Spirituality in Work............... 220
Taking Lies Prisoner 223
An Empire of Lies................................... 232
Thank God for Bill Maher......................... 237
Want to Ruin the World? Start with White Guilt 240
White Guilt Part Two 247
Paradise Lost: the Search for Justice Concept 254
Critical Theory 259
Three Things Every Journalist in
America Should Read Right Now................... 265
Don't Inhale.. 274

UNIQUENESS OF 2020...............................281
Christianity Yesterday Suggests
Tyranny Tomorrow................................... 282
The High Cost of Non-Discipleship............... 286
Political Cleavage Among Evangelicals........... 290
Chaos and the Sliding Scale of Morality......... 293
Should a Christian Leader Flee a Deadly Plague? 301

Impeached but not Convicted 305

Take the "Babble" out of Babylon 309

It's Thursday. It Must Be the

Stockholm Syndrome 317

That Hideous Strength 325

CONCLUSION: FOLLOW JESUS 333

Capturing Reality 334

Making Disciples in Dystopia.................................... 340

DIETRICH BONHOEFFER: A CASE STUDY 347

No Longer A Bystander 348

The Forming of Dietrich Bonhoeffer 355

Seeds of Greatness: The Character of

Dietrich Bonhoeffer 359

The Cost of Discipleship: *Nachfolge*, The Book 363

Is Contemporary Discipleship a Myth or

Can It Actually Take on Crisis and Suffering?............... 368

Bonhoeffer on Obedience 373

Bonhoeffer: Pastor? Spy? Traitor? Coward?................. 377

Bonhoeffer: Prison 382

Bonhoeffer in Crisis.. 386

The Last Days 390

Bonhoeffer Wanted More and So Do We.................... 394

ABOUT THE AUTHOR 401

Introduction

"Silence in the face of evil is itself evil and God will not hold us guiltless. Not to speak is to speak, not to act is to act."[1]

Dietrich Bonhoeffer

"The philosophers have only interpreted the world differently; the point is, however, to change it."[2]

Karl Marx

The great disparity between Christlikeness and contemporary Christian conduct derives not from what we are not teaching but precisely from what we are teaching—that you can become a Christian and not follow Jesus. It leads to a gospel of just getting by and just getting into Heaven. In this crevice called disparity, faith is nothing more than agreement with dogma and conversion is the mere recital of a formula, a rote prayer that has a bit of white magic to it. Say it and rub the top of your head and you are "saved." Salvation becomes a forensic justification that replaces regeneration, a religious status that has replaced new life. What do you get? A declining church desperate for relevance

---

[1] This quote is widely attributed to World War II martyr Dietrich Bonhoeffer though it has not been found in any of his writings. Eric Metaxas, *Bonhoeffer, Pastor, Martyr, Prophet, Spy* (Nashville: Thomas Nelson, 2010).

[2] Mark Murphy, "What Did Marx Mean by Thesis Eleven?" *Social Theory Applied*, (August 10, 2013). https://socialtheoryapplied. com/2013/08/10/what-did-marx-mean-by-thesis-eleven/

and so needy for affirmation from its culture that it is willing to accommodate almost anything to be liked.

We are in decline as a cultural force for several reasons. Some are spiritual; some are cultural; and all are reflected in our politicians and the cognitive elite. I have been a witness to this decline during the past fifty years. I cannot say I saw it coming, or coming this fast, but we have been left standing at the station. The ideological left owns the culture. Culture, for the record, is what we as a people do without question and without thinking. It also includes the arts, academia, social networks, media, sports leagues, and major corporations. Censorship is not unconstitutional when it is enforced by private enterprise. It simply does the government's dirty work for it.

The cultural train has left the station and we are not on board. "We" are those who hold a conventional worldview based on a historic exegesis of the biblical text. That historic text has been the foundation for an objective moral order on which Western civilization has been built. Friedrich Nietzsche, the nineteenth century philosopher and author, was fearful of the declaration of his day that God was dead. He agreed that for all practical purposes, God had been rendered useless. His concern was very logical. Once God was declared dead, humans would need to replace the moral order God left behind.[3] Nietzsche was doubtful that even his Superman, or Ubermensch, could pull it off. If God is dead, there is no moral base. There is only the will to power, the survival of the fittest.

The contemporary cultural juggernaut with "Love Train" written on its side left the station, and on board they have little idea

---

[3] Friedrich Nietzsche, *The Genealogy of Morals: A Polemic*, 1887.

of what love means.[4] The cultural elite are attempting to make up morality as they move toward their destination of a utopian dream world that rejects an objective moral order founded on the belief that a God who is sovereign and personal responds to his followers in daily life. They have rejected the world of the Ten Commandments, a world where it is wrong to steal, lie, cheat, commit adultery, and to commit crimes and be punished for them. They have rejected a world that is based on the family, where personal responsibility, hard work, and merit are the measure of goodness.

The saddest part for the Love Train is that their destination of a utopian paradise does not exist. After all, utopia itself means "no place." It is a train to nowhere, but they do not plan to slow down or turn back. Their "beautiful" socially engineered cities will be riddled with crime because no one will be willing to arrest, punish, and jail the criminals. They will not be able to muster an army to protect themselves because potential soldiers will have been taught from childhood to hate their country in the belief that it is basically evil. The family will disintegrate because it is the primary carrier for traditional values that must be snuffed out. Whenever the family rather than the state educates children and passes along the values of personal integrity, definitions of right and wrong, and specific ideals about the roles of mother and father, the population is more resistant to the erasure of such notions.

The last thing I will say about the Love Train is that 99% of the people on board are not privy to the plan. They are not driving the train. They are just happy to supposedly be leaving behind an

---

[4] "Love Train" was a popular 1970s anthem recorded by Cat Stevens and others that has come to represents a utopian idealism that love as a wish or aspiration will win over all societal problems.

evil, regressive, and repressive world they deem to be unfair—a world with too few having too much and too many having too little. They do not find it ironic that the train is being driven by a rich and largely white elite who love the power and privilege they have more than anything. They are a cut-flower generation who are ahistorical and simply believe what they have been told. They have bought into the narrative that the worst kinds of people are religious bigots who believe in absolute moral truth. This is acutely believed regarding personal sexual identity and behavior. Any restriction whatsoever on sexual freedom is to be considered evil.

No Longer a Bystander

So what to do? I know some Christians would say we must be disciples before we can make disciples. This is a tired approach which suggests contemplation before action. Passiveness and silence sprinkled with a dash of nice is why we find ourselves standing on the train platform, left behind and left out. Faith's primary attribute is to obey and to act.[5] Any spirituality worth having leads to obedience. The best habitat for personal change is action. That is why most great advances in medicine, in warfare, or in learning to love are discovered in the crucible of pressure-packed mission. The church encountered a perfect storm in 2020 and early 2021. Victor Davis Hanson summarized it by saying that in modern times, 2020 was unique.[6] We were confronted with a global pandemic, a national quarantine, a self-imposed shutdown of the economy, a presidential election, an attack on the U.S. Capitol building in Washington, D.C., and months of riots

---

[5] John 14:15; Jas 2:17-18.
[6] "Victor Davis Hanson on Citizenship," Western Conservative Summit 2021 https://www.youtube.com/watch?v=Y66u_zSNolE. Posted June 24, 2021.

and looting with no consequences for rioters who were granted immunity from prosecution. Essentially, we faced a national failure demonstrated by a weak-willed, undisciplined populace dominated and abused by its leaders. Basic freedoms were violated, law and order were suspended, and the government purchased Americans' obedience with an unprecedented flood of money.

Censorship practiced by the media and big tech cancelled free speech. "Misinformation," as Twitter and Facebook called it, simply was information with which they disagreed. The present government formed an alliance with the mainstream media and big tech to control the speech that is permitted to be spoken and discussed in the United States.

What does this have to do with the church? The church is about the truth, telling it and living it. It is the only way to freedom.[7] It is also about, regardless of the price, the freedom to tell the truth about the world, reality, and the purpose of human beings, including what makes them flourish.

This truth-telling issue confronted the church in Germany in the early 1930s. The German government controlled the flow of information that the German public was allowed to see and hear. There are some significant differences between then and now, between Germany and the United States. The most glaring is that the United States has 250 years of history in freedom, and people over forty know something about living free. Enter Dietrich Bonhoeffer who, in the context of his government's attempts to control the thoughts and actions of the German population, famously said, "Not to speak is to speak, not to act is to act."[8]

---

[7] John 8:32.
[8] See page 4, footnote 1.

Bonhoeffer referred specifically to government's treatment of the Jews in the early to mid-1930s. Even more pointedly, as a young clergy/pastor/scholar, Bonhoeffer was convinced that the church was not the church unless they were willing to stand between the oppressor, the government in this case, and those oppressed, namely, the Jews.

The German Evangelical Church chose appeasement toward the elite and powerful. Hitler appointed his syncopate Ludwig Mueller as their new bishop. Pastors were required to restrict Jews from important roles in the church and to sign a document pledging alliance to the government. The majority signed the document. They went along. They signed away their voice and their independence. They relinquished their spiritual authority. They were unwilling to pay the price for discipleship.

The Confessing Church was birthed as a protest against the government's desire to control the church. Karl Barth authored the Barmen Declaration, which stated that the church was free to preach the gospel without restraint.[9] Subsequently, the Confessing Church separated itself from the Nazi-controlled German state church, and it cost them dearly. They lost all funding, pastoral salaries, and benefits, for the government would not fund a renegade church. Bonhoeffer taught in an illegal seminary for Confessing Church pastors. The Confessing Church's founding documents were not about the Jews. They were about the Nazis and the freedom to preach and practice the gospel. The church in America must now take this same mindset if our discipleship is to mean anything at all.

If the church is to, in Lesslie Newbigin's words, "establish a missionary encounter with the culture" conflict will be required—

---

[9] "The Barmen Declaration," 1934. https://www.ekd.de/en/The-Barmen-Declaration-303.htm.

not in spirit, but in truth. This does not mean that the church needs to go and look for a fight. In fact, our purpose is to love the world as Christ loved the world.[10] Jesus was not looking for a fight, but all would admit that he found one. It means that we are to give ourselves to engaging the culture in order to save it. We do this by taking the good news to the nations, cities, neighborhoods, and to our friends and associates. We do this with peace in mind, but we must not be fooled. The Scripture tells us emphatically that we have an enemy. Lucifer and his disciples are prepared to destroy our mission and are committed to our failure. [11]

The focus of my effort for the past forty years has been to call the church to put disciple making at the center of its effort. I have played by the rules set by our culture. I have stayed in my lane, the clerical lane—the pastoral space—which means I have steered clear of public policy and politics. The only obvious exception has been abortion. I believe the taking of innocent human life to be America's greatest sin and the clearest violation of both moral responsibility as well as the United States Constitution. But now more is required because the theological, political, and ideological left have broken the system, changed the rules, and are hell-bent on destroying the world in which we live. They have sacrificed the First Amendment on the altar of power. They have formed a communication cabal that is censoring speech and cancelling anyone who speaks truth to their power. They have sold out the nation with open borders and the refusal to arrest criminals and hold people accountable for crimes. They do not seem to get or care that some Americans will insist on protecting themselves and, therefore, violence will increase. They have decided to waste the nation's wealth by irresponsible spending and, in the process, make people more dependent, less disciplined, less productive, and members of a permanent underclass—a new

---

[10] John 13:34; 2 Cor 5:13-14.
[11] John 10:10; 1 Pet 5:4-7; Eph 6:10-18.

serfdom. They are insisting on lowering academic standards, thus wasting the minds and lives of the young. By their beliefs, they make policies which are creating a nation of victims, of "can't do" types of people, who wait to hear from their leaders on what to be offended by next. In the meantime, they tear down national symbols that represent the truth about our history. They are ahistorical wanting to rewrite our historical narrative and rebuild the nation on the sand of falsehood. This may seem political, but as a person who is committed to a biblical worldview, I would oppose any political party or group doing these things.

I do not need to travel to the nation's capital or enter politics to take a stand. I will simply stand up, speak up, and refuse to shut up. And when I speak up, there will be conflict. I can no longer stand by and simply shake my head. I must do what I can. Martin Luther reportedly said, "If you want to change the world, pick up a pen and write." This is my effort to do just that.

I believe that the gospel itself is controversial. It calls us to live for others and to live a life committed to truth, justice, and order rather than chaos. The spirit of this age is quite hostile to these values. The gospel is about unifying a people from every tribe, language, and nation.[12] The present climate is about dividing people by tribe, language, race, gender, and many other ways. More than anything, the present zeitgeist denies what is plainly true and what you see with your own eyes. Hopefully, the cognitive elite's recent establishment of Orwell's Ministry of Truth and its convenient memory hole is a temporary phenomenon.[13]

---

[12] Gal 3:28; Rev 5:9.

[13] The Ministry of Truth was a department of the government in George Orwell's novel, *1984*. The memory hole was located next to hundreds of editors' desks where they would discard facts of history they wanted to destroy. If history is rewritten or forgotten, then the present leaders can define reality for society.

However, it could become permanent if we are quiet about what is true about life. Edmund Burke is famous in our time for his statement, "All that is necessary for evil to triumph is for good men to do nothing."[14]

The following pages represent my effort to speak to the problems we face. They include essays on the decline of our culture. They dissect various contemporary trends and prescribe actions for followers of Christ to take. You may have heard the statement, "You shall know the truth and the truth will make you free, but first it will make you miserable."[15] The final word before you plunge into the material comes from Dallas Willard. It keeps us on target regarding how we will make progress:

> But what we must never forget, in moving toward the faith "on the rock," is that our "doing" comes—or fails to come—from what our beliefs actually are. Hence, if we would train people to do "all things," we must change their beliefs. Only so can we change their loves. You cannot change character or behavior and leave beliefs intact. It is one of the major illusions of Western culture, deriving from a form of Christianity that is merely cultural, that you can do this. We cannot work around that illusion, but must dispel it.[16]

---

[14] Attributed to Edmund Burke (1729-1797) but never found in his works. Some trace it to *Thoughts on the Cause of Present Discontents*, April 23, 1770.

[15] James A. Garfield, 1831-1881, President of the United States from March – September 1881. https://www.goodreads.com/author/quotes/327289.James_A_Garfield.

[16] Dallas Willard, *The Divine Conspiracy: Rediscovering Our Hidden Life in God* (San Francisco: Harper & Row, 1998), 313.

PHILOSOPHICAL
FOUNDATIONS

Defining Reality

Two men have argued about the truth of Christ for two hours while traveling together. At the end of the conversation, one man says to the other, "Well, of one thing I'm certain, there is no such thing as absolute truth." The other man smiled and quipped, "Are you absolutely sure?"

My wonderment and befuddlement are on display daily as I watch secular humanism gain ground in America. My wonderment is my awe at how people with fallible arguments seem to dominate. My befuddlement is how the general population can be gullible enough to deny reality. This plays out daily in the public and political realm. If I attempted to explain it here, in this space, I am not sure it would help. Maybe you sense the same thing. The world has lost its mind: fiction is truth; narrative has replaced history. You are told not to believe what your "lying eyes" tell you is true. The most frightening aspect is the bold censoring of what is in front of you while being told, "There's nothing to see here."

I am not sure how much of what people say is true or, in the long run, real. But I do know this: reality has its own voice, and when reality knocks you to the ground, you can no longer ignore it. It took seventy years, but this is what happened to communism. China will likely defeat the United States, not in a shooting war, but through a slow demise of our democracy via economics and education. We will become a third-rate nation. Like the Roman Empire, the ground on which Americans live could be broken down into feudal states run by princes. However, in the end, countries like China will fail, just like the Soviet system did, because they are built on false ideas that humans ultimately refuse to live under.

The United States may fail, or at least become third rate, if we continue along the same path we are on now. Unprincipled and undisciplined democracy eventually falls because it gradually becomes more inclusive and permissive to the point where standards are lowered to accommodate those who would be left out and left behind if life's rewards were distributed through merit.

The two extremes of societies are oligarchy on the right and pure democracy on the left. The United States sits in the middle of the extremes as a republic. The concept of a republic protects a society from the democratic excesses and temptations that destroy it. That is why the Electoral College, two senators from every state, the separation of powers, an independent judiciary, and the Bill of Rights keep the country from being run by a simple majority of the most populous states. It saves America from power grabs and mob rule. I will be surprised if the United States does not fade away in future generations, as many other societies have, because of our failure to live with the truth of competition, merit, hierarchy, and the difference between equality of opportunity and equality of result. Heaven itself is filled with crowns, rewards, and differences.[17] People think it is a good trend that our world is becoming more Orwellian or the Brave New World, but we should prepare for a long and anguished societal

---

[17] Biblical passages that speak of rewards and gradations of living in Heaven: Mt. 5:12, 17-19; Mt. 16:27; Mt. 19:29; Mt. 25:21; Luke 18:22; Rom. 2:12-14; I Cor. 3:13-15; 2 Cor. 5:12; Col. 3:23-24; Jas. 1:12; 2 John 1:8; Rev. 2:26; Rev. 22:12.

lament[18] I am unlikely to see it, but a great anxiety and regret will come to whatever configuration this good land finds itself in the future. The great anxiety will precede the great awakening in that misery and a sense of futility usually precede people seeking divine help. Once a people have rejected their heavenly visitation from the incarnate God, the gradual departure of good takes a few generations. This normal deletion in history takes time, but globalism, technology, big tech domination, and control of information will speed up the process.

Norway is held up as a godless society that is clean, nice, and prosperous. It is all those things, but research shows that Bible reading in the home is still a national tradition and the fixtures of Norwegian culture have been laid by Western civilization based on the morals of Christian theology. Norway is living off the Christian dividend even though secularization is squeezing it out. This same process is in progress in the United States. However, we are far more embedded in the Christian narrative than Norway.

Norway became Catholic around the eighth century when Vikings returned home from war and brought the faith with them. Scandinavian Christianity became property of the state, and the country was divided into geographically determined parishes. People then were born into the faith, and it became the state religion. America was founded on ideas, one of which was the freedom to worship without state involvement. This led to a free market of religious choices which created competition and,

---

[18] Orwellian implies that freedom will be lost through a "Big Brother" type government that will control its population through disinformation, behavior, and thought control. Brave New World is a different approach with the same result. Neither the government nor the cognitive elite will burn your books. Instead, they will amuse and entertain citizens to the point of valuing pleasure more than freedom.

therefore, a more robust and improved religious experience. The church in America is more resilient and will respond and reform more aggressively. But with the now cultural dominance of the secular narrative, the future for the church looks to be difficult. The theological and philosophical left in America have now taken control of our universities, schools, media, and popular culture. Their Long March is nearly complete.[19]

This is primarily about academia and the cultural elite who control the levers of power. A few may profess to be Christian, and it may be true that they are in some sort of way, but they are not Christian or Bible believing with regard to worldview. They do not believe in absolute truth or that religious knowledge is absolute and equal in status to science. They live in a two-story world. The upper story is where faith, religion, personal experience, and subjectivity are. Knowledge of UFOs, ghost stories, Noah and the ark, Jonah and the great fish, Jesus and the resurrection, heaven, Mother Theresa, the Dali Lama, and The Lord of the Rings resides here. The lower story houses science, reason, objectivity, engineering, chemistry—the hard side of knowledge.

Living While Losing

How do we go about life when it looks like we are losing the battle for the mind and soul of America? Research shows that the church is in decline, our society is growing more secular,

---

[19] The Long March is an allusion to the 1934 four-thousand-mile Long March of Chinese Communists when they fled from their headquarters in southwest China and broke through Nationalist enemy lines. Mao Zedong became the established leader of the Chinese Communists as a result. "Long March," *History.com*, December 16, 2009. https://www.history.com/this-day-in-history/the-long-march.

leaders are weaker, people are softer, and big tech is controlling information. The goal defies reality and common sense.

In the 1970s, theologian Francis Shaeffer asked in a book and film series *How Should We Then Live?*[20] I have always sensed that the church and common sense would win out. I am still holding on a bit to that idea, but I am about ready to let go. I am joyful. I sleep well. I go about my day delighted with God. But the idea that my worldview is now in the minority has begun to set in. It is hard to swallow that more people now disagree than agree with how I see the world. Have the majority of my neighbors adopted the belief of Immanuel Kant without ever hearing his name? Kant taught that ultimate reality is unknowable—that we can only know the appearances of things but that we cannot go beyond appearances to know ultimate reality.[21] Jesus saying, "I am the truth, the ultimate reality," or "You shall know the truth and the truth shall make you free" are unattainable according to the prevailing worldviews in society today.[22] If that is so—if we are in a knowledge minority—then the question Francis Shaeffer asked as he walked through a scene of desolation in the aforementioned film *How Should We Then Live?* must be asked again.

How should I then live? I have decided to look down at my jersey and see what team I am on. I am on the human team. There are billions of us on that team. We are human; we are fallible; we are

---

[20] Francis A. Schaeffer, "Episode I: The Roman Age," *How Then Should We Live: A Ten Part Series*, Gospel Films, 1948, https://www.youtube.com/watch?v=w6c8EOyAg1U&list=PLBtCqYJcR2R0cOnm_M_ScQZk17UmfH7Xx, posted July 17, 2019.

[21] Immanuel Kant's ideas can be found in his three works: *The Critique of Pure Reason*, 1781; *Critique of Practical Reason*, 1788; and *Critique of Judgment* 1790.

[22] John 8:31-32.

mortal. In that sense, we are all in this together, regardless of our differences. I am also on the American team. This team is special in that we live in the most remarkable place on earth. We live in a land that is an idea: the idea that God created all of us equal and gave to us the right to life, liberty, and the pursuit of happiness. Faithfulness to this quest is lived and sorted out between the people and their government. There has been and always will be a tug of war politically about the meaning and application of these words. It is in this sense that we are losing and watching the country we love slip away.

Then I peel off that jersey and underneath I am wearing the Christian jersey. I know that my team is the winning team because in the end God brings peace and justice to the world, and he does so impartially. I conclude that the kingdom of God is different than any earthly kingdom.

1. The kingdom of God is composed of his authority and power and is a kingdom where his will is done.
2. The kingdom of God spreads through witness, and my role is to be a faithful witness of Christ my Lord.
3. The kingdom of God is international, composed of every nation, tribe, language and people.[23]

The winning and losing are God's business. Mine is to joyfully and with intention to represent him faithfully every day.

---

[23] Matt 6:10; Acts 1:8; Rev 7:9.

What Will Win, Civilization or Anarchy?

You probably think I am talking about the 2020 election, but I am not. The presidential election is merely a symptom of what is going on in the soul of America.[24] I am talking about order versus chaos, liberty versus a faux freedom that only applies to the cognitive elite. I am talking about freedom of churches to fully exposit the teachings of the Bible versus censorious government and industry beginning to punish the church for its beliefs.

To answer this question, America will first need to be convinced it has a soul—that it is not merely a random gathering of cells—and that its people are not just ex machina meat puppets.[25] Basic questions need to be answered, such as what the purpose of human beings is and what utopia, perfection, or heaven look like. Joseph Stalin, Mao Tse Tung, Adolf Hitler, and Fidel Castro all had some goal dancing about in their heads that steered their actions.[26] Their utopia, an imagined realm of perfection, became a dystopia, an imagined realm of evil. I would love to

---

[24] I am referring to the November 2020 presidential election between incumbent Republican President Donald J. Trump and Democratic challenger Joseph R. Biden, Jr.

[25] The soul of a nation simply means that a nation is composed of individual souls, a collective conscience, and a set of moral values.

[26] Joseph Stalin, leader of Russia from 1927-1953; Mao Tse Tung, leader of China from 1954-1976; Adolf Hitler, leader of Germany from 1932-1945; Fidel Castro Leader of Cuba from 1961-2011.

have five minutes of their time right now to get their post-death perspective. At least I know where to find them.

There has never been a time when casting a vote was more theologically or philosophically based than in this election because this one is about worldview. It is about whether we keep our Judeo-Christian ideological foundation and improve it or tear it down and rebuild from the ground up. Civilization means to have something walled in. There are rules, gates, and laws, and people do not need to waste time fighting about basic belief systems.

Civilization is having a law and order. This requires the collective will of society to make the law, the population to obey the law, the police to enforce the law, and the courts to punish those who break the law. If someone breaks the law, then they are fined or indicted, a trial is held, and a jury decides. People can have differing opinions and still eat dinner without being harassed, shouted at, assaulted, or worse. In too much of America now there are movements led by anarchists who believe the keys to change involve riots, destruction, fear, striking terror into ordinary life, and doing anything that will get internet clicks or clips on the news. It is as simple as Public Relations 101. It is also about money. Black Lives Matter, a Marxist-socialistic, anti-Christian, anti-family organization, is raking in millions of dollars from individual Christians, churches, and other Christian-based organizations. There's nothing like white guilt to fuel the donor ATMs of America.

However, the battle is not actually about politics. Chaos is Lucifer's tool for getting his way.[27] He is dedicated to destroying what is good, promoting what is evil, and tearing apart God's creative

---

[27] John 10:10a.

order piece by piece. He knows he can't win. He understands that he will spend eternity chained to the floor of Milton's abyss, Dante's inferno, and Revelation's lake of fire.[28] But fight on he will, because, like all anarchists, if he would win, he loses because he never thought he would win. He has no plan and no good ideas of how he can improve life on the earth.

The battle we are in is a spiritual one: "We are human, but we don't wage war as humans do" (2 Cor 10:3).[29] The collective called out ones, the εκκλησιά (the church), do not engage in this war in the same way other groups do. We use many of the same weapons, such as logic, persuasion, and argumentation, because we are called to knock down strongholds of human reasoning and destroy their arguments. Anything that keeps people from knowing God is our enemy, and we must fight against those adversaries.

"We use God's mighty weapons, not worldly weapons" (2 Cor 10:4). It is important to know what this means because its meaning determines what we do and do not do. The immediate context of Paul's remarks is one of answering his critics in the Corinthian church. Corinth was a city that was cosmopolitan, corrupt, and bawdy. Paul's first letter to Corinth makes it clear that philosophers, leading thinkers, and great apologists for every strain of thought from the Greek Classics to Hellenistic Judaism were in play in the streets of the city.

Some of the church members sided with eloquent spokesmen who held forth in the streets of Corinth, and, more dangerously,

---

[28] John Milton, *Paradise Lost*, 1667; Dante Alighieri, *The Divine Comedy*, 1320; Rev 20:10.
[29] Unless otherwise noted, all biblical quotes are from *The New Living Translation* (Carol Stream, IL: Tyndale House Publishers).

in the church itself.[30] Paul made it clear that the power of the Holy Spirit, the power of his apostleship, and the very hand of God would be in play and would overpower his critics when he returned to the city. A later statement in the text makes this clear. "And after you have become fully obedient, we will punish everyone who remains disobedient" (2 Cor 10:6). Clearly this means that Paul would settle those issues and church discipline would come to people who refused to submit to his apostolic authority.

The question then remains about us and here and now. The battle is broader than the local church, but the church cannot stay out of the wider battle. The church does not have authority outside of itself. It is highly unusual for local congregations to practice discipline of any kind on their own, so what authority does the church have in general culture? The official answer is none, but it actually has a great deal of authority.

The church's power is moral authority gained through a good example. The first order of business is to become the kinds of disciples who reflect the goodness that Christ exhibited, taught about, and gave a pathway for—the narrow way he called it—to become the kind of people who will love the world as God did in that he gave himself to it.[31]

---

[30] 1 Cor. 4:12-16.
[31] Matt 7:14; Eph 5:1-2.

Soft Totalitarianism

"A totalitarian society is one in which an ideology seeks to displace all prior traditions and institutions with the goal of bringing all aspects of society under control of that ideology. Wherever totalitarian philosophy has ruled, it has begun to destroy the essence of man."[32]

Hanna Arendt

"Soft totalitarianism has the same goal, but it is therapeutic. It comes to you under the guise of helping and healing . . . Many conservatives today fail to grasp the gravity of this threat, dismissing it as mere 'political correctness'—a previous generation's disparaging term for so-called 'wokeness.'"[33]

Rod Dreher

"Did God really say you must not eat the fruit from the trees in the garden? . . . You won't die!" the serpent replied to the woman. "God knows that your eyes will be opened as soon as you eat it, and you will be like God, knowing both good and evil."

Genesis 3:1c-4

Hard totalitarianism is easy to see. It is Soviet tanks rolling through your streets. It is the secret police in the former East

---

[32] Hanna Arendt, *The Origins of Totalitarianism* (New York: Harcourt, 1973), viii.

[33] Rod Dreher, *Live Not by Lies: A Manual for Christian Dissidents* (New York: Sentinel, 2020), 7.

Germany bugging your home, following you, arresting you, torturing you, and imprisoning you with a show trial or no trial. Soft totalitarianism, thanks to advances in technology, is coming to us via the surveillance culture. It is sort of a cross between George Orwell's *1984* and Aldous Huxley's *Brave New World*.

In the novel *1984*, there was a telescreen in each home that could monitor residents' lives 24/7. Winston Smith, the central character, often retreated to a small corner of his apartment where the camera could not see. There he engaged in the very subversive activity of reading. Big Brother, or those in power, wanted to dictate what people read and ultimately what they thought. In Huxley's *Brave New World*, no one cared to read because they had substituted pleasure and comfort for thinking. They, as Neil Postman wrote in the 1980s, were amusing themselves to death.[34]

Soft totalitarianism will not be enforced with prisons. It will punish you in more subtle ways by grading you according to the controlling societal narrative. If you support it, you will be rewarded with better opportunities, such as jobs and loans. However, if you are considered a racist, sexist, or homophobe, many of these benefits will slowly but surely be taken from you via algorithm. This is not primarily from the government. It is controlled more by major corporations, such as Google, Facebook, YouTube, Twitter, Instagram, Apple, and other mega companies that now have our data and know how to use it to socially engineer their definitions of a good person, a good life, and a good society. What might happen to Christians and the church?

---

[34] Neil Postman, *Amusing Ourselves to Death*: *Public Discourse in the Age of Show Busines*, (New York: Penguin Books, 1985).

The majority of people in these companies are not necessarily attempting to destroy Christians or the church, but their actions have ramifications for Christ followers, some of which are painful. For example, the loss of advancement or the necessary boycotting of a product you need that is produced by a company you cannot support is costly.

When Nobel laureate and Russian dissident Aleksandr Solzhenitsyn was released from prison in 1974 and exiled to the United States, he gave a parting exhortation to Soviet citizens that can be summed up in the title of his article "Live Not by Lies!" His point was that most people did not have the power or position to stand up and defeat the then colossal Soviet state. But they could resist by not living the lie that was the communist narrative. He suggested a few simple things they could do.

- Do not say, write, affirm, or distribute anything that distorts the truth.
- Do not go to a demonstration or participate in a collective action unless one truly believes in the cause.
- Do not take part in a meeting in which the discussion is forced and no one can speak the truth.
- Do not vote for a candidate or proposal one considers to be dubious or unworthy.
- Do walk out of an event as soon as "the speaker utters a lie, ideological drivel, or shameless propaganda."
- Do not support journalism that "distorts or hides the underlying facts."[35]

How a Christian interprets the above guidelines is based on everything from one's understanding of Scripture to one's conscience. One thing is for certain. What you read, buy, watch,

---

[35] Dreher, *Live Not by Lies*, x.

"like" and say on social media or via your phone, and what you tell Siri or Alexa will be recorded, stored, and finally graded not by a person but by an algorithm. This is not personal, but it is punitive if you persist with your biblical viewpoint.

At this point, the collection of your information is primarily commercial and monetized for the business sector's profit motive. If you watch a John Wayne movie on Saturday morning, by Saturday afternoon your social network will be trying to sell you chaps and spurs. But be assured that the more moralizing these organizations engage in, your "score" will be kept, and it will make a difference. I think we already have ample evidence that the prevailing, growing national narrative is moving away from the biblical narrative. The media and the government are pushing a narrative that is creating an aristocracy of victims. False victims are becoming society's new royalty who require special treatment for life.

We cannot hope to resist the coming of soft totalitarianism if we do not have our spiritual lives in order. This was Solzhenitsyn's belief. He argued that the core of the crisis that created communism was spiritual, not political.[36] In his famous 1978 Harvard commencement speech, he proclaimed, "We have placed too much hope in political and social reforms, only to find out that we were being deprived of our most precious possession: our spiritual life."[37] He went on to claim that the West had lost its will to fight, its willpower in general, and its moral courage in particular. His call for repentance for sin was not well-received by the secular elite. He taught a spiritual reality or kingdom that was behind the societal battles.

---

[36] Ibid., xi.

[37] Alexandr Solzhenitsyn, "A World Split Apart," speech delivered at Harvard University, June 8, 1978. https://www.americanrhetoric.com/speeches/alexandersolzhenitsynharvard.htm.

Christians must never forget that behind, beneath, and above all human activity are two kingdoms at war: the kingdom of God and the kingdom of darkness led by Lucifer disguised as an angel of light. What is Lucifer's goal? To destroy what God most loves, his creation and his people. Satan's goal is to oppress, kill, and destroy what is good about life.[38]

God made us free to choose what we say, believe, and think, who we love, who we marry, and where we live. We may not be able to change the opinions of the leaders at Google or Facebook or of the editors at *The New York Times*, but we can be faithful witnesses of Christ our Lord by following Solzhenitsyn's advice and taking those six simple actions to protest the lies we hear. Yes, we will be punished. We may suffer and lose advantages, but we will gain inner peace and reap satisfaction and joy like the members of the early church. "The apostles left the high council rejoicing that God had counted them worthy to suffer disgrace for the name of Jesus. And every day, in the Temple and from house to house, they continued to teach and preach this message: 'Jesus is Messiah'" (Acts 5:41).

In this case, it was the actual name "Jesus" that offended the Jewish Council. In our case, it might be less his actual name that offends but rather something that cuts through the prevailing narrative. It would be more likely walking out of an important dinner or disagreeing with a person who has power over you in a company. Moments of taking a stand are small but important. Dietrich Bonhoeffer said, "Not to speak is to speak, not to act is to act."[39] You do not have to take to the streets. Just live your life and refuse to live by lies.

---

[38] John 10:10.

[39] Eric Metaxas traces this statement to an article that Bonhoeffer wrote. See page 4, footnote 1. .https://www.goodreads.com/quotes/601807-silence-in-the-face-of-evil-is-itself-evil-god.

Misunderstanding the Kingdom of God is Normal

The world can no longer be left to mere diplomats, politicians, and business leaders. They have done the best they could. But this is an age for spiritual heroes—a time for men and women to be heroic in faith and in spiritual character and power.[40]

Dallas Willard

Many of us have trouble explaining the kingdom of God. Dallas Willard defined it as "The realm of God's effective will, where his will is being done."[41] We at the Bonhoeffer Project break down what we call the "gospel Americana" and examine why it is deleterious to making disciples.[42] We explore the "gospels" of forgiveness only; the left, old and new; the right; prosperity; consumer; and the one we favor, the Gospel of the kingdom of God. Everyone nods their heads, and we move forward in a theological maze because we are only clear on what we are against, not on

---

[40] Dallas Willard, *The Spirit of the Disciplines: Understanding How God Changes Lives* (New York: HarperSanFrancisco, a div. of Harper Collins Publishers, 1988).

[41] Ibid.

[42] The Bonhoeffer Project is a one-year cohort-based community that "Turns Leaders into Disciple Makers." You can learn more at thebonhoefferproject.com

what we are for. That is the reason Ben Sobels and I wrote *The Discipleship Gospel*.[43] We wanted to explain the kingdom Gospel in terms that contemporary Christians could understand. We simply said that the operative words of the discipleship Gospel are "Follow Me." Everything else is superfluous.

It is this kingdom Gospel that Jesus preached and that we find Paul still grinding on in the last chapter of the Acts of the Apostles. But why do I say this idea of kingdom is confusing to us and that it is normal not to understand it? Because the apostles themselves did not seem to get it after spending three years with Jesus. After his resurrection, Jesus spent forty days with them, giving them his time, and "he proved to them in many ways that he was actually alive. And he talked to them about the Kingdom of God" (Acts 1:3).

Does it get any better than this? Being in Christ's presence, having him as your teacher, and proving he is resurrected. "Come on!" we say. "How could you miss it?" But they did, and so do we. "They kept asking him, 'Lord, has the time come for you to free Israel and restore our kingdom?'" (Acts 1:6).

It must have been frustrating to Jesus. They missed it because they thought the kingdom included a political and military victory. To Jesus' disciples, the kingdom of God meant freedom from Rome—something like what was enjoyed during the Maccabean period two centuries earlier. They were right in a way because releasing the captives was something Jesus talked about. He also spoke about all the promises made to Abraham, David, Moses, and those spoken through the prophets. The Messiah would reign over the kingdom of Israel from Jerusalem. They, however,

---

[43] Bill Hull & Ben Sobels, *The Discipleship Gospel* (Nashville: Him Publications, 2018).

did not know the time and place. Jesus claimed neither did he and that this was not his business nor theirs.[44]

Things are similar now. We often confuse our national blessing with God's blessings and what the kingdom is all about. Recently, a movement called "The Return" held a six-hour meeting on the National Mall in Washington D.C.[45] I streamed about four hours of it. One dignitary after another got their two minutes at a microphone. Many prayed a prayer of repentance. Others preached via a prayer. Some simply yelled stuff. It was like some churches: grand, wonderful, glorious, grotesque, embarrassing, and partisan. I was with them on our sins as individuals and as a nation. I found that refreshing and cleansing. I was with them in regard to abortion. Even when they mentioned the latest Supreme Court justice's nomination, I was hanging in. But then it went sideways into a Republican rally.

What bothered me was not that the political veils came off and eliminated half the nation. I was disturbed at the idea that the group equated revival and God's return with establishing God's kingdom via a conservative America. I am conservative, so the idea of a conservative America did not bother me so much. I simply thought that they, like the first century apostles, were getting the idea of kingdom and rule wrong. They turned toward the Capitol building and prayed and toward the White House and prayed. It seemed that they looked to politics and governing officials as an essential element in national revival. Revival could include such a turning by government officials, but such a political turn, in and of itself, is not the kingdom of God.

---

[44] Luke 4:18; Acts 1:7.
[45] https://thereturn.org.

If the meeting would have been run by Jim Wallis rather than Franklin Graham, they would have made the same mistake, just with the lions of the left.[46] They would have prayed to their version of God and called for policies and governmental intervention through the righteous actions of their version of God. Everyone has a right and a duty to go forward as they see fit. After all, we believe in the First Amendment guarantee of freedom of religion and freedom of speech. However, there is a temptation to see the kingdom of God on earth only through our own worldview.

It would be truly remarkable to see Jim Wallis and Franklin Graham shoulder to shoulder praying together for the same thing. I wonder what would bring them together? Some things they might agree to would be what Jesus told his disciples just prior to his ascension.

1. The kingdom of God is the exercise of the Holy Spirit's power, not human power

"Do not leave Jerusalem until the Father sends you the gift he promised, as I told you before. John baptized with water, but in just a few days you will be baptized with the Holy Spirit" (Acts 1:4).

Jesus was saying, "No. I am not establishing the kingdom now. Don't go anywhere and do anything. I want you to wait because if you go and make disciples right now, you will fail." This led to confusion and questions. Waiting is hard; waiting is boring. Waiting makes activists fidget, and they get frustrated.

---

[46] Jim Wallis is an ordained minister, founder of Sojourners Publications, and a Democratic political activist. Franklin Graham is president of the Billy Graham Evangelistic Association and the relief organization Samaritan's Purse. He is also a Republican political activist.

Those disciples felt out of control. Their anxiety was real, and it was revealed through their repeated questioning of Jesus. However, Jesus' logic was perfect. "You will need power. You will have no power unless you wait, and you will fail; so trust me and wait."

2. The kingdom of God spreads through witness

"But you will receive power when the Holy Spirit comes upon you. And you will be my witnesses, telling people about me everywhere—in Jerusalem, throughout Judea, in Samaria and to the ends of the earth" (Acts 1:8).

God's kingdom is spiritual with a material element. Jesus in his resurrected form could be seen and touched. He could eat and speak. He looked real. At the same time, he could pass through solid objects.[47] He could not rule in the new heavens and new earth with transformed humans unless there was some material element to the spiritual dimension. But the primary power and reality of God's rule and reign is in the hearts and minds of his followers. It is to be found residing in our immaterial nature—the one that cannot be weighed or seen on a CT scan. It is the soul, conscience, mind, heart, will, and spirit of a person. The way the kingdom is to be spread is not through governments, armies, or political intrigue. It is through the daily and ordinary witness of his followers. Every one of us is to be a witness. We are not all evangelists, teachers, or leaders, but all of us are to be witnesses. Between Pentecost and Parousia there is witness.[48] And yes, kingdom morality and values will collide with secular values and even with different interpretations within biblical worldviews. We are human, and we do not see clearly yet. We look to our King

---

[47] John 20:19.
[48] Acts 1:8; 2 Cor. 5:15-21; Eph. 4:11-16.

for truth. Politics involve argument. In God's kingdom, there is obedience to his commands.[49]

When the Holy Spirit came, the disciples spilled out of that room and did what only the Holy Spirit could cause them to do. They preached the gospel without restraint to thousands of their own countrymen. Suddenly they had a church of more than three thousand, and the Acts of the Apostles tells the story.[50]

3. The kingdom of God is international
We are told that the church will include every tribe, nation, people, and language standing before the throne of God in heaven.[51] Part of getting the kingdom wrong is to limit it to your nation. The apostles were right and wrong on this issue. They were right in that it started in Israel with the promises and prophecies to Abraham, Moses, David, and the prophets. But they were wrong in that they did not understand that one day they would be outnumbered by Gentiles in the great promise to Abraham. All those stars that Abraham saw in the night sky were not all Jewish.[52] In fact, in raw numbers, very few were Jewish. The spread of the Lord's kingdom would begin with the Jews, but it would soon leave Jerusalem, Judea, Samaria and leave the shores of Israel to every other land in the world. When this gospel of the kingdom is preached to every nation, the end will come.[53]

The kingdom of God is the realm where his will is being done, and it is done among individuals who will spread it gradually

---

[49] Matt 6:10; John 14:23; Jas 1:22.
[50] Acts 2:11-41.
[51] Rev. 7:9.
[52] Gen 22:17; Rom 9-11.
[53] Matt. 24:14.

throughout the entire globe. This is what Dallas Willard called the Divine Conspiracy: the kingdom growing silently, hidden in plain sight, as it penetrates every domain on earth.

The secular society in which we live has control of the levers of power. The way to wrestle it away is not by political or military might but through the power of witness. One day it will triumph. When that will culminate is not ours to know, but oh how certain it is! As my church prays every Sunday when we leave the gathering, "And now, Father, send us out to do the work you have given us to do, to love and serve you as **faithful witnesses** of Christ our Lord. To him, to you, and to the Holy Spirit, be honor and glory, now and forever. Amen" (emphasis added). [54]

---

[54] *The Book of Common Prayer*, Anglican House Publishing (Newport Beach, CA : Anglican Church in North America, 2019), 137.

Would You Like It in Heaven?

Christians in America seem to have been schooled in the gospel Americana.[55] One of its main features is an obsession with meeting the minimal entrance requirements for admission to heaven. Every time I have watched *Monty Python and the Holy Grail*, I recall the scene when Arthur and his band are trying to cross a giant abyss to enter the castle. There is a bridge keeper, and he asks them three questions to see if they can cross the bridge and enter the castle. If they get any of the questions wrong, they will be cast into the abyss.

The first knight is told, "State your name," and he does. Then, "State your quest," and he does. Then the bridge keeper asks, "What is your favorite color?" The knight says "red," and he is amazed that he is allowed to cross the bridge and enter the castle.

The second knight is asked the first two questions, and he answers them correctly. Then he is asked who won the World Cup in 1948. The knight says, "I have no idea." He is cast down into the abyss.

The third knight is confused and frightened. He also answers the first two questions correctly. Then he is asked, "What is your

---

[55] This concept is more fully explained in *The Cost of Cheap Grace: Reclaiming the Value of Discipleship*, Bill Hull and Brandon Cook (Colorado Springs: NavPress, 2020), 67.

favorite color?" He nervously says "Red. No! Blue." He too is thrown into the abyss.

Arthur is the last one. The bridge keeper asks him to state his name. "I'm Arthur, King of the Britons."

"What's your quest?"

"The Holy Grail"

"What's the air speed velocity of an unladen swallow?"

"Well, that depends. An African swallow or European swallow?"

The bridge keeper says, "I don't know that" and he casts Arthur into the abyss.[56]

Absurd, right? Most people think the big question is, "How do you know you will get into heaven?" But the real question is, "If you went to heaven, would you like it and would you want to stay?" Christian philosopher Dallas Willard was an expert at forcing us to wrestle with a different viewpoint. Here is what he says about getting into heaven, wanting to stay there, and the idea of being able to turn to God whenever one gets the desire. The "them" he refers to are those who have thus far rejected Christ but think Christ is always at the ready. Christ may be always at the ready, but what makes us sure that we would be? Willard describes them as already in "hell." But they are there because that is what they want.

---

[56] This dialogue is a cross between the 1975 film *Monty Python and the Holy Grail* and Dallas Willard, *Living in Christ's Presence: Final Words on Heaven and the Kingdom of God* (Downers Grove, IL: IVP Books, 2014), 53.

One should seriously inquire if to live in a world permeated with God and the knowledge of God is something they themselves truly desire. If not, they can be assured that God will excuse them from his presence. They will find their place in the "outer darkness" of which Jesus spoke. But the fundamental fact about them will not be that they are there, but that they have become people who [so] locked into their own self-worship and denial of God that they cannot want God. A well-known minister of other years used to ask rhetorically, "You say you will accept God when you want to?" And then he would add, "How do you know you will be able to want to when you think you will?" The ultimately lost person is the person who cannot want God. Who cannot want God to be God. Multitudes of such people pass by every day, and pass into eternity. The reason they do not find God is that they do not want him or, at least, do not want him to be God. Wanting God to be God is very different from wanting God to help me."[57]

During a crisis many people turn toward the transcendent. They seek high and low for God or a god that will help them cope with something unpleasant. When I hear that someone has turned to Christ, I automatically rejoice, but I do wonder to which Christ they turned. Was it the one who claimed to be God, who challenged the religious institutions and the hubris inherent in the human race? Was it the Christ who said, "Repent of your sins, believe the good news, and follow me?" (Mark 1:12-18). Or was it some selective Christ figure or principle that would accommodate one's lifestyle and worldview? Willard states it well in his last sentence: "Wanting God to be God is very different from wanting God to help me."[58]

---

[57] Willard, *Divine Conspiracy*.

[58] Dallas Willard, *Renovation of the Heart: Putting on the Character of Christ* (Colorado Springs, CO: NavPress, 2002), 57.

Hell is an existence. It could even be a place where all those who insist on their will instead of God's will being done will reside.[59] It is God's best solution for those who do not like him, who oppose him, or have put him on trial and found him to have failed. It is for all those who do not want the peace and tranquility that come with submission, repentance, forgiveness, and reconciliation.

I recall the repulsion that came from the late Christopher Hitchens, author of the best-selling *God is not Great*, at the existence of an all-knowing God who would surveil you for eternity. He saw it as a violation of his dignity as a human. He mistook sovereign care and love as surveillance. That is just one way in which people who insist on having it their way end up in a place separated from God. They do not want God to be God. They want to be their own god.

---

[59] Hell is a place where God chooses not to be. There may be a way, beyond our comprehension, in which God is there and not there at the same time. I believe the fire of hell presented in a few Scriptures to be metaphorical and meant to communicate the hideous nature of life without God.

Evil

*"Silence in the presence of evil is itself evil.
Not to speak is to speak, not to act is to act."*[60]

Dietrich Bonhoeffer

Remember when evil was evil and good was good? Bonhoeffer was not confused about evil. Box cars of Jews being transported to extermination camps was evil. Isn't it interesting, however, that many German Christians didn't think so? This blindness, or confusion, or ignorance was not unique to mid-twentieth century Germans. Americans who were highly educated and part of the ruling class defended Joseph Stalin and communist ideology from the 1920-1960s.

Both Nazism and socialism are utopian in nature. They insist on purity of thought, cannot abide dissent, and require state control to manage society. People finally catch on when the body count gets high and corpses start piling up in the streets.

Evil often appears as a fiery angel of light inhabiting human minds, institutions, and communications. Philosopher Hannah Arendt went to Jerusalem in 1961 to report for *The New Yorker* on the trial of Adolph Eichmann. Eichmann was the Nazi bureaucrat who organized the transportation of millions of Jews to concentration camps, a project called the Final Solution. Arendt found Eichmann

---

[60] See page 4, footnote 1.

to be an ordinary, rather bland, bureaucrat, who, in her words, was "neither perverted nor sadistic" but "terrifyingly normal." She published *Eichmann in Jerusalem: A Report on the Banality of Evil* in 1963.[61]

Her term "banality" is still debated today. The left did not like her conclusion because they like to explain evil as absent in most people and resident in only a special few who should be excised from our societies—a mutation that must be cast off on humankind's grand ascent into enlightened morality. This is what some mean when they say a conservative-minded person is on the "wrong side of history." Once again, this aversion to Arendt's interpretation is the secular left's flight from personal sin, human fallenness, and great potential in each person for great evil. Arendt said (and it remains a thorn in the liberal side):

> I was struck by the manifest shallowness in the doer which made it impossible to trace the uncontestable evil of his deeds to any deeper level of roots or motives. The deeds were monstrous, but the doer—at least the very effective one now on trial—was quite ordinary, commonplace, and neither demonic nor monstrous.[62]

In other words, given the right circumstances, any one of us could have done it.

Evil is not primarily located in systems or societies. Evil resides in every human heart. It is through individuals that it escapes

---

[61] Hannah Arendt, *Eichmann in Jerusalem: A Report on the Banality of Evil* (New York: Penguin Books, 1963).
[62] Kathleen B. Jones, "The Trial of Hannah Arendt." *Humanities* 35, No. 2 (March/April 2014). https://www.neh.gov/humanities/2014/marchapril/feature/the-trial-hannah-arendt.

human restraint and then multiplies and metastasizes among families, neighborhoods, institutions, and societies. That is why German Christians could sing hymns loud enough to cover the cries for help from Jews as the trains passed by their churches on Sunday mornings. We humans have a way of protecting ourselves from harm by rationalizing our support for the systems that provide protection to us. "I was just following orders." "I didn't know about it." "I trusted my government" "I believed the propaganda." "The church needs to stay out of politics and preach the Gospel." Bonhoeffer put it well, "Not to speak in the presence of evil is itself evil."

It all seems so clear looking back to Nazis, Germans, and Jews. But it gets a bit more sticky when we start talking about Donald Trump, Joe Biden, Black Lives Matter, Antifa, media bias, abortion, same-sex marriage, trans women competing against biological women, and so on. Where is the evil? Who is most evil? More importantly, how do you choose good from this pile of evil? It is always more difficult when you are up to your eyeballs in it. The only recourse for the Christian is the Bible itself.

Biblical Evil

The Bible separates moral evil from physical evil. Moral evil is what people do; physical evil is what nature does: earthquakes, floods, disease, death, mudslides, fires, hurricanes, tornadoes and so on. Physical evil is because of the Fall which includes the entire realignment of a fallen earth versus what was a pre-fall earth.[63] Human evil or moral evil when carried out is considered a sin. The Ten Commandments are addressed to human decision and will. Keeping the Sabbath; honoring parents; avoiding idolatry, misuse of God's name, murder, adultery, false testimony, and coveting

---

[63] Gen 3:14-19.

another's house, spouse, or property all involve acts of human will.⁶⁴ The Old Testament moral and ceremonial laws sort it all out for Israel's daily life and religious practices. Jesus summed up the Ten Commandments and the Law of Moses when he said, "You must love the Lord your God with all your heart, all your soul, and all your mind. This is the first and greatest commandment. A second is equally important: 'Love your neighbor as yourself.' The entire law and all the demands of the prophets are based on these two commandments."⁶⁵

Getting more specific

The human conscience, factory installed by God, agrees with its creator's moral design.⁶⁶ The basis of law in Western civilization is built on the biblical narrative as experienced by humans for thousands of years. But to answer our question, we need a deeper dive into the New Testament on contemporary practices.

As a people, we are separated at birth from God. We are made in his image, but that image is effaced. The remainder of life is about restoration from that separation beginning with reconciliation with our creator.⁶⁷ The degree to which we enter into evil is determined by how far away from God we stray. The New Testament provides several general lists of evil for our understanding.

---

⁶⁴ Exod. 20:3-11.
⁶⁵ Matt. 22:37-40.
⁶⁶ Gen 1:27 states that God made humans in his own image. Our bodies, brains, and particularly our conscience and sense of right and wrong are part of the human package. This is why a toddler cries out, "That's not fair" in the sandbox.
⁶⁷ 2 Cor. 5:15-21; Eph. 2:1-10.

Wickedness is a category of behavior that violators knowingly practice:

> Their lives became full of every kind of wickedness, sin, greed, hate, envy, murder, quarreling, deception, malicious behavior, and gossip. They are backstabbers, haters of God, insolent, proud, and boastful. They invent new ways of sinning, and they disobey their parents. They refuse to understand, break their promises, are heartless, and have no mercy (Rom 1:29-31).

This reads like a political party's unofficial playbook. Do we know any political party that is free of these sins? The candidates themselves swim in the same moral cesspool. Here is more Scripture for your reading pleasure:

> When you follow the desires of your sinful nature the results are very clear: sexual immorality, impurity, lustful pleasures, idolatry, sorcery, hostility, quarreling, jealousy, outbursts of anger, selfish ambition, dissension, division, envy, drunkenness, wild parties and other sins like these. Let me tell you again, as I have said before, that anyone living that sort of life will not inherit the Kingdom of God" (Gal 5:19-21)

The thought that immediately comes to mind is Romans 3:23: "For all have sinned and fall short of the glory of God."

Is anyone inherently qualified to lead our country, cities, counties, churches, schools, industries, or even our homes? Whoever is chosen to lead a church or a country is a sinner and has a checkered past. Their lives will have inconsistencies. Mistakes they have made will be published and accentuated. Everyone gets vetted now. There is opposition research, and, of course, much of our lives are now recorded.

A compromise must be made. We must use our best judgement and common sense to define exactly what decision needs to be made, whether a person is a right fit, and what the person represents in person and policy. Calling a pastor to your church is very different than choosing a mayor or school board superintendent. A Baptist church will not call an Episcopal priest or a Jewish rabbi to be their pastor. A really nice man who runs the hardware store might be a good fit to be the part-time mayor of a hamlet of three hundred people but not the leader of General Motors. Whoever is selected to be president of the United States will be flawed. The question really comes down to what is best for the United States. The word evil is thrown around a lot by partisans when describing the candidate they oppose. Both candidates have committed numerous sins listed in the aforementioned verses. As Bonhoeffer said, "It is better to do evil than to be evil."[68]

By the time you read this, the 2020 U.S. Presidential election will have been decided. I would suggest that after digesting the result, as a Christian, pray for that person, support them when you can, and remember that evil is resident in all of us. As Jesus said:

And why worry about a speck in your friend's eye when you have a log in your own? How can you think of saying to your friend, 'Let me help you get rid of that speck in your eye, when you can't see past the log in your own eye? Hypocrite! First get rid of the log in your own eye; then you will see well enough to deal with the speck in your friend's eye. (Matthew 7:3-5).

---

[68] Aleksandr Solzhenitsyn, *The Gulag Archipelago*, (Nashville: HarperCollins, 1985), 75.

The line separating good and evil passes not through states, nor between classes, nor between political parties either— but right through every human heart . . . even within hearts overwhelmed by evil, one small bridgehead of good is retained. And even in the best of hearts, there remains . . . an uprooted small corner of evil.[69]

---

[69] Ibid.

PROGRESSION
OF DECLINE

The Intoxicated Mind

G. K. Chesterton argued that new ideas are most dangerous to those who have not studied them. Due to the lack of a mental filter, a new idea will "fly to his head like wine to the head of a teetotaler."[70] I am still in a search to learn how our culture has lost its collective mind. Chesterton's thesis is as good as any for a starting point.

Intoxication has its virtues (euphoria, temporary illusions of grandeur, openness, and laughter) and its penalties (sickness, regret, crumbled documents signed while under the influence, and more serious maladies as well). Thinking and intoxication are not friends. There is a reason you do not want your pilot or surgeon to be chemically "just a little more relaxed" before they go to work.

A poorly educated populace is easy prey for new ideas because they have no filter. That filter should be the ability to do critical thinking. That is what good teaching and instruction are supposed to achieve in educating the young of a society. But today's general populace and its younger generations are poorly educated. They do not think critically, and, therefore, their minds are easily intoxicated with new ideas. However, most destructive ideas are not new. They are old ideas recycled for younger more defenseless minds. That is one of the reasons morality is in decline. It might seem that we have hit moral bottom, but as we think about Paul's three-stage societal decline defined in his letter to the Romans, I am afraid we are not at bottom.

---

[70] G. K. Chesterton, *Heretics*, (Radford, VA: Wilder, 1905, 2007), 115.

You mean it could get worse? Yes. "Since they thought it foolish to acknowledge God, he abandoned them to their foolish thinking" (Rom 1:28). This is the third, but I'm not sure the final, cascade into the moral confusion which precedes cultural collapse. Paul labeled it "foolish thinking." That is human thinking without divine assistance. Reasoning without revelation always leads to foolish thinking, particularly when it is about moral foundations and conduct.

What is even worse is the lack of moral restraint—the inability to curb the human appetite for power and advantage: a better place in line, a more comfortable seat on the airplane, to be a U.S. senator rather than state representative, a president rather than a secretary of state. There is such a thing as healthy ambition. Without it, nothing would get done and especially great things would never be accomplished. What Scripture opposes is selfish ambition.

What makes it all worse is the little add-on to Paul's description that unleashes an ugly catalogue of pathology designed by Lucifer to destroy humanity: ". . . he abandoned them to their foolish thinking and let them do things that should never be done" (Rom 1:28).[71]

Let your mind explore the category "things that should never be done." This statement refers back to what Paul has already described and then moves forward to the moral cesspool he plans to name. It is compounded in that human creativity becomes a trigger for inventing new ways of sinning. This is all supercharged by the unrestrained exercise of humanity's destructive abilities. God does not force behavior on any soul. He simply takes his hands off and allows a person to exercise their will.

---

[71] John 10:10 identifies Lucifer's purpose for human beings: "To kill, steal and destroy."

Not very long ago, pedophilia was thoroughly rejected in our culture. Across the political spectrum from far left to far right, child molestation—adults taking sexual advantage of children—was considered the bottom of the moral barrel. Historically, it would have been considered repugnant for a person like Jeffery Epstein to exploit underage girls, and when photos of said girls were found on his property, most people would have been sickened and considered the photos proof of his guilt.[72] Recently, however, the unthinkable has become thinkable. There is evidence to show that many in the media and politics covered up Epstein's sins for political reasons.[73]

There is also controversy over the new Netflix series *Cuties*. Critics call the series a sexploitation of pre-teen girls. Advertising incudes a poster of girls in skimpy dance outfits and "twerking." Many are outraged, but its defenders say we are all just too exercised about this whole thing and if we would settle down, it too shall pass.[74] They are right. If critics and, of course, those prudes who care about their children would just cool it, pedophilia will become acceptable in due course. Before you know it, sexual child abuse will no longer be a crime, and perpetrators will go to therapy instead of jail. They will no longer be considered incurable and

---

[72] James B. Stewart, "The Day Jeffrey Epstein Told Me He Had Dirt on Powerful People." *The New York Times*, 12 August 2019. https://www.nytimes.com/2019/08/12/business/jeffrey-epstein-interview.html

[73] Khaddeja Safdar, Rebecca Davis O'Brien, Gregory Zuckerman, and Jenny Strasburg, "Jeffrey Epstein Burrowed into the Lives of the Rich and Made a Fortune." *The Wall Street Journal*, 25 July 2019. https://www.wsj.com/articles/jeffrey-epstein-burrowed-into-the-lives-of-the-rich-and-made-a-fortune-11564092553

[74] Just as an aside, whenever an apologetic is being put forward for a previously morally outraged work of art, the term "French Film" provides some air cover. Somehow smut is more acceptable if it comes from France with the proper wine and cheese.

no longer required to register as sex offenders. You won't know they live next door. Just imagine a world where the only place left where justice can be done on earth as it is in heaven will be a federal prison where the prisoners take justice into their own hands and administer punishment.

This is an example of how the unthinkable becomes commonly believed and eventually encouraged. It qualifies under the rubric "things that should never be done." They are working with a knowledge that understands but rejects the truth. "They know God's justice requires that those who do these things deserve to die, yet they do them anyway" (Rom 1:32). But yes, it gets even worse. "Worse yet, they encourage others to do them, too." (Rom 1:32c).

"Their lives became full of every kind of wickedness, sin, greed, hate, envy, murder, quarreling, deception, malicious behavior, and gossip. They became backstabbers, haters of God, insolent, proud, and boastful" (Rom 1:29).

I hate to say it, but I have witnessed all this behavior among church leaders. This is not a special depravity reserved for the non-religious. It comes down to the difference between a community or society accepting these qualities as normative versus a culture that rejects them. If they are officially rejected in a church, and people are cautioned and disciplined, then the behavior is restrained. This is obviously what Paul is saying because the first sentence of Chapter 2 says so. "You may think you can condemn such people, but you are just as bad, and you have no excuse" (Rom 2:1). No one gets a pass on this behavior. Condemnation is on those who openly practice such things, approve of them, and encourage others to do the same. Paul says they deserve to die.

The word that describes the world in which we are living is nihilism. Nihilism means "nothing." It essentially proposes that there is no absolute truth. Basic questions about good versus bad and truth versus falsehood are routinely dismissed. Nineteenth century German philosopher Friedrich Nietzsche had it logically right when he concluded that nihilism leaves only the will to power. The future would belong to the Ubermensch, the superman who dares to exercise his will and power. He is the one who will conquer. Morality becomes utilitarian. "Does it work?" rather than "Is it right?" becomes the question.

American religion in particular has focused on pragmatics rather than theology, and we are poorer for it. I heard only yesterday that focus groups have concluded that the ongoing riots in the streets are hurting the Democrats in the polls forcing their candidate to come out against violence, looting, and destruction. Isn't the logic interesting? Your reason for taking a moral stand against violence is a concern for loss of power. I am not saying the Republicans would not do the same. They are utilitarian as well. This is an example of nihilism at work. Morality, justice, and what you speak up about is determined not by conscience but by personal and party advancement.

I sit at night rubbing my eyes and shaking my head. What I see on television or read online makes me wonder how much worse it could become. It causes me great concern for our future, for my children and grandchildren. The world is becoming a morally confused cesspool. Because we do not know history, we are not teaching accurate history to the young thus dooming them to repeat its mistakes. It is unfair to expect young people to behave much better than they do since, in many cases, we have failed them. We have failed them in our public schools, in our churches, in the arts, in films, the theater, and print media. Media sources are no longer are neutral referees. They wear jerseys of a particular party or worldview.

How many fingers am I holding up? As many as the controlling elite says I am.

The Spiral of Silence[75]

On July 14, 1789, 156 years to the day before I was born, thousands of French citizens stormed the Bastille in Paris. Actually, only about nine hundred people stormed the Bastille. Numbers vary depending on what cable news channel Parisians watched. Citizens were fed up with King Louis XIV. He must have been worse than his thirteen predecessors. His wife, Marie Antoinette, reportedly snorted and said of hungry Parisians, "Let them eat cake." Apparently, she never said it, but let's blame her anyway. It fits the narrative and that is all that counts these days. She was arrested, tried, and beheaded on October 14, 1792. Reports vary as to whether or not head and body were buried together.

The Bastille armory, fortress, and political prison symbolized raw power and tyranny of the monarchy. Revolution was necessary, but before the revolution was possible, defending the king had to go out of fashion. Revolutionaries would need to employ a strategy that would change public opinion. In more modern terms, public sentiment necessary to make the monarchy tenable would need to be crushed. Storming the Bastille is a study in public opinion and mass psychology. It also teaches us about the power of free speech and the squelching of it. Before a mob could storm the Bastille, a spiral of silence would be required.

---

[75] The title of this article and the germ of its idea stems from Elisabeth Noelle-Neumann, *The Spiral of Silence: Public Opinion—Our Social Skin*, 2nd ed, (Chicago: University of Chicago Press, 1993), 107-14.

Once the crowd turned into a mob and found its way to Les Invalides, the square near the Bastille, it had grown to several thousand. For a large crowd to turn into a mob, individual moral judgements must be deferred to the group and the group itself becomes a living entity. Normally rational individuals defer both judgment and individual morality, turning their wills over to self-appointed leaders. Often, when questioned later, members of a riotous mob will deny any personal responsibility for the destruction of property, injury, or even the death of others. They have become convinced that there is a "greater good" which transcends all normal forms of morality.

A very interesting dynamic is the movement of a crowd. The French crowd shoved its way toward the Bastille, but it was only able to move in that direction because it was allowed to do so. The authorities allowed the crowd to proceed, and soldiers trained to squelch such a mob cooperated. The mob shot at the Bastille from 10:00 a.m. until 5:00 p.m. The walls were forty-five feet high and thirty feet thick. The mob could have shot endlessly for days and no real damage would have been done.

Soldiers in the Bastille were careful to not harm the crowd. The crowd made demands, and the Bastille commander withdrew the cannons from the firing port. Then he invited a deputation from the mob to have breakfast with him before ordering his soldiers to not fire on the crowd, even if attacked. He finally allowed his soldiers to fire but only after alerting the crowd that he had given that order. The commander had already lowered the first bridge into the fortress, possibly as a show of accommodation.

The commander's opinion was shaped by forces other than conventional convictions that previously had protected the monarchy from threat. He and his soldiers no longer believed in those convictions. They had changed their minds. Public opinion had changed. In the end, one of the fighters put it well: "The Bastille was not taken by force. It surrendered before it ever could be attacked." In the end, a soldier inside the Bastille lowered the bridge and allowed the mob to enter and begin the destruction. What appeared to be all of Paris outside the fortress to the 120 soldiers inside was less than one thousand active revolutionaries. There were thousands more gathered, but witnesses reported that most were spectators—well-dressed men and women stopping to watch on their way to do something else. Like most corrupted leaders or ideologies, the cultural elite eventually crumbled under the weight of their own failures.[76]

The interesting aspect to this was the behavior of the onlookers who vastly outnumbered the actual people storming the Bastille. They went along with the mob. They knew that in order to avoid isolation, rejection, and criticism, they would need to show approval. Crowd hysteria is a manifestation of public opinion. It is somewhat like when an out-of-state vehicle enters your neighborhood and runs over a child. Outraged residents attack the vehicle, drag the driver from the automobile, and beat him or her in a "righteous rage."

Through a large part of 2020, the United States had this same dynamic at work. It is not my purpose to take a political side in this article. We have, however, seen how officials have ordered police to stand down in the face of peaceful protests that deteriorated into looting, destruction of property, rioting, and physical abuse. How is this possible? It is possible because public opinion has changed. On this, I will take a side.

---

[76] For an extensive treatment of the Storming of the Bastille, see Charles Rivers Editors *The Storming of the Bastille: The History and Legacy of the Most Famous Flashpoint of the French Revolution*, 2014.

Public opinion is being falsely shaped by the censorship of big tech and big media backed by big money. I do not have a problem with all sides being represented by Google, Facebook, and Twitter. But I do have a problem when they suppress free expression and undermine the First Amendment. The sad result is that a good share of Americans have no opportunity to make truly objective sourced decisions regarding their leaders and representatives because correct information is unavailable through electronic and print media. In fact, alternative views to those of people in power have been censored. This has also led to the "cancel culture" movement, and then, either out of malice or ignorance, publicly protected, non-partisan platforms curating news and shaping it to fit their narrative. It has become clear from their employees' and leaders' voting and charitable giving habits that they are quite partisan.[77]

There is a larger point to make here. Freedom of speech is a moral issue based on an absolute truth.

The Contemporary Argument against the First Amendment

"Congress shall make no law respecting an establishment of religion or prohibiting the free exercise thereof; or abridging the freedom of speech, or of the press; or the right of people peaceably to assemble, and to petition the Government for a redress of grievances."

First Amendment, Bill of Rights, United States Constitution.

---

[77] "Supreme Court Rules in Favor of Cheerleader in Free Speech Case." *ny1.com*, 23 June 2021. https://www.ny1.com/nyc/all-boroughs/news/2021/06/23/supreme-court-snapchat-cheerleader.

Some simple exegesis interprets the relevant phrase "or abridging the freedom of speech." To abridge is to limit, shorten, or curtail a right or privilege. There is a movement among less enlightened or historically ignorant generations that says some speech is so heinous, wrong, or misleading, it should not be seen by the American people or allowed on public platforms. This is an argument that has been put forward since the earliest time of humankind, and it has been soundly rejected in the United States again and again.[78]

The First Amendment's speech provision is to protect all speech, especially the kind that is heinous, incorrect, and crazy. Unless all speech is protected, none of it is and that which does get protected is decided by whoever is in power. We must hear from the extreme right and left as well as those in the middle. We are responsible to sort it all out. It is the only way truth can remain center stage. Without that, we are not a free people.

The press too is free to be as partisan and crazy as they have become. They are free to lose the confidence of the American people, as they have. The people of the United States are free to turn them off, criticize them, and even replace them. The free market will replace them when the citizens ignore them and stop watching, listening to, and reading them.

Earlier I stated that freedom of speech is a moral issue. That claim centers around the basis upon which we say that free speech is

---

[78] There have been numerous Supreme Court cases that have upheld free speech in America. The most serious challenge to free speech presently is censoring by big tech companies Facebook and Twitter and major media outlets, who restrict and eliminate the free exchange of ideas with which they disagree. The motivation is primarily political power, social engineering, and, for big industry, financial.

not merely a political right but a moral right bestowed upon all humans.

The Materialistic View

I propose that the idea which says the existence of humans, the heavens, and the earth is a cosmic mystery or mathematical improbability is a lie. A universe without a guide, a mind, a strategy, or a purpose is an absurdity. It defies logic, any sense of reason, and science. Science requires reason and logic to exist. The mind itself cannot be trusted to work a problem if it is not designed to comprehend laws of the universe that are logical. Matter and mind must match up for anyone to make sense of what is happening around us.

The easiest lie to expose is the one that repulses all of humanity: there is no God; your life is an accident, and you are nothing more than a mere puppet. You live; you die; nothing really matters. As Paul put it so simply:

> They know the truth about God because he has made it obvious to them. For ever since the world was created, people have seen the earth and the sky. Through everything God made, they can clearly see his invisible qualities—his eternal power and divine nature. So they have no excuse for not knowing God (Rom 1:19-20).

Here is the link to free speech. The materialistic view held by many in the ruling class aasserts that we are simply consumers. The rulers can censor and edit out reality from the consumer class because ensuring the latter's conformity to the alleged greater wisdom of the ruling class is a higher value than freedom of speech. The government makes the decision as to what is true and false, right and wrong, and they have the power to confer limited freedoms on the population in concert with what the ruling class thinks is best for the underclass. This is how the majority of nations have conducted themselves for most of history, except in the United States.

The Spiritual View

This is the most simple and clear point because it is profound. Our founding fathers, some Congregationalists, some Baptists, some Methodists, and yes, even agnostics and Deists agreed on this point: we are made in God's image and our rights come from the divine, not from man or government. "We hold these truths to be self-evident, that all men are created equal, that they are endowed by their Creator with certain unalienable Rights, that among these are Life, Liberty and the pursuit of Happiness"[79]

The first amendment to the United States Constitution, ratified in 1791, gave the right of free speech to every citizen. While the Constitution and Bill of Rights do not specifically mention God, many involved in writing and signing the Declaration of Independence assumed a Divine as evidenced by their making the above statement.

However, this goes even deeper. God made man in his own image and that image goes to man's immaterial nature—the personality traits such as mind, spirit, will, conscience, and soul. We are so valuable to God that he became a man in the person of Jesus the Christ and died for our eternal souls. Jesus' visit to earth was the most powerful word or statement that could possibly be made as to the value of persons. He gave himself as a sacrifice that ensured our freedom and our dignity.[80] This also means that

---

[79] United States Declaration of Independence, 1776.
[80] Gen 1:27; John 3:16; 2 Cor 5:21; Phil 2:5-8; John 8:36.

every thought and word that a human being has is valuable to God and every person has a right to be heard. We are told that one day every word we speak will be remembered by God, and we will be held accountable for those words (Matthew 12:36).

The fight for freedom of speech is one worth having. It is temporal in the sense that it is decided by the powers of government, but its source is the dignity and authority that comes with being a child of God. It also permits our culture to be a better place to live with a high probability that its citizens can live a life based on reality and truth. Without it, censorship rules, elites rule, and the powerful can punish those who do not obey.

Do not give in to the spiral of silence that has already begun. Step up instead of shutting up.

I leave you with the words of Dietrich Bonhoeffer: "Not to speak is to speak, not to act is to act." Pray for the courage to speak the next time you are told to pipe down and not create a ruckus. What you say matters. Don't go with the mob. Don't fold in the face of the ruling class or as a citizen of the secular city. You are a citizen of the kingdom of God. Jesus is listening to you, recording what you say, and, unlike Siri, will be there to reward you on judgment day.[81]

---

[81] 2 Cor 5:10.

The Wasting of the Evangelical Mind

Responsible Christians face two tasks—that of saving the soul and that of saving the mind . . . No civilization can endure with its mind being as confused and disordered as ours is today. [82]

Charles Malik

The above title was the subject of an article in *The New Yorker* magazine written by Editor Michael Luo on March 4, 2021. If there is one thing I noticed from the start, the author did not understand the Christian mind nor did he have an evangelical mind. He drew heavily from Historian Mark Noll's polemic issued twenty-seven years ago, *The Scandal of the Evangelical Mind*. Luo's article was informative for young readers who have not lived through the last fifty years of evangelical development and decline as Luo has. But I must take issue with the author's premise and overall purpose in writing the article.

Put simply, the article tries to present a connection between the lack of serious intellectuals in the evangelical community to

---

[82] Charles Malik was a Lebanese scholar and founding member of the United Nations General Assembly. He delivered these remarks in a 1980 speech at the dedication of the Billy Graham Center in Wheaton, IL. Charles Malik, "The Two Tasks," *JETS* 23:4, (December 1980), 289-96, 295. https://www.etsjets.org/files/JETS-PDFs/23/23-4/23-4-pp289-296_JETS.pdf.

the attack on the nation's capitol building on January 6, 2021, specifically because some of the more prominently dressed and vocal rioters said prayers and invoked the name of Jesus Christ. Somehow all this supposedly could have been avoided if real Christians had graduated from Harvard, or at least a private Eastern Seaboard college. Maybe if these people knew the differences between the philosophies of Socrates, Plato and Aristotle, they could have avoided going down the biblical rabbit hole. Because of this ignorance, these limited-in-mind, wooden-headed biblical literalists have fallen prey to QAnon conspiracy theories.

Anyone who has ever attempted to research the origins of QAnon or the identity of Q will find that the only solid answer is actor John Cleese, who played Q in a James Bond film. I think Cleese would enjoy being the founder of QAnon and could ridicule the idea better than anyone I know. QAnon consists of a few crackpot ideas perpetrated on the internet by a variety of people—usually some moderate to low IQ people who have been wronged by the government or brilliant minds who recite great soliloquies into broken mobile phones and then post them on a social network. The idea that QAnon represents any organized group with a leadership structure is not supported by the evidence.

For an insurrection to take place, there needs to be someone behind the attack to take over the government. There is no evidence that this conspiratorial line of thought has one. The idea that the church or any of its credible leaders had a hand in the attack is preposterous. I do not know one Christian or Christian leader who supported the attack or even sympathizes with any of it.

I agree that Donald Trump bears some responsibility because he went too far in challenging the election results. I also agree that the gathering in Washington D.C. on January 6th consisted of many Christians. But 99% of those of gathered did nothing illegal, and they peacefully left the area. It seems obvious from subsequent research that whatever was being planned was pre-planned and that 1% of the overall group, and only a small fraction of them, had bought into a conspiracy theory.

These statistics weaken Luo's premise that conservative Christians do not think critically and have abandoned reason for faith. It also demonstrates an obvious oversight in that he missed the huge growth in the evangelical field of apologetics, both practical and philosophical, in the past fifty years. He also has confused Christianity with a few guys in bunkers and basements posting rants on social networks.

Luo states, "The intermingling of religious faith, conspiratorial thinking, and misguided nationalism on display at the Capitol offered perhaps the most unequivocal evidence yet of the American church's role in bringing the country to this dangerous moment."[83] Notice how the First Amendment has been flipped. Instead of the state being dangerous to the freedom of religion, religion is deemed dangerous to the health of the state. The state becomes the victim. The state, not the people and their God-given rights, is what is to be preserved. This is the same line of argumentation used by the Catholic Church to start the Inquisition in the twelfth century. It is the consistent apologetic for tyrannical governments who intend to silence any challenge to their power. This is the state turning its attention to the dangers of free religion.[84]

---

[83] Michael Luo, "The Wasting of the Evangelical Mind." *The New Yorker*, 24 March 2021. https://www.newyorker.com/news/daily-comment/the-wasting-of-the-evangelical-mind.

[84] The press is free as well and protected by this same amendment to be as crazy as they have been.

There may be some churches who have been captured by conspiracy theories. There always have been and always will be. But this is not a serious or prevailing presence among evangelicals or any churches of note. Luo quotes studies by The American Enterprise Institute and others, but the analysis lacks precision. For example, the idea that 75% of people surveyed thought that there was widespread voter fraud in the 2020 presidential election is not news. Most seasoned political watchers know that there has always been voter fraud. The issue was how much. Most concluded, as the courts did, that there was not enough to change the election results. If fifty thousand people show up for a rally, what percentage is that of seventy-four million people who voted for Trump?[85]

The Antifa question is laughable. This is the height of journalistic hypocrisy. The leadership elite and press were silent during the summer of 2020 concerning the riots, destruction of public property, injury to police, and the beating of citizens clearly led by Antifa, but they lost their minds when it came to the Capitol riots. This is because the press has been swallowed by their own political views. They have ceased to be a trusted source for information. They, not the church, have lost their souls.

The Evangelical Mind

Luo's article presents a short history of some of the church's great minds: Thomas Aquinas, Martin Luther, Jonathan Edwards, and C.S. Lewis. But it falls off a theological cliff with Reinhold Niebuhr, T.S. Eliot, and W.H. Auden. I do not mean to speak ill of Niebuhr, Eliot or Auden, but they are from a very different kettle of fish than those previously mentioned.

---

[85] The answer is .0006 – far less than even one quarter of one percent.

Luo is correct in his statement that the most popular and influential pastors have tended to give publicly palatable messages that sell on television. They preach a gospel with plenty of Americana in it that makes the message a product that can be plucked out to help those in pain and special need.

This trait is found in virtually every field of endeavor. Journalism as practiced in the early 20th century up through Watergate is dead and gone. Bob Woodward and Carl Bernstein in *All the President's Men* were both the apex of classic journalism as well as the start of its decline.[86] Woodstein, as the two were called by their editor Ben Bradlee, became famous. Their investigative reporting on Watergate made their careers. Journalism became the thing, and people went into it to became famous—to practice a journalism that sells.

This is no more obvious than in present day cable news and in the scramble among print media sources to survive. Interviewing Prince Harry, who is estranged from Great Britain's Royal family, is done because it sells, not because it is important. The tendency to extract the fashionable from the serious and to market it for profit is human. It is also very much Americana and part of the competitive nature. Religion does it. All humans do it for themselves and for profit. Just like the partisan cable news hosts who call themselves journalists, some religious people

---

[86] Watergate was the name of the hotel in Washington D.C. that housed the Democratic Committee presidential campaign offices. It was broken into by five burglars who worked for the White House. Over a two-year period, it was learned that President Nixon covered up many illegal campaign activities and, as a result, he was forced to resign from office in August of 1974. *The Washington Post* reporters Bob Woodward and Carl Bernstein broke the story, became national heroes, and won the Pulitzer Prize for their work.

take the Gospel and corrupt it for personal gain while still calling themselves godly.

The Pastor as Scholar-Theologian

Luo quotes historian Richard Hofstadter: "The Puritan ideal of the minister as an intellectual and educational leader was steadily weakened in the face of the evangelical ideal of the minister as a popular crusader and exhorter."[87] Religion became part of the marketplace. It is competitive and "may the best salesman win." Yes, true enough, that is what made American Christianity robust and aggressive. This is quite different than the parish idea that led to the great decline among higher sacerdotal Christianity with a European base. But whose pews are empty?

The answer is found in those groups, schools, and denominations that have adopted progressive deconstruction of the biblical text to accommodate and appease a fast-changing culture. This deconstruction has been led by once great universities, such as Harvard, Yale, and Princeton.[88]

Scholarship among evangelicals has grown substantially in the last fifty years. The growth of new and outstanding seminaries

---

[87] Luo, "Wasting of the Evangelical Mind," *The New Yorker.*

[88] Harvard was first established to train ministers. When the school became too liberal, Yale was founded as a more conservative alternative. Princeton was next for the same reasons. Jonathan Edwards was appointed the first president of Princeton but died before he could take office. These universities were once great in the sense that they started for the purpose of furthering the kingdom of God. Now it would be fair to say they are enemies of same.

and conservatives involved in leading academic circles and organizations has exploded, but this is limited to those who operate within the academic society and who are willing to give their careers to such work.[89]

The majority of people are not academics. Pastors as humans are apportioned in giftedness and interest just like practitioners in any other profession. There are a few select ones who become scholars. There are others who are hybrids: academic in orientation and careful exegetes who focus on the average person as their student. To this is added a sense of pastoral care and responsibility. A third group can be categorized as biblically based, thoughtful, and action oriented. They would rather spend twenty hours a week with people than in their studies making sure their sermons reflect the latest in cultural niceties and have appendices on the Medes and the Persians. Hopefully these three tiers together provide a balanced faith community, and the collective knowledge of the scholars, the pastor-theologians, and faithful practitioners will edify the entire church. But the notion that the ideal would be a church led strictly by scholarly contemplatives does not square with reality.

There is, sadly, a fourth tier of pastors made up of abusers, exploiters, and charlatans who give the Christian faith a bad name. It seems those who oppose or have a prejudice against conversative Christians use this group as a rationale to attack. I would suggest that journalists, media leaders, and big tech

---

[89] The last fifty years has seen the acceleration of evangelical scholarship with the establishment of institutes and the training of young scholars at colleges and universities such as Trinity Evangelical Divinity School, Calvin College, Fuller Theological Seminary, Biola University, particularly in Apologetics, and many more.

executives take the words of Jesus seriously here and first look at the timbers in their own eyes before trying to remove the speck out of another person's eye (Luke 6:1-42).

Whose Mind is Wasted Now, Evangelical or Secular?

To waste something means to fail to use it for its intended purpose. "What a waste," everyone says about the person with great intelligence who could have been a scholar but instead became a drug addict. A person with special athletic talent who will not go to class disqualifies him or herself for collegiate competition and exits the university with no degree. Again, "What a waste."

There has been and will continue to be great waste in the church. What the church has been in the past two thousand years has been enough to inspire billions, create great art and literature, lift millions out of poverty, and educate the masses. However, it has also contributed to the misery of millions. When it comes to waste, clergy flying around on private jets funded by donations and fully robed priests saluting Adolf Hitler with uplifted right arms has no rival.[90]

We turn our attention again to Michael Luo's *The New Yorker* article "The Wasting of the Evangelical Mind."[91] I am confident the problem with the church has not been nor ever will be

---

[90] Ezek 34:10: "This is what the Sovereign Lord says: 'I now consider these shepherds my enemies, and I will hold them responsible for what happen to my flock."

[91] Luo, "Wasting of the Evangelical Mind," *The New Yorker*.

primarily intellectual. If you and your heroes are intellectual and most of those intellectuals are secular minded, then, of course, all problems with religion will be perceived as intellectual in nature.[92]

Anti-intellectualism is a problem but a very small problem for the existing church. Yes, it is writ large in conventional academia, but in most local congregations in America, the variety of minds and levels of minds are as varied as humans are unique from one another. The minds of most people are sufficient to understand the necessary principles and nuances of spiritual life. Furthermore, even though most have not been schooled in streams of intellectual categories or vocabulary, their minds joined to their souls provide wisdom to live good lives every day. Possessing the correct worldview is much more important than sheer brain power. If a person believes that "In the beginning God created the heavens and the earth," he or she has a clear advantage over the person who has no clue about who is behind everything or what the meaning of created life is about.[93] If you start with the wrong premise, or no premise at all as atheists, agnostics, and skeptics do, or you start with a premise of, "We don't really know much, but we are working on it," then regardless of how smart you are, one can only say, "What a waste."

It reminds me of the two men arguing on an airplane ride. When the plane landed the skeptic told the Christian, "One thing I

---

[92] "Intellectual" is defined here as the properly degreed elites or public intellectuals who agree with and support the power centers of the ruling elites and their major organs. These organs are *The New York Times*, *The Washington Post*, the mainstream media, big tech, big corporations, major league sports, and the entertainment industry.
[93] Gen 1:1; 1 Cor 1:25.

am sure of is that there is no such thing as absolute truth." The Christian smiled, "Are you absolutely sure about that?"

His point was made. All opinion, even scientific theory, is faith-based belief. The skeptic does not grasp that his logic is self-contradictory. A scientist can only do science and draw any meaningful knowledge that could be placed into a category called truth because he or she has faith in their brain and in the order and the repetition of physical laws of the universe.

The Bible makes a claim about minds that are out of alignment with their creator.

> The message of the cross is foolish to those who are headed for destruction! But we who are being saved know it is the very power of God. As the Scriptures say, "I will destroy the wisdom of the wise and discard the intelligence of the intelligent." So where does this leave the philosophers, the scholars, and the world's brilliant debaters? God has made the wisdom of this world look foolish. Since God in his wisdom saw to it that the world would never know him through human wisdom, he has used our foolish preaching to save those who believe.[94]

I am enthralled with scholarship and have spent my life in pursuit of knowledge endeavoring to follow the evidence. My conclusion, provisionary of course, is that intellectual pursuits without a suitable starting point are fool's errands. If you start with something, the universe, for example, and say it sprang from nothing, then everything you build on that premise will crumble. This is because you have no viable starting point to build on except, "I don't know." If you posit some order, some mind that

------

[94] 1 Cor 1:18-21.

has created enough order to do science itself, and that mind is not a person, you have gotten yourself into a philosophical pickle. You find yourself advocating an unscientific theory that itself denies any principle of science. If you have no material, no mind, no person, no guiding force with design, you have a faith-based position with less evidence than a Pentecostal snake-handling preacher dancing on an altar two miles down a red dirt road.

Historian Mark Noll, who taught at Wheaton College in the mid 1990s when *The Scandal of the Evangelical Mind* was published, seemed to argue that evangelicals needed to integrate themselves into institutions of power and prestige to get a seat at the cultural leaders' table. He also advocated their creating of journals and other serious organs of communication in the academic societies to stem the tide of secularism and provide a continued presence for the Gospel. The purpose was missional. If we are to be salt and light and fulfill our mission regarding the Gospel, we need to be taken seriously by cultural leaders. "On the one hand there is enormous growth of the Church, and on the other its almost complete lack of influence."[95] That is a worthy goal, but I must fast forward to a world that has changed far faster and in even more dastardly ways than he feared.

There is an absolute frenzy in popular culture, which has now become the controlling narrative in American life, to purify and strip the culture of political incorrectness. It is Orwell's *1984* where Big Brother controls what you read, say, and think. A surveillance society is created with new technologies. If you conform, you

---

[95] John C. Green, "The Fifth National Survey of Religion and Politics: A Baseline for the 2008 Presidential Election." Ray C. Bliss Institute of Applied Politics, University of Akron, 29 September 2008. https://www.uakron.edu/bliss/research/archives/2008/Fifth_National_Survey_Religion_Politics.pdf.

will be miserable at first, but you will grow accustomed to soft totalitarianism which will be followed by hard core control and punishments. You will be cancelled, stripped of certain careers, privileges, and societies, and money-making opportunities will be denied you. This will not be done by the government. Orwell envisions that private industry more powerful than government will do the dirty work. The government will stand by and let it happen. Or worse, they will collude with media companies to censor "misinformation" and then lie about it. In exchange, big tech, big entertainment, and big corporations will fund the feckless politicians who will look the other way.

While Orwell's vision of dystopia involved tight controls, Aldous Huxley's *Brave New Word* feared not the burning of books, such as *Dr. Suess*, or the removal of Uncle Ben's rice and Aunt Jemima's pancake syrup from store shelves.[96] It feared a society transformed from facts, news, and responsible journalism to one of all communication becoming entertainment.[97]

Evangelicals have lost the culture war, and we have been out discipled by the advocates of progressivism. In 2011, Carl R.

---

[96] Dr. Seuss is a series of children's books. Aunt Jemima and Uncle Ben are food products that present Black stereotypes in the brand logo. Pressure from advocate groups caused the companies to change their branding. Robert Hart, "Six Dr. Seuss Books Won't Be Published Due to 'Hurtful and Wrong' Racist Images," *Forbes*, 2 March 2021, https://www.forbes.com/sites/roberthart/2021/03/02/six-dr-seuss-books-wont-be-published-due-to-hurtful-and-wrong-racist-images/?sh=602ef2966e34; Annie Gasparro and Michah Maidenberg, "Aunt Jemimah and Uncle Ben's Rooted in Racist Imagery to Change," *The Wall Street Journal*, 17 June 2020, https://www.wsj.com/articles/pepsico-unit-to-retire-aunt-jemima-brand-citing-origins-in-racist-stereotype-11592398455.
[97] Aldous Huxley, *Brave New World*, (London: Chatto & Windus, 1932), 161.

Trueman proposed that the actual scandal is not that there is no mind but rather that there is no evangelical because evangelicalism has no well-defined theology and, therefore, no clear understanding of the Gospel.[98] In other words, the entire discussion concerning the evangelical mind is impossible because an evangelical is more of a way of thinking than a group with agreed-upon doctrine.

More importantly, evangelicals do not have an agreed-upon ecclesiology like Lutherans, Anglicans, Catholics, Presbyterians, and the Eastern Orthodox Church. Each subset of the evangelical community holds to different versions of church purpose, polity, and authority. There is no one to keep them in line except for individual congregations, book publishers, conference planners, and Christian music companies. In my opinion, this could explain the reason that theological capitulation has been so easy for the movement and its falling apart as a definable entity.

There is some truth to the latter premise, but "evangelical" has become a convenient term to gather around for people who are Christ centered, who believe the Bible to be authoritative, who hold to the idea that conversion is a needed event or process, and who believe that all Christians are to be a part of Christ's mission to make disciples. But evangelicals got tangled up in partisan politics starting in the 1980s. Now many younger evangelicals want to disassociate themselves from the movement and declare themselves "not guilty" of its sins of secularizing the church's mission and worshipping at the altar of prestige and power.

However, after saying all of this, the facts remain the same. The progressive train has left the station bound for utopia, and most

---

[98] Carl R. Trueman, *The Real Scandal of the Evangelical Mind*, (Chicago: Moody Publishers, 2011), 110.

evangelicals are not on board. This is partially evangelicals' own fault. What Noll wrote and part of what Luo claimed is true. The church has opted out of the academy as a primary strategy for world evangelization. Even Bonhoeffer made the mistake of thinking an intellectual elite, a spiritual nobility, could save Germany or at least rebuild it after the war.[99]

Yes, the church must engage with the intellectual elite. Yes, it will take a hundred years to turn it around. But it is a long slow process that will yield great fruit in the long run. Its importance is that what your philosopher says that is laughable today is eventually believed by the cogitative elite who run the nation in as little as two generations. This elite controls the levers and pathways of communication to the general populace. When this idea the philosopher had many years ago becomes accepted at the street level, it becomes plausible and something people accept without challenge. For example, review the history of the definition of sexual morality or the definition of marriage. What if scholars with a biblical worldview would have had the necessary standing among the intellectual elite to knock down such erroneous philosophy years ago?

At the same time, the overall strategy for the fulfillment of the Great Commission must be multi-faceted and aimed at all levels of society. Jesus, for example, wired around the elite by working with and preaching to the average person. The power brokers in the religious and political worlds eventually heard of and encountered him.

The first century church was populated with some of history's sharpest intellects, such as the apostle Paul, but the church was

[99] Charles Marsh, *Strange Glory: A Life of Dietrich Bonhoeffer*, (New York: Alfred A. Knopf, 2014), 278.

not in power and was persecuted regularly for three hundred years by those who were in power.[100] What put Christians into a position of prominence in the Greco-Roman world was not strategy. It was spiritual power that cannot be accounted for by IQ or cultural acceptance among the ruling elites.

Whatever mind has been given to you, love God with all your mind.[101] If you are elite in your mental abilities, then your mission should be to the academic world. Intellectuals matter. They shape the minds of those who become leaders in every facet of society. If you have other loves such as business, arts, sports, or mechanics, then love God with all you've got in those fields. Start companies and movements to compete with big tech, corporate America, and the media and entertainment elite. The wasting of the evangelical mind would be to allow those who do not have the mind of Christ to set the ground rules, remain the gate keepers, and control the narrative of what is true or false, good or bad, ugly or beautiful. Do not waste the mind God has given you. Put it to work and put aside the advice of those who minds are blinded to God's truth.

---

[100] Paul was student of the well-known Jewish scholar and Pharisee Gamaliel. The latter appears appears in Acts Chapter 5 as a defender of logic and reason regarding how the Jewish leadership should handle the success of the early church. Paul studied with Gamaliel for an unknown length of time in his youth. He mentions that he grew up in Jerusalem and later moved to Tarus (Acts 5:33-40, 22:3).

[101] Matt 22:36-40.

Hath God Said?

*"The least dramatic place on earth was the Garden of Eden.
Then Eve met the Serpent, and the rest is history."* [102]

Michael Walsh

"Now the serpent was more subtle than any beast of the field which the Lord God had made. And he said unto the woman, 'Yea, hath God said, ye shall not eat of every tree of the garden?" (Gen 3:1)

Then the discussion ensued, and the woman gave the party line: "God told us we could eat of every tree but the one tree, if we eat of that tree we will die." The serpent had a comeback.

"No, you won't! Come on now. Are you sure that is what he meant? He doesn't want you eating from that tree because then you will know what he knows. And if that happens, you will be a god like him, and then he will no longer be your God" (Gen 3:2-4, paraphrased).

---

[102] Michael Walsh, *The Devil's Pleasure Palace: The Cult of Critical Theory and the Subversion of the West* (London: Encounter Books, 2015), 17.

"And when the woman saw that the tree was good for food, and that it was pleasant to the eyes, and a tree to be desired to make one wise, she took the fruit thereof, and did eat, and gave also unto her husband with her; and he did eat" (Gen 3:4, KJV).

"What's for dinner?" Adam asked. Eve winked and said, "I've got something special tonight, Honey. Fruit." Adam partook, and the rest is history." [103]

Adam and Eve's original sin was reaching for the Godhead. That of course is what makes us human. Two people who had it made living in an actual utopia were enticed to give it up for the allure of another utopia.

That is exactly what is being offered to the American public right now: a Marxist utopia, a world free of racism, hate, and corruption where you get peace, justice, and equality. That is what is promised, but it is not what has been or will be delivered. People who are disgusted by injustice are being sold a utopian dream that will crash down around their ears like Adam and Eve's expulsion from the Garden of Eden into a world that became a dystopian nightmare. [104]

Socialism has never worked. It will never work. It cannot work because it violates human nature, and one thing that has not changed since creation until now is human nature. Humans are selfish and ambitious, but they also have a sense of fairness and

---

[103] Dialogue based on Gen 3:1-7, KJV.
[104] Gen 3:7-24.

equality. They are insistent that they deserve what they work for and do not like being forced to share what they have earned with someone else.[105]

We creatures who have been endowed with free will and who are superior to the angels long for peace, but because of our desire to get ahead, we choose to be fallen with the ensuing drama and conflict inherent with it. We are sinners. Our natural state is not peace but conflict and war. We are at war with ourselves and others.[106] However, we long for redemption, so we seek a way out in hope of finding a better life.

The Marxist promise of socialism is not a solution and is anti-human. There is no chance of redemption. It is nihilism, which literally means "nothing." "Utopian" literally means "nowhere." Nothing and nowhere—that is why it is satanic. There is no redemption in it. But Marxism is rarely presented as such. It is normally espoused as equality of result where everyone shares the goods and services that laborers produce. The goal is a stateless society where sharing is primary. The rich share with the poor, and the poor are lifted out of poverty by the redistribution of wealth.

This has never worked because Karl Marx's thinking along with Friedrich Engel's theory of economics created a monstrous

---

[105] Some obvious examples of socialism's failures include Cuba, Venezuela, the Soviet Union, the Berlin Wall, and the prison camps in North Korea. The prosperity of the democratic republic of South Korea stands in great contrast to poverty-stricken Communist North Korea. Historically, there has been a trend of citizens feeling to America from nations ruined by Marxism, but hardly a soul wishes to leave the United States. Some Christians buy into socialism in the name of the Bible's admonitions to help the poor, but, in Scripture, benevolence was handled privately through the church, never through the government.
[106] Matt 10:17-25; Rom 7:14-25; Eph 6:12.

system where productive human beings have their wealth taken from them by the state and given to those who do not work.[107] The highly productive members of society resist the system and always find themselves cancelled, imprisoned, or killed. Then people flee the country or region only to be captured, imprisoned, or executed. If anyone attempts to write or speak against the power structure, they are silenced.

This, of course, is what is happening at this very moment in the United States. Anyone on a major communications platform who, in the government's opinion, says anything that is "misinformation," will be silenced. President Biden himself has accused any company or person who speaks "misinformation" about Covid 19 of "killing people."[108] Speech becomes violence and murder, and a federal court with powerful prosecutors can throw you in prison. Behind this very dangerous belief system is Karl Marx.

Naïve evangelicals need to drill into our heads that the truth does not matter to our enemies. Jesus said that you are either for him or against him. Jesus is committed to the truth for it is the only thing that sets us free.[109] The truth does not matter in public debate with those whose purpose is to defame and destroy the Christian faith. The goal of the radical left is to advance Marxist socialism under the banner of social justice. Most of its advocates

---

[107] For further information on the socialist economic philosophies of Marx and Engle see Karl Marx & Frederick Engels, *Collected Works: Vol. 48* (New York: International Publishers, 1974-2004).

[108] Matt Viser, Rachel Lerman, and Tyler Pager, "They're Killing People:' Biden Aims Blistering Attack at Tech Companies Over Vaccine Falsehoods." *The Washington Post*, 16 July 2021, https://www.washingtonpost.com/politics/biden-vaccine-social-media/2021/07/16/fbc434bc-e666-11eb-8aa5-5662858b696e_story.html.

[109] John 8:32.

are simply pawns, but their leaders intend to lead an insurrection to divide and conqueror Americans and discredit the church and make it irrelevant. They want the entire culture to follow the serpent and ask, "Hath God said?" When Americans see the U.S. flag, they want people to think the same thing they think when they see a Confederate flag: "America is a bad country and a bad place. Let's totally change it." This is why the National Football League agreed to play a second "National Anthem" before games in 2021.[110]

The left's Long March through the academy in the United States is rooted in Marxism and Critical Theory, a Pandora's box that has released swarms of thought demons into the American mind. Those demons have now found a home in religion, culture, and politics. British Theologian James Lesslie Newbigin had this to say about Critical Theory. The critical principle claims that all truth claims must be subjected to critical examination. Of course, this is where the real issue arises because the critical faculty can only operate on the basis of beliefs which are held uncritically. When someone criticizes a proposition, one has always to ask, what are the assumptions which are not criticized when that critical move is made. If you examine the critical statements that are made, they are made on the basis of what everyone assumes to be true.[111]

---

[110] "ArLuther Lee, "NFL to Play Black National Anthem at All League Games in 2021." *The Atlanta Journal-Constitution*, 16 July 2021, https://www.ajc.com/news/nfl-to-play-black-national-anthem-at-all-league-games-in-2021/2UJEBV5NLBBF3DO3QDKPEJXYPU/; Leandra Bernstein, "Reported NFL Decision to Play Black National Anthem Before Games Faces Pushback." *ABC13 News*, 2 August 2021. https://wset.com/news/nation-world/nfl-decision-to-play-black-national-anthem-before-gaes-faces-pushback.

[111] Lesslie Newbigin, "Nihilism," https://www.youtube.com/watch?v=5WyrC-7JVd5Q

Critical Theory advocates would say that divine revelation is not real knowledge and therefore is to be rejected. However, these same people would claim to know their spouses, children, and friends, even though such knowledge is subjective and would not stand up against Critical Theory itself. To remain true to Critical Theory, knowledge of these persons would also need to be rejected. But most would not admit to that.

Another assumption of the Critical Theory is that doubt is superior to belief even though all thoughts begin with belief, not doubt. One can only doubt what one has already believed. If we doubt everything, we will never know anything. It is impossible to begin by doubting. Doubt has its place but only as secondary to belief. Faith is primary; doubt is secondary. The Critical Theory will eventually destroy itself because in the end it advocates the destruction of all society that is built on faith, belief, and the transcendent—all the things that make life worth living. Newbigin tells a story that helps us here:

> I remember a friend telling me that he'd been on a plane with someone with whom he got into conversation. At the end of the conversation, the other man said, "Well, of one thing I'm certain, there is no such thing as absolute truth." My friend said, "Are you absolutely sure?" . . . It is of course logically absurd.[112]

The best-known figure in the development of the Critical Theory and contemporary nihilism is Friedrich Nietzsche. He saw European thought as moving to a point where it would be impossible to say of anything that it is true or false or good or bad. All you have is the will to power, and the future lies with the Ubermensch, the superman. Those who control history are those brave or cynical enough to exercise their will.

---

[112] Ibid.

Nietzsche did sound a warning. He doubted that the basis for basic morality would disappear once society discarded divine revelation and the religious foundation of Western civilization. He worried whether humans would be able to construct a new morality without a moral foundation. He said that God is dead and there is not enough water to wash the blood off our hands.[113]

That is exactly where we find ourselves right now in America. Radicals, leftists, and anarchists want to burn down the foundations of America—its morals and religion. They want to take down its statues, blow up Mount Rushmore, erase the country's history, and stand in triumph on the rubble. Just like Satan, they destroy without offering a better solution. The serpent told Eve she would become like God when she took a bite from the forbidden fruit, but what she got was alienation from God, expulsion from paradise, a murderous son, and a dead son.[114]

Any utopian worth his salt will promise peace and love, but what he delivers instead is dystopia and piles of corpses: one hundred million plus in the twentieth century. China's Cultural Revolution, the former Soviet Union, the repression and tyranny of communism that continues today in China, Cuba, and Venezuela—these are always one assassination away from "utopia," meaning they believe it just takes ridding themselves of a leader who is in the way of achieving their goals. They are willing to commit a crime to advance their "holy" cause. It all starts with that phrase, "Hath God said?"

---

[113] Friedrich Nietzsche's most complete work on the "God is Dead" theory can be found in *The Gay Science* which he first published in 1882 followed by a second edition in 1887.
[114] Gen 3-5.

Order and Chaos

Let us not be afraid of the fact that the Church is different from the world, that the reality that we celebrate, that we share, that we rejoice in, our worship, is a reality that the world treats as an illusion.[115]

Lesslie Newbigin

Conservative Christians in America are living in moral chaos. There is confusion and disorientation regarding their social surroundings. They are asking, "What kind of country am I living in? Where are we headed? Has the moral order collapsed?" Before the pandemic of 2020, conservative hopes were riding high. A prosperous economy, strong military, and socialism on the run pointed to bright days ahead. Then came the Covid 19 pandemic, the protests and riots, and, of course, Donald Trump's war against big media, big tech, big industry, big sports, and big everything. A scorned and angry left ganged up on him and, in the end, defeated him. Unprecedented division now exists in the nation, and no one knows what is going to happen next. What seemed in great order has now become chaotic.

America is not divided by religion and race. Racial tension is pro-moted as a major crisis, but it is not a crisis. It is a problem. Global climate change is not a crisis; it is a problem. Government spending is an actual crisis. If we do not do something now, nothing else we do will matter. We will no longer be a powerful nation.

---

[115] https://twitter.com/lesslienewbigin/status/1337764429446995971?s=10.

Problems do exist, and they have long-term solutions. Race is a major victory for America. We are the least racial society on earth. We have repented of our sins. We have changed, and it shows. There is the obvious example of the Civil War where six hundred thousand white men died to end slavery. There are numerous examples such as the Civil Rights Act of 1964 and the Freedom of Housing Act of 1965. We have actually gone overboard with the Great Society of Lyndon Johnson in that we helped create a permanent dependent underclass. We have made great strides in addressing climate issues. The United States contributes the most funding in the world for global climate accords. Unfortunately, while we are the least culpable in our practices, countries like China, India, and Russia continue to violate those accords while contributing very little. We are doing better than most nations. Solutions are long-term in nature.

The greatest divide in America is philosophical. It is worldview. It is about moral authority. Around that issue, there is chaos. For example, Donald Trump was not known as a Christian before he ran for president. Some reported that indeed he had become one just before he became president. To many Christians, this seemed a bit convenient. Progressive Christians in particular saw it as a political move. One thing was clear to conservative Christians. Trump seemed to favor a more conservative interpretation of the Bible. He was pro-life. He supported a more traditional view of marriage, and he was a law-and-order advocate. He also supported religious liberty, freedom of speech, and the Second Amendment.[116] The capstone was his appointment of originalist judges to federal courts and three new conservative judges to the United States Supreme Court.

---

[116] The Second Amendment to the United States Constitution states that the government will not infringe upon citizens' rights to keep and bear arms in regard to well regulated militias, considered necessary for the security of a free state.

Our new president, Joseph Biden, is also a religious man. It could be argued that Biden is more spiritual, more consistent, and more faithful to his religion than Trump. While Trump is a bundle of chaos looking for a place to happen. Biden represents, at least in his demeanor, order—a sigh of relief for an emotionally exhausted nation. He and many of his fellow progressive Christians possess and read Bibles. Prior to the pandemic, fewer liberal Christians attended weekly services than conservatives.[117]

President Biden's Bible reading somehow has commanded him to expand abortion rights, even though his church, the Catholic Church, abhors it. His compassion has been saved up for immigrants, even criminals, and his executive orders have been so far left that they defy common sense. His decree that allows transmen to compete against biological women in athletics will ruin women's sports and set back the women's movement by decades. He seems to be a reed blowing in the political winds. We should all prefer that he be guided by inner conviction, and I pray that he will be. We are wondering what is at his core. What seemed calm is actually a storm of radical actions that will exacerbate our differences and create even more chaos and moral confusion.

Philosophically, President Biden is taking the nation in a more systemic Liberation Theology direction. Classic Liberation Theology joins liberal theology with liberal political theory, primarily socialism that reorders society. It is another utopian ideology that denies actual reality and human nature in general and always requires authoritarian government to institute it.

This is understandable in that the left has historically dismissed personal sin and focused more on systemic cultural sin. When

---

[117] Jeffrey M. Jones, "U.S. Church Membership Falls Below Majority For First Time." *Gallup*, 29 March 2021. https://news.gallup.com/poll/341963/church-membership-falls-below-majority-first-time.aspx

Dietrich Bonhoeffer attended Union Theological Seminary in New York City for one year in 1930, he did not agree with their liberal deconstructive approach to the biblical text that led to the erosion of biblical authority. Bonhoeffer did not get along with the Lion of the Left, Reinhold Niebuhr. Niebuhr believed that societal sins that led to racism and poverty were the greater sins.[118] He was a brilliant proponent for such a view. His ideas flew in the face of orthodoxy and made him the darling of the secular left. He made fun of Billy Graham which put him on the cover of *Time Magazine*, and he joined Graham and C.S. Lewis as a "cover story."[119] The intellectual elite and ruling class despised fundamentalism and its cornpone spirituality.

The ruling class remains arrogant and superior, both left and right, according to their own words. Many are calling for a deprogramming of people who disagree with them. Again, they have a secular worldview. Worldview is shaped by theology,

[118] Christine Firer Hinz, "The Drama of Social Sin and the (Im)Possibility of Solidarity: Reinhold Niebuhr and Modern Catholic Social Teaching." *Studies in Christian Ethics*, 22.4, (2009), 442-460. https://www.luc.edu/media/lucedu/dccirp/pdfs/articlesforresourc/Article_-_Hinze,_Christine_1.pdf.

[119] C.S. Lewis was a highly respected Anglican layman and a prestigious Oxford University professor. He wrote several fifteen minutes addresses aired on the BBC at their request to present a non-clerical explanation of what it would mean to know God in Christ "Religions: Faith for a Lenten Age." *Time Magazine* VI, No. 10, 8 March 1948. content.time.com/time/subscriber/article/0,33009,853293-1,00.html; content.time.com/time/covers/0,16641,19480308,00.html; "Billy Graham: A New Kind of Evangelist." *Time Magazine* LXIV, No. 17, 25 Oct. 1954, content.time.com/time/subscriber/article/0,33009,823597,00.html, content.time.com/time/magazine/0,9263,7601541025,00.html. "Don v. Devil," *Time Magazine*, 8 September 1947, content.time.com/time/subscriber/article/0,33009,804196,00.html; content.time.com/time/covers/0,16641,19470908,00.html.

religion, and philosophy combined with life experience. The power of snobbery cannot be underestimated. You can forget the Latin, Greek, and art history you studied at your university or left-wing seminary, but being a snob stays with you for life. This was beautifully put by George Orwell:

> When I was fourteen or fifteen, I was an odious little snob, but no worse than the other boys of my own age or class. I suppose there is no place on the world where snobbery is quite as ever present or where it is cultivated in such refined and subtle forms as in the English public school. Here at least one cannot say that English "education" failed to do its job. You forget your Latin and Greek within a few months of leaving school—I studied Greek for eight or ten years, and now at thirty-three, I cannot even repeat the Greek alphabet—but your snobbishness, unless you persistently root it out like the bindweed it is, sticks to you till your grave."[120]

This short history puts the real divide on the table. It is between the interpretation of Scripture which proposes that the Bible is true and has moral authority in a person's life and the view that this ancient book on which our society has been built needs to be reinterpreted and re-applied to American life. A progressive interpretation of the Bible dismisses these key doctrines of the historic Christian faith:

1. Jesus Christ is God incarnate and the only way to heaven.
2. Any sex outside of marriage is immoral and a sin.
3. Hell is a real place where those who reject salvation will spend eternity.

---

[120] George Orwell, *Road to Wigan Pier* (Boston: Mariner Books, HarperCollins, 1936), 128.

4. Ideal marriage is between one man and one woman.
5. God created the world and universe and one day will set up his kingdom from which he will reign.
6. People rather than the physical universe are eternal.

Where are conservative Christians to turn for order while the chaos swirls around us? When Moses went up the mountain to meet with God and was gone for forty days, the people waited under the supervision of Moses' brother Aaron. The people didn't pay much attention to him. Genetics does not necessarily mean that the mantle of power and authority is passed on in a family. When it seemed Moses had been gone a bit too long, what once was order turned to chaos. The people's sentiment was summarized as "Come on, make us some gods who can lead us. We don't know what happened to this fellow Moses who brought us here from the land of Egypt."[121]

Moses would have gone into his tent to seek the Lord, but Aaron said, "Take the gold rings from the ears of your wives and sons and daughters and bring them to me." Then Aaron melted the gold and made the golden calf. When the people saw it, they exclaimed, "O Israel, these are the gods who brought you out of the land of Egypt." Aaron then announced that day there would be a festival the next day with feasting and drinking that would please their lord.[122] Obviously, Aaron was a political pawn, not a leader, and certainly not a brother who could be trusted with power. He melted like butter.

Meanwhile on the mountain, God told Moses to quickly get down the hill. He described the problem and entreated Moses to step back while he destroyed the lot. Moses tried to pacify the Lord by

---

[121] Exod 32:1.
[122] Exod 32:2-5.

taking up the people's cause and asking for mercy. "So the Lord changed his mind."[123] This is the kind of leadership that is needed. That leader broke up the party and restored order.

When Moses saw what God told him about, Moses burned with anger and smashed the tablets God had given him which contained the Ten Commandments. He took the golden calf and ground it into powder, threw the dust in the water, and made the people drink it. He did not stop there. He had the Levites go through the camp and slay even their loved ones until three thousand were dead.[124] A bit strong for modern sensibilities, but order was restored. Without that, there was no going forward in any meaningful way. Restored order finally came through the law of God found on those smashed tablets, historically known as the Ten Commandments. They hang today in the Supreme Court of the United States and form the basic morality of Western civilization. When a society breaks them, leaves them behind, and starts indulging their pleasures via their own gods, chaos results. Christians, here is what to do:

- Read, study, memorize, and mediate on Scripture. It will provide stability, focus and a comforting reminder that God is knowledgeable and in ultimate control. This fact does not ensure that life will be less difficult or without tragedy. But it will provide the required knowledge and hope necessary to move forward with courage.
- Find purpose and mission. The Bible tells us that God has a purpose and plan for each human life and directs us as to how to discover that plan. Passages such as Ephesians 2:10 say that we are the work of God's hands, his masterpiece, created to do good works as a result of

---

[123] Exod 32:7-14.
[124] Exod 32:19-28.

salvation. That mission in general is to be a disciple and to make new disciples who also reproduce. This is the assignment until Jesus returns (Matt 28:18-20).

- Connect with a group of believers and live in community with them (Heb 10:25). Hopefully you will find a community of like-minded individuals who live by covenant. That means you have leaders, rules, discipline, and order.

How We Got
What We Have

In 410, Saint Augustine received news that his beloved Rome had fallen to the barbarians. He was shaken and went into a period of mourning. But almost immediately he was constrained to construct a philosophical and theological ark—what we call orthodoxy—wherein his church could survive the days ahead. He went to work on his massive theological masterpiece *The City of God*—a work that occupied him for seventeen years. It is a great treatise on what man owes to God and what man owes to Caesar.

Augustine was a great scholar and professor of rhetoric, eventually ascending to the University of Milan in Italy where he came under the influence of the great Bishop Ambrose and began to study the Scriptures. His conversion took place in a garden in Milan. As he sat in the garden, he heard the singsong of a child in a nearby home: "Take it and read it; take it and read it." So he opened his copy of the Gospels to Saint Paul's Epistle to the Romans and read, "Not in revelry and drunkenness, not in lewdness and lust, not in strife or envy, but put on the Lord Jesus Christ, and make no provision for the flesh, to fulfill its lusts"[125]

Augustine became disillusioned calling his position at the University the "Chair of Lies." Very much like our present conditions, he found himself, as revealed in his *Confessions*, addicted to luxury, violence, and self-indulgence. Augustine was

---

[125] Rom 13:13-14, NKJV.

particularly addicted to sexual pleasure, which, he concluded, offered a fraudulent ecstasy—joys that expire when the neon lights go out.

He returned to North Africa to pursue a new career. He planned a private monastic life with a few close friends, but his gifts were too great, his reputation too big, and the need for his leadership too precious for a cloistered life. He went to Hippo because they already had a bishop, but the church there snapped him up and made him a priest and then their bishop by the age of forty-three.

Augustine's city is set against Rome, the City of Man. The city he loved was flawed, and it fell. The City of God, however, would never fail or fall. He wrote: "The Heavenly City outshines Rome, beyond comparison. There, instead of victory, is truth; instead of high rank, holiness; instead of peace, felicity [state of well-being] instead of life, eternity"[126]

The City of God was written to counteract the accusation among disappointed Romans in 410 that Christians and their theology of non-violence had been responsible for the fall of their country. Rome had ruled for one thousand years, and now their walls had been breached and their once great kingdom had been broken up. The Mediterranean Sea was no longer a Roman pond. Many Romans blamed the abandoning of the traditional gods and goddesses. Augustine answered with an alternative worldview and also gave Christians a vision for the future—as said before, an ark to get the church through an uncertain period.

Augustine once called his "Chair of Rhetoric" a "Chair of Lies." It is demonstratively true that we now live in an Empire of Lies. How do we get through?

---

[126] Malcolm Muggeridge, *A Third Testament* (New York: Orbis Books, 1976), xii.

The Shift and Decline of Moral Authority

Moral authority is what an African American has in any discussion with a white person regarding race. The poetic truth erases the distinction between fact and narrative. A poetic truth is something that might as well be true for the sake of narrative coherence, regardless of whether or not it is actually true to the facts. For example, the facts say that nineteen Black people were shot by white police officers in 2020. Poetic truth is that Black men are being hunted by white cops. Racist officers do exist, but it is not true that most cops are racist. But then again, what makes a racist is unclear. It is normally defined by a Black person's opinion based on lived experience, which is a moving target, subjective, and almost impossible to define.

To my point, a Black person can make all kinds of statements that people from the white or oppressor race cannot make. The white oppressor is considered guilty and has no authority to speak. The best example I have seen lately is a young Black activist with some conservative views who was debating a white ruling class elite from a popular magazine. The young Black defended some very conversative views, and the white ruling class progressive was helpless to debate him because of the massive white guilt that weighed him down and kept his mouth shut. He did not think he had the moral authority to speak and thus he kept quiet. The Black man possessed a moral innocence coming from a historically oppressed race. This is normal operating procedure today. The public narrative conflates the pre-1960s racial policies with what is actually true today. But how did we get to the point of poetic truth replacing historical fact or even current research?

The National Hypocrisy

Five movements birthed in the 1960s revealed a good nation's hypocrisy. Our Declaration of Independence and Constitution were and remain aspirational. Our grand experiment as a nation with the people governing themselves had created the greatest society on earth, but we fell short, and the 1960s exploded around our shortcomings. The movements below represent the pathways that solved some problems, disrupted the national calm, and divided us philosophically.

1. The Civil rights movement
2. The Vietnam War
3. Women's movement
4. Sexual revolution
5. Environmental movement

The entire culture became aware of our hypocrisy in 1968. Shelby Steele put it this way. "Has there ever been a single year in all of American history in which the American way of life came so thoroughly under siege? It was hard for anyone to go into that year and come out the same person."[127]

In general, each of these movements exposed a hypocrisy, an issue where America needed reform. Movement leaders wanted the American people as well as the government to say "Yes, your grievance against America is legitimate, and it deserves to be taken seriously and resolved."

The Civil rights movement led the way. The problem was clear, easy to define, and the government could act, as it did, with the 1964

---

[127] Shelby Steele is an African American Senior Fellow at the Hoover Institute at Stanford University—a largely white elitist home for conservative scholars. In the late 1960s and early '70s he and his wife traveled to Algeria to get to know the Black Panthers. At that time, he was a classic 1960s liberal and civil right activist. Shelby Steele, *Shame: How America's Past Sins Have Polarized Our Country*, (Philadelphia: Basic Books, 2015), 81.

Civil Rights Act which made discrimination based on race illegal. The women's movement, the anti-war movement, and the sexual revolution all won the day in the face of American hypocrisy. By 1968, there was no longer legitimate support for racial oppression, sexism, and arrogance of power abroad with Vietnam. All the major institutions had failed to uphold their moral positions The nation was in moral crisis and the moral authority of the culture began to shift. It became more honorable to resist the rule of law than to submit to it. This led to the collapse of authority. In 1968, young adults questioned everything: their parents, their college, marriage, the military draft, sexual mores, and especially their religion. Rebellion made one authentic, somehow giving a person moral authority to speak truth to power.

1960s -2021

Having lived through this period from a college student to senior citizen, from a non-Christian to a serious and seasoned saint, I wonder what kind of ark Augustine would build now. I would say he would recommend, like Archimedes, a place for us to stand.[128] The shift in moral authority from a biblical worldview to the wide deconstruction of truth has created moral chaos. This train to destruction at first looks like Cat Stevens' "Love Train" but ends up being moral confusion barreling toward an abyss. The church salt has lost its savor because the contemporary church cannot capitulate fast enough to avoid being cancelled by the surrounding culture.

I would not have predicted the culture could fall apart as fast as it has in the last decades. At first, political correctness was something to ridicule. It provided a good laugh: micro aggressions on the college campus, safe zones, gender neutral bathrooms, suppression of free

---

[128] Archimedes was a famous mathematician and inventor in Ancient Greece circa 287 BCE.

speech, the harassing of and outright persecution of a conservative point of view. But the college campus has now become the general culture. Cancel culture, political correctness, suppression of speech from the university to big tech to big industry and big media—it is unworkable. There will eventually be a backlash because such suppression has never worked. But that does not mean it won't be tried for seventy to one hundred years or more. So where is our ark when we need it?

It is right here as it always has been: read the Bible, believe it, and obey it. I recently read about a group of Christians in India whose homes were surrounded by Hindu zealots. They came with torches and threatened to burn down the homes with the families inside. The Christians' response was, "Burn our homes with us in them, but we won't stop proclaiming Christ."

Our culture right now is about revenge and cancelling those with whom we disagree. But Christ taught us something else. He died by the hand of his enemies and asked God to forgive them because they did not know what they were doing.[129] As one of my favorite pastors said, "Jesus died for our enemies. He is only asking us to love them." Augustine's ark then is ours now. We believe not in the City of Man but in the City of God. And those who reside in that City of God are those who say, "We cannot stop talking about what we have seen and heard."[130]

---

[129] Luke 23:24.
[130] Acts 4:20.

The Church's
Secular Affair

"It is in the context of secular affairs that the mighty power released into the world through the work of Christ is to be manifested."[131]

Lesslie Newbigin

When two people love each other, it matters not if they are co-dependent drug addicts or the pastor of First Baptist Church and his wife. It is all God's love. Abraham Kuyper, prime minister of The Netherlands from 1901-1905, said it well: "There is not a square inch in the whole domain of our human existence over which Christ who is Sovereign over all, does not cry, 'Mine!'"[132]

God is love. He created love. When flawed humans experience it, it comes from him. That does not mean those people are Christian or that they are living in a way that pleases God. However, it does mean that the common grace of God and the specific graces of God run together in everyday life like syrup runs over and saturates pancakes. Join this idea with Newbigin's statement, and

---

[131] Lesslie Newbigin, *The Gospel in a Pluralist Culture* (Grand Rapids: Wm. B. Eerdmans, 1989), 230.

[132] Roger Henderson, "Kuyper's Inch." *Pro Rege* 36, No. 3, (March 2008), 12-14, 12. https://digitalcollections.dordt.edu/cgi/viewcontent.cgi?article=1380&context=pro_rege

it is clear that the church's task is to deliver its product of love to the people of the world through secular sectors of society. If it does not get to the secular sectors, then something is wrong with the church's delivery system.

Love has been sentimentalized. Like the romantic age overreacted to the age of reason, the power and practicality of love has been lost. "God so loved the world that he . . . "[133] "That he" means he did more than feel it, think it, ponder it, sing about it, or write a poem about it. He "gave his only son." The idea that God has a son, whatever that means, and that he gave him may or may not appeal to the secular mind. One could oppose such an idea with the retort, "It is not that impressive that an eternal, all-powerful God gave his only son if he knew in advance that his son would raise again and reign forever with all creation worshipping him. It would be much more impressive that a human father with limited knowledge and the frailty and doubt that comes with it would give his only son who would be executed with no resurrection and no second chance."

This alternative scenario played out in story of Abraham's willingness to sacrifice Isaac—a story that skeptics have excoriated for centuries.[134] It trashes their humanly resourced sensibilities. It would take conversion, the illumination of the Holy Spirit, and a new capacity to appreciate the mystery of God's action. This is the point: love is action and sentiment without action is empty. [135] The question on the table is how does the church, right now and right here, love the world? How do we deliver our product to secular society? Do we begin by making peace? If you do not see the problem, you may have already capitulated.

---

[133] John 3:16.
[134] Gen 22:1-19.
[135] 1 Cor 2:12-16; Eph 3:10-22; 1 John 2:11-17.

There is a line of thought among Christians that we should back up and make peace with the other side. Everyone acknowledges there is another side and that we have an enemy. The tricky part is the proper identification of the enemy. There is wide agreement that almost everyone is anti-Satan or Lucifer. But think about it this way: if we, as Newbigin says, are to deliver the work of Christ, his love, and subsequent transformed human beings to the world through secular affairs, institutions, and structures, how might the enemy come to us? Who is trying to shut up the church right now? Who is conducting the new Salem Witch Trials? Who wants to cleanse America of biblical Christianity and its followers? Who hates us?

No one can hate on conservative Christians like enlightened liberal Christians who have sold out to the political left. Sure they can accuse us of the same, but that does not make it true. I can only speak for myself. I do not in any way want to cancel, shut up, punish, or curtail the left's right to say and do whatever they want. In fact, I would defend their right with all my might. I would like it if they would not rewrite the First Amendment and punish us for disagreement. I do not want unity if I must join them. I do not want unity if I must agree with the state that I have six fingers on my left hand.

There comes a time when sane nations go through temporary periods of insanity. This is one of those times in America. The argument goes something like this: the peril of the moment justifies amending or suspending the Constitution to cleanse our nation of dangerous subversives. These subversives disagree with the bi-coastal elites who control the levers of power.

This has been, is, and always will be a totalitarian argument—the excuse to destroy institutions that protect people who are not in power.[136] The problem with such thinking is that one day those in power will be out of power. Alas, while in power, they destroyed the institutions that could protect them and when they find themselves out of power, there is no one to save them. This happened to many tyrants: Pol Pot, Benito Mussolini, and, of course, General Manuel Noriega of Panama. How do you take power away from people without taking their guns or using your guns? You silence them, cancel them. You punish them. You make it difficult for them to find work, publish their writing, appear on television, or use the internet.

This is the spiral of silence that is now descending on our nation and is coming soon to a church near you. Ryan T. Anderson's work, *When Harry Became Sally*, was pulled by Amazon.[137] One may agree or disagree with the book. Historically, this has not been the point in publishing and free expression. But now, obviously powerful people who disagree have censored the book.

One might argue that Amazon is a private company giving them the right to take such action. Correct. But if Amazon continues such totalitarian practices, it will not be long before they will not be a single company. They will be broken up into several divisions under governmental control. This will happen when they cancel one too many people who have more power than they do.

It used to be fantasy to think of Orwell's *1984* as reality. A surveillance culture in the United States was unthinkable. But it

---

[136] "Statement on Amazon's Removal of *When Harry Became Sally* Updated with Amazon's Response." *Ncac.org*. 16 March 2021. https://ncac.org/news/amazon-book-removal.

[137] Drew Harwell and Craig Timberg, "How America's Surveillance Networks Helped the FBI Catch the Capitol Mob." *The Washington Post*, 2 April 2021. https://www.washingtonpost.com/technology/2021/04/02/capitol-siege-arrests-technology-fbi-privacy/.

is now possible and is already in process. The genius and power of the internet makes it possible for the government to ask The Bank of America to run a check on all its credit card users to analyze the behavior of its customers regarding travel to and from Washington D.C. during the attack on the Capitol building on January 6, 2021. By law, this requires a warrant issued by a court, but in this case, the peril to the nation was so great, an exception was made.

It is not enough for the FBI to hunt down and arrest those who actually broke the law. Everyone associated with the rally, march, or conservative political views was scrutinized. Why? Because they disagree with the ruling class left. It is rationalized that their civil rights of freedom of speech and the right to assemble and petition the government for grievances need to be suspended to facilitate a national cleansing of disagreement. This civil rights suspension does not apply to those who agree with those in power. As long as you are willing to agree that you have six fingers on your left hand, then you are not in danger.

Instead of shutting up, it might be the time for the church to stand up and say, "Mr. Gorbachev, tear down this wall." [138] If any group should declare itself free from soft totalitarianism, it is the church. The glory of churches meeting unmasked in crowded sanctuaries is not that it is safe or a model of public hygiene. It is because they can choose it and can do it. It says something. "We are a free society, separate from the state, and if we choose to endanger ourselves, and our families, that is out business, not yours." Personally, I do not choose that particular form of free speech or truth telling, but I admire the courage and faith

---

[138] "President Reagan Challenges Gorbachev to 'Tear Down This Wall,'" *History.com*. https://www.history.com/this-day-in-history/reagan-chal-lenges-gorbachev-to-tear-down-the-berlin-wall

of those who do. Of course, skeptics can call it stupid, selfish, and not Christian, but skeptics know little about things Christian, faith, and courage. The entire country is fast becoming a "safety first" society. The United States of America did not become great by playing it safe. When we start doing so, we become easy prey for the predatory powers who will take us down at their first opportunity. We are fast becoming weak, flabby, fearful, and so preoccupied with political correctness, that we are destroying the very foundations of liberty and freedom.

In the face of all this is Jesus, the way, the truth, and the life.[139] It remains a fallacy that you can both appease those in power and speak truth to power. Power is fleeting and shifts from country to country, party to party, and person to person, except in the case of the power of Christ mentioned by Newbigin at the top of this article. Paul said, "For I am not ashamed of the gospel, for it is the power of God for salvation to everyone who believes, to the Jew first and the Greek."[140] In other words, it is the power of God to change a person's life. This is it—the power above all other powers. Paul prayed for us that we would get it.

> I also pray that you will understand the incredible greatness of God's power for us who believe him. This is the same mighty power that raised Christ from the dead and seated him in the place of honor at God's right hand in the heavenly realms. Now he is far above any ruler or authority or power or leader or anything else—not only in this world but also in the world to come. God has put all things under the authority of Christ and has made him head over all things for the benefit of the church. And the church is his body; it is made full and complete by Christ who fills all things everywhere with himself.[141]

---

[139] John 14:6.
[140] Rom 1:16, NASB.
[141] Eph 1:19-23.

But this power is not just a religious power separated from the rest of life. It includes all governments and all realms of the universal. It is inclusive of all the kings, armies, and kingdoms of this world. God's power through his church cannot be separated from other things, no matter how hard the church and the other powers of the world work to make it so. Our role is to be salt and light.[142] The salt slows the decay of culture, and the light illuminates the moral darkness that often includes the church itself. Political parties themselves are, at best, pockets of self-interest. Their hold on power is human, limited, and ultimately a fool's errand because God's truth and justice will decide in the end.

And I saw a great white throne and the one sitting on it. The earth and the sky fled from his presence, but they found no place to hide. I saw the dead, both great and small, standing before God's throne. And the books were opened, including the Book of Life. And the dead were judged according to what they had done, as recorded in the books. The sea gave up its dead, and death and the grave gave up their dead. And all were judged according to their deeds. Then death and the grave were thrown into the lake of fire. This lake of fire is the second death. And anyone whose name was not found recorded in the Book of Life was thrown into the lake of fire.[143]

Custodians of truth, the church of Jesus Christ, what dead gospel are we preaching that allows us to shut up about this? So much for a pristine Gospel that is separated from the actual lives we live. Stand up. Speak up. God will take care of the rest.

---

[142] Matt 5:16-17.
[143] Rev 20:11-15.

Justification of Sin, Not the Sinner

Most Christians do not knowingly begin their day by thinking of Reformation theology but revisiting the mind of Martin Luther through the words of Dietrich Bonhoeffer can be illuminating and possibly change our thoughts and behavior. Take, for example, the Bonhoeffer statement regarding Luther's reason for leaving the life of an Augustinian Monk.

> Luther's reason for leaving the monastery was not justification of the sin, but justification of the sinner. Costly grace was given as a gift to Luther. It was grace, because it was water onto thirsty land, comfort for anxiety, liberation from the servitude of a self-chosen path, forgiveness of sins. *The grace was costly because it did not excuse one from works. Instead, it endlessly sharpened the call to discipleship.* But just wherein it was costly, that was wherein it was grace. And where it was grace, that was where it was costly. That was the secret of the Reformation gospel, the secret of the justification of the sinner. [144] [emphasis added]

Bonhoeffer spoke often of justification of the sin rather than the sinner. In his context of the early twentieth century German

---

[144] Dietrich Bonhoeffer, "Discipleship," in *Dietrich Bonhoeffer Works,* Vol. 4, (IMinneapolis: Fortress Press, 2003), 49.

Evangelical Church, [Lutheran], it could be easily identified. Discipleship as Bonhoeffer saw it is daily following a living Christ who is active right now, today, and who will reveal to you his plan for your life.

The German Church was largely about thinking, creeds, and celebrating grand truths of the past in very rigid rituals. The growing pressure in Bonhoeffer's church was what to do about the Jews. An even larger issue arose about whether the church would step up and stand in the breach between the oppressive Nazi ideology and the Jews. Would they be independent of the state? Would they be disciples of Christ or disciples of the Third Reich?

The answer to the question became the failure of the German Church and ultimately the German people. They did not stand up to the government. They gave in to the prevailing cultural mood and opinion. They played it safe and thought they were right not to go to war with those who would make their lives hard. So long as it was the Jews and not them, they were safe. In protest, Bonhoeffer and many others formed their own church, the Confessing Church, which declared its independence from any government and its freedom to preach and live out the Gospel.[145]

The German church made two basic errors. First, they became progressive. They deconstructed both the Bible and traditional interpretations of biblical texts. They left Martin Luther far behind and became the mistress of the Enlightenment, of rationalism, and disciples of Critical Theory. Critical Ttheory was based on

---

[145] "Barmen Declaration," *United Church of Christ*, https://www.ucc. org/beliefs_barmen-declaration/.

German philosopher Georg Hegel's dialectic that saw truth as an evolving entity.[146]

The German church's second error was their abhorrent misapplication of the doctrine of justification by faith alone. They focused on justification by faith as a doctrine, part of a creed, and declared themselves forgiven based on agreement with that doctrine separate from any behavioral result from it. Therefore, they justified their continued sin against the Jews and their lack of obedience in daily life as covered by the great Reformation message of justification by faith.

Even though justification by faith alone has to do with the sinner, not the sin, for the German church it provided cover for sinners to continue to sin. Justification is something that happens to a person who is saved from their sins. It is a legal status applied to a repentant sinner with a new nature now dedicated to discipleship, to one who has begun to follow Christ.[147] This was both the excuse of the German church for not obeying and the reason as well. In other words, their mistake and sins were hidden from them by their theology and culture. Their sins became subtle, benign little sins—little lies, a bit of gossip here, a dash of avoiding needs there. "After all, it's not impacting our lives."

It did impact their lives. Slowly the Nazis dictated everything about the church even to the point of naming its bishop. Churches displayed swastika banners, and fully-robed clergy thrust out their arms in homage to their Fuhrer. The country went to war, six million Jews were exterminated, and by May of 1945, Germany

---

[146] Georg Wilhelm Friedrich Hegel, *The Phenomenology of Spirit*, 1807, https://www.goodreads.com/book/show/9454.Phenomenology_of_Spirit.
[147] Rom 5:1; Eph 4:21-24.

lay in ruins. There was a time early in Hitler's administration that the church had the power to resist, but they did not do so.

The Twenty-First Century American Version or The Sad Result of the Gospel Americana

The German mistake has been repeated again and again but nowhere more successfully than in the United States and other Anglophone countries. We would describe it in theological slang as the separation of salvation into conversion and discipleship. What is meant to be one thing, salvation which includes both conversion and discipleship, is made into a subtle but deadly ideology that makes conversion necessary but discipleship optional. When something is considered optional, it is rarely done. And if done, it is done sporadically because life can go on without it.

Just as the German Church had trouble seeing their sin, we do as well. We too justify the sin, but not the sinner. Larry Alex Taunton aptly describes it:

> Most of the evil committed in this world is of a subtle nature. It's committed by the Kempkas, that is, the many people who aren't the architects of evil. They are just indifferent to it unless it affects them at a personal level. Who are, I wonder, the army of people who don't actually kill babies? They just make the abortion clinics run efficiently. What of the myriad bureaucrats who daily obstruct, ignore, or inflict hardship on the people they are meant to serve? This is evil, subtle, but evil nonetheless. How many of us who have "never intentionally done anybody any harm" turn a blind eye to the poor, the sick, the elderly—those

whom Jesus called "the least of these"? How many of us ignore the larger narrative of evil—the persecution of our Christian brothers and sisters, the wicked curriculums being taught to our children in our public schools, the systematic suppression of dissenting voices—but are quick to note a slight?[148]

This may be what Hannah Arendt meant by the banality of evil that she saw in Adolf Eichmann, the Nazi bureaucrat who made sure the trains ran on time, fully loaded with Jews for their extermination in the camps. Eichmann, as Arendt contended, was not able to think, had little self-awareness, and was not particularly different than most people.[149] He is what the Bible would call a sinner, a person in need of salvation, but he was not endowed or cursed with any peculiar or special dose of evil. This makes us all uncomfortable because we want to assign the worst evil to a special category of lower humanity that we desperately need to dissociate ourselves from in our self-justification and claim of innocence.

As Christians, we do not want to be called names, but we are directly in the line of fire in today's cancel culture. The dissociation desire and claim on innocence is becoming common in both the legitimate church and the "woke" church as demonstrated with statements such as, "Yes, we know that amongst us white Christians there are racists, but not me! I've confessed my sins.

---

[148] Erich Kempka was Adolf Hitler's driver. He chaffered The Fuhrer for several years. His book *I Was Hitler's Chauffeur: The Memoir of Erich Kempka* only speaks of Hitler's good points, delightful habits, and how well he treated people. It makes no mention of Jews, death camps, and World War II. Larry Alex Taunton, "Ravi Zacharias: 'Who Can Know It?'" 21 February 2021. https://larryalextaunton.com/2021/02/ravi-zacharias-who-can-know-it/.

[149] Arendt, *Eichmann in Jerusalem*, Kindle version, n.p.

I've fired all my racist workers. I stopped supporting them, and I've started supporting the right causes. Most white rich people don't care for the poor, but not me! Most men are oppressors, but not me!"

All humans have flaws and hearts capable of great good and heinous evil. The prerequisite for doing evil is birth.[150] We all are guilty not because we have acted it out as much as because we are acting human. The most glorious words that one can hear and words which can provide the most hope are "all have sinned and fall short of God's glory."[151] In his book *People of the Lie*, the late Dr. Scott Peck tells a story of a women who approached him at a cocktail party. She said, "I need some hope, but don't tell me I need years of therapy. Tell me something hopeful like, you are a sinner." She found it hopeful because a sinner can repent; a sinner can change. A sinner is not stuck. A sinner can be redeemed, grow, and be transformed.

Justification by faith alone is not worth the effort to define if it does not describe the saving of a sinner. Using it to justify sin is evil and debilitating to all of us.

---

[150] Rom 5:12-13; Eph 2:1-2.
[151] Rom 3:23.

Roll Over Beethoven

In the 1960s, the Beatles covered Chuck Berry's classic hit, "Roll Over Beethoven." The lyrics are low-brow poetry or at least verse that challenge the elite: "Roll over, Beethoven, and tell Tchaikovsky the news. I've got a rockin' pneumonia. I need a shot of rhythm and blues."[152] What did the Beatles represent to the culture? The long-haired working-class boys from Liverpool were saying, "Move over high-brow elites. The working class is taking over."

The "Fab Four" took the world by storm. I recall the night I saw them live at the Indiana State Fairgrounds in the summer of 1966. I put down my five dollars, and my buddy Dean and I took our seats and waited for the Beatles' arrival. The girl seated next to me sat quietly for about an hour. Then the black limousine carrying the boys pulled onto the infield and behind the stage. The quiet young girl stood on her chair and began to scream along with seventeen thousand other people, mostly girls. I couldn't hear myself, Dean, or the music of the band. I doubt we heard one note that evening—only screams. Fifteen minutes into the concert, the girl was carried out along with half the people seated near us. All had hyperventilated and passed out. I don't think Paul, John, George and Ringo thought of themselves as telling the controlling elites to "move over," but they certainly took possession of the popular culture.

John Lennon in particular developed an anti-cultural narrative as he matured and then married Yoko Ono. His anti-war anthem,

---

[152] Chuck Berry, "Roll Over Beethoven," Entertainment One, 1956.

"Imagine," aspired to a world of peace and love. It was a feck-less and weak portrayal of a world void of the real conflicts that make us human with assumptions that humans have an innate ability to live in peace with one another, and corrupt govern-ments with their politics, interest in power, and armies are the only reason humans do not naturally live in this way. It was very much Jean-Jacques Rousseau, not Augustine. Rousseau saw the problem of evil not coming from a bad impulse but from a good impulse in trying to please or accommodate others.[153] Augus-tine saw the same problems, but he took responsibility because of a fixed human nature that was fallen. Rousseau saw the solu-tion as being in a person's quest to be their authentic self.[154] Au-gustine presented the solution as repentance, forgiveness, and reformation of the soul.[155]

"Move Over, Beethoven" is more apt than "roll over" because that is what we now face as the revolutionary 1960s critique replaces conventional ways. The 1960s rebellion happened against conventional society. Controlling elites have now come full circle. Those who were hippies in the 1960s are now in control and have become the very thing they hated. But now that they have the money and power, even though they loathe what they have become, they enjoy it. There is an important difference between what you rebel against and how far you are willing to go. What you plan to replace the present regime with is basic.

---

[153] Jean-Jacques Rousseau (1712-1762) was a self-taught philosopher whose *Confessions* set the individualistic framework for the French Revolution. It contradicted much of what Augustine taught about the individual and the meaning of life.

[154] Rousseau stole asparagus because it was an act of benevolence and that made theft virtuous. Jean-Jacques Rousseau, *Confessions,* Reissue edition (Oxford: Oxford University Press, 2008), 31-32.

[155] The story of the pears is in Book I. Augustine, *Confessions*, 397-400 CE.

Rebellion against a king, a political ideology, or an oppressive government has its place. America itself is a product of a rebellion against a king and governmental oppression. John Milton, who wrote *Paradise Lost,* a famous epic poem about the fall of man, participated in the English Civil War (1642-51), during which King Charles I was beheaded in 1649.[156] Milton approved of the beheading and barely survived the new king. In 1667, he published *Paradise Lost* about the rebellion of Satan against the King of heaven and Earth. Milton pointed out that rebellion against a human king can succeed due to that king's sinfulness, but successful rebellion against the King of heaven is impossible. Such action makes the rebellious satanic and evil.[157]

Rebelling against God is more than rebelling against the church. Milton was a Puritan. Puritanism was itself a form of rebellion against the Catholic Church. But rebelling against God is taking on the entire idea that nature has an ordained meaning. It calls into question the belief that humans have souls and life with meaning—that we live and die and are connected to the past through our parents and to the future through our children. One can rebel against the elites telling Catholics, or governments, or tyrants, to "move over," but challenging the fact of creation entails slipping into another realm.

This is the difference between the American Revolution and the French Revolution. The American Revolution was against the British elite and maintained the values and aspirations to be an elite culture, a good culture. The French Revolution was against the church, against God, and against the entire nature of creation.

---

[156] The 1970 film *Cromwell* starring Richard Harris gives further insight into the English Revolution.
[157] Thanks to novelist, playwright, and podcast host Andrew Klavan for his insightful explanation of *Paradise Lost* as it relates to revolution.

It was a paradise lost—a satanic revolution that ended the way such revolutions do, with bloodshed and murder

Where we are presently is with people who started out rebelling against the elite but who slipped into rebelling against their own humanity and the higher meaning of creation. In protesting police shootings of Black men, some insist on their pound of flesh prior to a full investigation thus violating the participants' civil rights. People get fired for insisting that the law be followed. Protesters are interested in the poetic truth, the truth of a narrative that may or may not be true in fact. People certainly have a right to peacefully protest, but what they are asking for violates their own civil rights and those of a society.

Nothing has been quite as extreme as Congresswoman Rashida Talib calling for no more arrests, no more prosecutions, and, I would say, no more understanding of human nature. She called for the restraints to be taken off the wicked and deceptive nature of the human heart. She has left the normal political protest and has moved into an insurrection against God and his place at the top of the created order.[158] Talib does not seem to understand that her call for justice has simply cast any hope of justice to the wind. She advocates a journey into moral darkness where self fulfillment is the highest goal. Without knowing it, when you arrive at this destination of yourself as the ultimate judge, you are lost along with all those who have followed you.

---

[158] Justin Vellejo, "Rashida Talib Calls For 'No More Police' Following Dante Wright Shooting." 13 April 2021. https://news.yahoo.com/rashida-tlaib-calls-no-more-221355507.html.

COURSE
CORRECTION

"What Have I Done?"

The Academy Award winning movie *The Bridge on the River Kwai* focuses on a battle of wills, strength of character, and the power of example. The battle of wills occurs between a Japanese colonel and a British colonel. The latter's soldiers have been captured by the Japanese, and they are compelled to build a bridge over the Kwai river in Thailand (Burma).[159] The Japanese colonel, accustomed to getting his way through fear and intimidation, does not hesitate to execute, starve, beat, and torture prisoners, including his own men, if it achieves his goals of maintaining his authority and getting the job done on time.

The first confrontation between the two military leaders occurs because the 1929 Geneva Convention exempts officers who are prisoners of war from manual labor. The British Colonel Nicholson refuses to engage in manual labor and is thrown into solitary confinement in a metal hut with nothing but water and a bucket. Burma's heat and humidity are nearly unbearable in normal conditions but deadly for someone confined to a metal hut. Periodically, Nicholson is dragged from his hut to stand before the Japanese colonel who offers him incentives to cooperate. Nicholson refuses to compromise.

---

[159] *The Bridge on the River Kwai*, directed by David Lean and starring Sir Alec Guinness, William Holden and Jack Hawkins, won the 1957 Academy Award for Best Picture. Guinness also took home the Oscar for Best Actor. Sessue Hayakawa was also nominated for an Oscar for his portrayal of the Japanese camp commander. A portion of the epic drama can be viewed at https://www.youtube.com/watch?v=tRHVMi3LxZE.

Meanwhile, the bridge building is slow, and, thanks to the shoddy work of the prisoners, portions of the bridge are literally falling. Pressure is increasing on Japanese Colonel Saito. He will be shamed if the bridge is not ready in time and will look weak if he gives in to the British colonel who is slowly dying in his tin cell. To make matters worse, Colonel Nicholson is admired by his men, but Colonel Saito's men loathe him. Every day of the standoff, Colonel Saito becomes more desperate until he eventually is a broken man. He considers suicide but instead gives in exempting British officers from manual labor and letting Colonel Nicholson out of his tin cell.

Then the story takes an interesting turn. Thus far the viewer of the film admires the British colonel. He wins the battle of the wills. He is a man of impeccable character and has an iron will. He is everything a man should be. He builds on that reputation when he takes control of the bridge construction and proclaims the British will demonstrate their superiority by showing the Japanese how to build a world class bridge. He allows his officers who are engineers to start over and place the bridge in the correct place. The work begins in earnest. The British colonel works harder than even the Japanese and drives his men to do great work. Over time, the Japanese Colonel Saito actually submits himself to his British counterpart. As they walk on the finished bridge together, they start talking like friends. Both achieved their goals. The bridge over the River Kwai is complete. It is a magnificent achievement. In a strange way, building the bridge brought two men at war together. What a way to end the film! If only the world could come together like these two. The viewer expects end credits to read, "A film by the United Nations."

But wait. We are not quite done.

American POW Commander Shears is everything that Colonel Nicholson is not—a soldier willing to cut any corner, break any rule, take every pleasure, and avoid suffering and sacrifice like the plague. He escaped from the prison camp where he was quite cynical about Colonel Nicholson and his high and mighty principles. He made it through the jungle, wounded, and ended up as a patient in a very nice hospital on the beach. A beautiful nurse becomes Shears' girlfriend, and he develops a somewhat cushy life while waiting to be released from military service so he can return home. He lied about being an officer and had no interest in an assignment offered to him that would take him back into the jungle.

That assignment was to blow up the bridge over the River Kwai— blow up the bridge that could transport troops and prisoners and give the Japanese great strategic advantage in the war. Only Shears knows the way and is familiar with the terrain, but he does not want to go. However, the Army tells him they know about his ruse, and he has no choice but to return and help destroy the bridge.

Under the command of Major Warden, the small band of men return to the bridge, plant explosives, and run wires to plungers hidden behind rocks about one hundred yards from the bridge. The small platoon goes to sleep and waits for dawn when the train arrives. At just the right time, they will push the plungers that will blow the bridge to smithereens.

The next morning is fresh and bright. A ribbon cutting ceremony is conducted and Colonel Nicholson surveys the bridge one last time before the Japanese dignitaries arrive on the train. The reason the two colonels are now men of mutual respect is that they both feel a sense of partnership in their accomplishment. Colonel Nicholson in particular has fallen in love with his accomplishment and will stop at nothing to protect it. His strength of character, iron will, and reputation as a man of his word have driven him to a place where his personal pride in his and his men's achievement has caused him to lose the big picture. He has become so immersed in the work and getting the job done that he forgot about being in a war. He used his substantial gifts to assist his enemy. He has built something wonderful, but it put him on the wrong side of the war.

The platoon members awaken to a disastrous fact. The waters of the river have receded overnight and the explosive wires connecting the charges to the plunger are now visible. Colonel Nicholson spots it and is startled by what he sees. He tries to process what it means. He cannot quite believe that someone is attempting to destroy his wonderful creation. Who could it be and why? He descends from the bridge to the riverbed and picks up one of the wires slightly embedded in the riverbed sand. He pulls on the wire and follows it where it leads. At the same time, Shears jumps up from behind the protection of the boulders to beat Nicholson to the plunger. Someone needs to blow up the bridge. It is now a race to the plunger between Shears and Nicholson. Japanese soldiers begin to fire, and they cut down Shears just about the time he reaches the Colonel. They recognize each other from the prison camp. There is mutual hatred, but then the Nicholson recognizes his error. His final words are "What have I done?" as he falls on the plunger, blowing up the bridge and sending the train into the river.

"What have I done?" What was the meaning of those words? A question arises here. Who shot the Colonel? Was he shot by a stray Japanese bullet or one from the small platoon? Was he cut down by an Allied soldier who now saw him as the enemy, as a traitor to the mission? He was shot because he was desperately trying to keep the Allied soldier from depressing the plunger. He was shot by the Allied platoon members because he was working for the other side. His last words were an acknowledgement that his pride in the bridge's construction had blinded him to his military duty.

What Does This Mean?

Christian leaders can fall in love with our achievements, such as building a magnificent ministry or church. That is not what Christ commands us to do. This is not a black and white issue; it is some shade of gray. We all enter into a project or ministry assignment with a conscious motivation to please God and to help people know him. But being human is a very dangerous thing. We are not qualified to understand our own hearts and motivations. God claims that he alone understands our hearts. We want to know our own hearts. We pray and ask God to show us the truth, but in the final analysis, God will do the sorting of the soul.[160]

I must admit that there have been times where I, like Colonel Nicholson, have sought to keep my creations and achievements alive, causing me to get confused in my mission. My mission is to make disciples of Christ. Disciples are not robots living in a sterile, untroubled world. They are real, imperfect people who struggle with knowing and believing God and who work through the culture in which they live with its challenges and troubles, often helplessly watching their cultural leaders either build or destroy the society in which they live.

This has been the story of most humans throughout history. American Christians at least have a vote, but that is of little consolation if you lose. It is crucial that a person knows his mission. To make disciples is our mission. Building ministries, churches, or businesses come along with that mission, but we must not

---

[160] Jer 17:9, Ps 139:23-24; 1 Cor 3:12-15; 2 Cor 5:10.

confuse the two. The only thing that Jesus commissioned us to do and authorized us to do was to introduce people to Christ, teach them to obey everything that Christ commanded, and give them the vison to do the same.[161] The rest of it is optional. If we maintain that focus, when we come to our end, we will not have to face the truth with the agonizing lament, "What have I done?" It will be, "Thank God for what I have done—exactly what he asked of me."

---

[161] Matt 28:18-20.

Replacement Culture

*"The difference between truth and fiction is
that fiction needs to make sense"* [162]

Spoken by actor Armin Mueller-Stahl in
The International

Are you happy with America right now? As a proponent of a
biblical worldview and the moral foundation it is built upon, I am
not. Most of us are looking at our land through a political lens at
this moment. At the time of this writing, the 2020 presidential
election has just concluded, but it will not be settled until the
new Congress is in place in January 2021. As the months go by,
the politics will fade, and we will begin to think about how our
lives changed with a new government. We will also reflect on the
pre-Covid 19 world and compare that life with the one we will
have with a vaccine available.

What concerns me most about the election result are the reasons
people had for a presidential change. For most partisans, the
reasons were ideological—a fixed worldview that is about power
and a political agenda. But for several million, it was emotional
and personal. Something moved them to vote for the first time or
to change their vote from the last election. They said something

---

[162] *The International* is a 2009 action thriller directed by Tom Tykwer.
The plot centers around an Interpol agent endeavoring to expose a
high-profile financial institution's role in international arms dealing.

like, "We hate Donald Trump. We don't care how much he accomplished. We find him immoral and odious." Or they said, "We liked what Trump did. He has been good for the country." Millions more were first-time voters. I wonder how rational their votes were.

People's votes are often irrational—not irrational in that they were stupid or not thought out, but irrational in that they were emotional and passionate with reason playing only a supporting role. The losing side, in this case, conservatives cannot believe it happened. As one commentor said:

> It should be the other way around. It's so irrational they should believe it happened. Humanity is not a rational race. It never was, and there's no reason to think it ever will be. Feelings don't care about your facts. Humans see situations and make moral decisions about them and fill in the reasoning later.[163]

Eve's desire for the attractive fruit that was pleasant to her eye caused her to take an irrational action. Adam engaged in the same foolishness. Adam and Eve's son, Cain, after a counseling session from the Almighty himself, still went out and killed his brother.[164] Not a good start for the human race.

It seems that humans are easily influenced by many factors, some so deeply seated in the human personality that reason alone cannot and will not control them. Right now, we live in a culture that is shaping its inhabitants' opinions and sentiments.

---

[163] "Democrats Are a Criminal Organization." *The Andrew Klavan Show*, Ep.938, premiered July 29, 2020. https://app.podscribe.ai/episode/48527078; https://www.youtube.com/watch?v=w994YjfJbqk.
[164] Gen 4.

The sentiment it is producing is increasingly secular and separated from the biblical narrative. By way of review, the biblical narrative is that man is fallen and sinful, separated from God, and is without ability to save him or herself and the society in which they live. "Save from what?" you might ask. From the self-destructive tendency to serve self, to take more than they need at the expense of others, to punish and rid themselves of those with whom they disagree, who are different from or in any way threaten them. This includes saving themselves from the greatest problem of all which is death—what the Bible calls "sin and death."

The human race wants to live. It is made to live. No one under normal conditions wants to die or cease to exist. People have done everything in their power to extend life, delay death, and even avoid discussions about death. We have come up with various euphemisms for it such as passing way, transitioning, buying the farm, kicking the bucket, biting the big one, and the big sleep—anything but the raw reality of death, skeletons, and rotting flesh. Humankind would nearly unanimously welcome being saved from that. Even our atheist friends might give a nod to this kind of saving. But you will not hear any of this kind of talk in the impolite exclusive society of the national media.

Existing western culture is laboring under the false impression that reason and science will save them. For the ruling class who control the flow of information in the culture, religion is premodern and primitive in thought. Only the uneducated, graduates of state schools, and the lower classes find any real solace in such ancient enchantments. Many of those who voted for the first time in the last election voted based upon a sentiment developed by the controlling secular narrative. I do not mean to say that anyone who voted for Biden was misguided or not Christian. What I am saying is that if their vote for Biden was to bring order to the chaos, calm to the storm, or peace to the conflict, they were guided by a false narrative. That desire for something more normal was developed on a foundation of irrational thought.

This is not surprising. We are irrational beings. It is just as irrational to believe that a vote for Trump was any more rational. He fueled fire and resentment in the American public concerning the ruling elite, the press, and claimed they all were fake, crooked, and corrupt. Yes, they were corrupt. Yes, they were fake at times, but so was his going back to the birther claim against Obama, the size of his own hands, and the size of his inaugural crowd. Trump discredited himself in ways that were self-destructive. Here is my point: if you do not like the culture the way it is, then replace it. We should have started about thirty years ago. How does one go about such a gigantic task?

Building a Replacement Culture

Ideally, we would simply observe how the philosophical, theological, and political left shaped the culture and replace it with a more biblical approach. Their most fundamental means was the university. What rose out of the ferment of the 1960s sexual revolution and the anti-war movement was a concept of freedom that had been twisted and malformed by Critical Theory.

Critical Theory fundamentally questioned the basis of all forms of knowledge. Its primary tool was Hegel's dialectic of thesis, antithesis, synthesis.[165] For example, a thesis would be that the story of Adam and Eve is true. The antithesis would be that it is not true. The dialectic is to argue, to go back and forth about it,

---

[165] Terry Pinkard, *Hegel's Dialectic: The Explanation of Possibility* (Philadelphia, Temple University Press, 1988).

to reach a new or more advanced truth called synthesis. In this case, the synthesis would be that the Adam and Eve narrative is instructive and helpful and lives in all of us but is not real history. This dialectic is to continue through time with each generation gradually discovering an advanced, more refined truth. Critical Theory applies to any belief system, particularly moral truth, and the beliefs that undergird institutions such as family, church, government, business, industry, and, of course, the academy.

For Christians, the first step then is to form alternative educational systems that compete with the universities and big tech companies who control the flow of information and who have become more powerful than the government. The latter censor based upon their largely anti-Christian, secular worldviews and how that is reflected in politics. They bury stories that they do not agree with while protecting their favorites. They play up what they are for and destroy what is contrary to their wishes. It is dishonest and will eventually kill democracy and divide the country even more because when no one knows who to trust and what is true eludes us, anarchy will reign. As one friend told me, "We will go from 'I'm right and you're wrong' to 'I'm right and you're evil.'"

Every major institution and force in the culture will need to be infiltrated and transformed or simply replaced. I believe that many of the major media companies will be passe in four years. CNN, MSNBC, FOX, and even the major networks will be dissolved, absorbed, or radically changed because they will be discredited. The alternative media as represented by podcasts and new media companies that are more open and honest will rise and replace them. *The Daily Wire*, a conservative online news service, now has more traffic than CNN, MSNBC, *The New York Times*, and *The Washington Post* combined. I would recommend the church to flood the zone with bright and young journalists who will return to actual journalism. Do the work of reporting. Get two sources before reporting the news and stop giving an opinion. Journalists are supposed to be the referee, not the participant.

The same strategy goes for films, books, magazines, public schools, and private schools. The sports industry in particular needs to be cleansed of its political bias. This is about fairness, truth, and integrity. Without it, we are lost.

I write about this need because it all has such a powerful influence in how we think, even what we feel. The less we read and believe the Bible, the more we are controlled by the culture. We are losing the battle right now. People are less educated in the most important ways, primarily in basic subjects like history, English grammar, foreign languages, mathematics, and basic civics. We are vulnerable to what we are told. Confusion about the Covid 19 virus is an example. Are lockdowns effective? Who is safe and who is not? What about wearing a mask? Every day there are conflicting reports from the Centers for Disease Control or the World Health Organization and various studies. Who can be trusted? It would help if we could trust our leaders and what they say.

My replacement document is beside me on my desk. It is tattered a bit and really marked up. It is a New Living Translation of the Bible—the document I really trust. I believe what I read in it.

The grass withers and the flowers fade,
But the word of our God stands forever.
(Isaiah 40:8)

Convincing the Contemporary Mind That Redemption is Needed

"If sinners be damned, at least let them leap to Hell over our dead bodies. And if they perish, let them perish with our arms wrapped about their knees, imploring them to stay . . . and let not one go unwarned and unprayed for."[166]

Charles Spurgeon

"If the biblical story is not the one that really controls our thinking then inevitably we shall be swept into the story that the world tells about itself. We shall become increasingly indistinguishable from the pagan world of which we are part."[167]

Lesslie Newbigin

"If God created the world, then fixing the problems it has falls squarely on his shoulders. If anything needs redemption it seems to me its him or her or it. He should focus on saving himself and quit blaming us for his mistakes. When he gets his act in order, then he can come calling. At least he should stop blaming us for his problems by telling us all we are sinners who must repent in order for him to forgive and not destroy us. Who does he think he is trying to run that line of philosophical tripe by us?"

Zeitgeist "spirit of the age"

---

[166] https://www.goodreads.com/author/quotes/2876959.Charles_Haddon_Spurgeon.

[167] https://twitter.com/LesslieNewbigin/status/1344449742370181121.

The first statement was issued in the 1800s by English preacher extraordinaire, Charles Spurgeon. It was largely non-controversial in nineteenth century London, graphic in its depiction, desperate in its spirit. The meaning of words and the belief that truth was a category that could be trusted were still intact. Life was tough in a world with plagues and no antibiotics, oxycodone, penicillin, or good anesthesia. It kept everyone focused on the reality of pain, death, and of the second death.

The second quote came one hundred years later from a missionary statesman and scholar who spent thirty-seven years working in India. He was a rousing success in that enchanted land, writing and preaching with eloquence in the language and dialects of that land. This Englishman adapted to a culture in which Western logic and its commitment to the law of non-contradiction was frowned upon and rejected. There could be more than one way to understand the universe, to establish truth, and to find God. For that matter, numerous other gods were not personal or particularly interested in the human problem. Yet Newbigin returned to Birmingham, England some forty years after his departure with his orthodoxy, intellect, and integrity intact. He released his seminal work *The Gospel in a Pluralistic Society* in 1989—a masterpiece of philosophical navigation through our skepticism and confusion.

I wrote the third statement to depict the "spirit of the age." There have always been skeptics, but now, another forty years after Newbigin, skepticism prevails. It is in the philosophical air we breathe. It is not a formally held position as much as an attitude that we humans have problems. We know the world is broken, but who broke it? Was it ever unbroken? To believe it was once perfect and not broken means believing in a very convenient fairytale-like story about Adam and Eve.

A 1990 conversation with a young physician alerted me that a benign, non-combative skepticism was coming. I was seated on a plane next to a young M.D. who had just graduated from medical school and was starting her career. We had a couple of hours to discuss all things "religious" on the flight. She seemed fully engaged and was very cordial as I worked through her list of intellectual problems with Christianity. After answering many of her questions, it was clear that I had thought a great deal more about the issues than she had. I thought I was in the driver's seat. "Now she is ready to pray with me to commit to Christ."

When I asked her if she had ever considered committing her life to Christ, she said that she had thought about it, and then she said the oddest thing: "But it really doesn't matter because no one can really know the truth. If I become a Christian, it becomes just a place holder until more information comes along in the evolutionary cycle." She presented to me that truth as a category was no longer something to be taken seriously and certainly not to dedicate one's life to. She went on to say was that it was God's responsibility to make things right. Her personal guilt or sin was rooted in a false narrative presented by the church. You can only imagine how much this attitude has grown in the decades since and how much more work God allegedly has to do now than then.

Newbigin warned of this: "Every missionary path has to find the way between these two dangers: irrelevance and syncretism. And if one is more afraid of one danger than the other, one will certainly fall into its opposite."[168]

As people on mission with Jesus, we endeavor to make Christ relevant. The temptation I faced in the conversation was to

[168] https://twitter.com/lesslienewbigin/status/1269254539972087809.

capitulate and fall into syncretism. Syncretism means to be sympathetic to several contradictory religious ideas co-existing like the common bumper sticker suggests. This is becoming one of the church's fastest growing sins—the idea that accommodation, agreement, and compromise with the "spirit of the age" will help the church be relevant. One sage warned, "Do not marry the spirit of the age, for you will soon become a widower." How do we find our way back to a place where the contemporary person sees their redemption as necessary?

First, I will attempt to deal with why the human mind has trouble with this concept. Why is the Gospel not good news to the Jews or the Greeks? Essentially, in Pauline categories, this includes everyone. To the Jews it is foolishness, as Paul stated in First Corinthians 1:23: "So when we preach that Christ was crucified, the Jews are offended and the Gentiles say it's all nonsense."

William Blake expressed the powerlessness of the human being thrown into the world:

My mother groan'd, my father wept;
Into the dangerous world I leapt,
Helpless, naked, piping loud;
Like a fiend hid in a cloud.[169]

Blake was aware of good and evil.

Every Night and every Morn
Some to Misery are Born;
Every Morn and every Night,
Some are born to Sweet Delight;
Some are born to Sweet Delight,

---

[169] Muggeridge, *A Third Testament*, 47.

Some are born to Endless Night.[170]

Blake powerfully conveyed the mysteries and inequities of life. He lived a life of joy, accomplishment, maltreatment, poverty, and sadness. He was a Romantic Era poet and artist trying to find meaning after the despair of the Enlightenment, much like the idealist in the twenty-first century who seeks a utopia.

Communist China knows socialism does not work. That is why they have abandoned it for capitalistic fascism. Marx has lost credibility with Russia, China, and the former USSR. The only holdouts are Cuba, North Korea, and the powerful ruling class in America, largely in the upper one percent of wealth holders. It will crumble quickly once the reality of the human condition comes to visit their lives and penalize them for being stupid and foolish. Then the private university will fall because it is too crazy to help anyone. Even tenured professors in English departments will repent when all they own can fit into a stolen shopping cart.

The real trouble starts when the confused, such as Blake, are thrown into this veil of tears without a good story that explains it. If humans do not like the story because it requires repentance and submission, they start thinking, "If I were God, then I would do this." From that very high place, where the air is thin and the dangers are many, the best and the brightest proceed to prosecute God. The difference between the idealist and Lucifer is the devil did not know about or would not face his limitations. Three times during the wilderness temptation, he offered power, bodily comfort, and the kingdoms of the earth to Jesus if Jesus would only kneel down and worship him.[171] Jesus already had

---

170 Ibid.
171 Matt 4:1-11.

what Lucifer offered to him, but not then and there. Jesus knew about and took the long view.

According to the Bible, Satan never will repent, accept his limitations, or change his mind. Therefore, he will spend eternity outside of God, completely destroyed.[172] However, the idealistic and confused human can repent, change his mind, and find reconciliation with this supposedly hideous, capricious (to some) God who in reality is the only one with a solution—more accurately stated, with the only one with a solution that can be accomplished.

People have come up with their own ideas, such as just put it back like it was in the first place. "If things were perfect in the pre-fall days, God, just take us back and let us start over." Erasing history and all its injustices, miseries, and wars has an appeal. But that would also necessitate erasing all the good, which far outweighs the evil. Also erased would be all people, their families, their histories, and their accomplishments. That sounds like a great deal of work and there would be no one left to care whether any work had been done at all.

Could we all agree that whatever perfect is, we do not have it? It is smashed and gone. We are fallen, alienated from our creator and from one another. Maybe a clean start that included the admission of our responsibility to the problem would help. But where do we start? This God that so many blame and hold responsible for the awful world in which we live, already made his move. Since he went first, he may convince us to join him in his redemptive work.

---

[172] Rev 20:10.

The Argument for Redemption

"We are so damned different, that we are all still the same."[173]

Joe Walsh

Imagine a Greek citizen in 300 BCE struggling to get through his short life in Athens. He was susceptible to various plagues and diseases. He worked as a farmer, soldier, teacher, or craftsman. His sons may have been required to fight in wars locally or against other nations. He could be envious or angry at his politicians. He was tempted to cheat, steal, commit adultery. He basically faced the same problems that citizens of the United States encounter today.

The Greek citizen walked or used a horse or donkey for transportation. Today's typical citizen owns a Honda Accord, a Mercedes, or even a Ford. Both men have the same nature, the same immaterial nature housed in a human body. Human life has changed dramatically regarding transportation, medicine, and ease of communication, but people are still beset with the very

---

[173] The lyric at the start of this essay has been somewhat altered from an Eagles concert referring to the Eagles themselves over the many years. Eagles, *Farewell 1 Tour: Live from Melbourne* DVD, 2005. Original lyric was "Everybody's so different, I haven't changed." Joe Walsh, "Life's Been Good," Spirit Music Group, Sony/ATV Music Publishing, 1978.

same human conflicts. Human progress has not fixed whatever it is that is broken in us.

There are those who have staked their careers and reputations on the myth of human progress. By progress, they refer to amounts and kinds of knowledge. Knowing that the earth is not flat but somewhat round and rotates around the sun has changed our lives a great deal for the good. Ulcers have been proven to be bacteria, not the result of worry. Bulls do not become angry at the color red. House flies live longer than twenty-four hours. Knowledge has increased and improved our lives, particularly in medical and other technologies.

However, the increase of knowledge has also brought plagues of information that have threatened, and, in some cases, ruined the lives of millions. Television, the most powerful force in modern life before the internet, infused the minds of billions of people around the world with ideologies. Once a culture ingests bad ideas, those philosophies are then lived out in society voluntarily rather than by governmental decree or some other official mandate.

When I was a child, Robert Young played Jim Anderson, husband of Margaret and father of Kathy, Bud, and Betty on the beloved television series *Father Knows Best*. They all had the same last name, which is not as common today. Jim Anderson was a man of routine. He was reliable, stable, and had no vices. He was the nation's role model for a father for a decade. Try to find such a father on television or in films today. Homer Simpson comes to mind as modern alternative. Homer is clumsy, fat, lazy, immature, and stupid. He cannot stay committed to newly found passions. Such massive changes in what the culture admires makes a huge difference in what is acted out. I would assert that American culture has not improved. It has declined. What we once admired is now considered evil, and what we once thought evil has been declared good. Some day in the future, people will combine marvel and disgust when they describe the barbaric practice of abortion.

Elite culture leaders seem to be the spiritual blind leading the spiritually blind. They ignore what is plain to see. For example, the fatherless child rate is 70% in the Black community. The crime rate among African Americans has grown in direct proportion to the rate of increase in fatherless homes.[174] Everyone who wants to see it can see it. However, those who could lose power and credibility by admitting the problem refuse to take off their blindfolds.

This is most obvious in the political realm where legislators continue to blame the other party for racism and for deeper pathologies created by the funding of a culture of dependance. Such willful blindness belies anything they may say about caring for this vulnerable population. The continuing problem of bad schools, a struggling economy, and danger in the streets are all ignored or blamed on white supremacy—a term they refuse to define or offer a solution for. They are living in a milieu that is four hundred years old, or, at best, a pre-civil rights movement understanding of the problem. They will not own the problem they have created through the failed War on Poverty.[175] Proponents of this failed philosophy continue to treat African Americans as inferiors who need the "white man's" help and resources. To hear

---

[174] John Gramlich, "What the Data Says (and Doesn't Say) About Crime in the United States." *Pew Research Center*, 20 November 2020. https://www.pewresearch.org/fact-tank/2020/11/20/facts-about-crime-in-the-u-s/.

[175] Robert Rector, "The War on Poverty: 50 Years of Failure." *The Heritage Foundation*, 23 September 2014. https://www.heritage.org/marriage-and-family/commentary/the-war-poverty-50-years-failure.

them tell it, Black people are not intelligent enough to find an ID so they can vote, get a vaccination, open a bank account, or buy concert tickets. How long are Blacks going to put up with this patronizing nonsense that continues to oppress them?

Racism is not curable by laws. If it could be, it would not exist at all. Racism is a matter of the heart and is found in every tribe, tongue, nation, and ethnic group.[176] Racial discrimination is already against the law in the United States.[177] Many crimes against the law are committed daily, which is the reason we have police, courts, jails, and prisons. We are selfish and rebellious, and, if not watched and policed, we will commit illegal acts against others.

People who disassociate themselves from such things need to recognize that we are all guilty, not just some of us. All Americans are free; we need to encourage one another to act free. Some might object that we are not free and blame others for their inability to excel. Just because someone does not feel free does not mean they are not actually free. They may be disadvantaged, have been dealt a bad hand, and have a lot to overcome, but

---

[176] At the root of racism is the belief that by origin of birth one race, usually the one you are in, is superior to other races or tribes. Tribes here refer to ethnic origin. With this in mind, it should be noted that most national populations are ethnic or tribal. The former Yugoslavia is an example of a nation ripped apart into several countries by racial division and war. Racism does not require slavery or the partitioning of populations. Racism does not require a difference in skin color. The continent of Asia would prove the point that people who have similar physical characteristics can refuse to live at peace in the same physical space because of ancient bigotries.

[177] The Civil rights Act of 1964; Voting Rights Act, 1965; Fair Housing Act of 1968; The Fourteenth Amendment to the Constitution of the United States of America 1789, revised in 1992.

they still are free to break out of the victim mentality and at least attempt to improve their lives. Some might only get halfway to their intended goal, but that may be enough to encourage the next generation to continue to close the gap.

Those who believe someone owes them something are doomed to failure and to passing that failure on to the young. A nation of victims, of consumers who are not producers, will eventually destroy the nation. More legislative or governmental decrees will only make matters worse. All that "help" does not actually help but instead continually feeds a lie to the recipients of special help that they did not earn it and are not capable of achieving it on their own.

When I speak of the myth of human progress, I refer to moral progress. Philosopher Fredrick Nietzsche warned his generation in the nineteenth century that if they destroyed the biblical moral code, they risked not being able to replace it.[178] This is precisely what has happened in America. People are seeking redemption, and they are looking for it to come from one another. Western culture is morally confused. People are struggling with identity. It is in vogue to question your gender, your religion, authorities, and the foundational institutions that give a nation stability. The left's Long March through our institutions has turned universities into breeding grounds for socialistic ideals that have never worked to help people. They have only led to utopian dreams and dystopian disappointments. The only way you can force this on people is to punish them, to surveil them, and finally to prosecute them through the courts and lock them out of normal daily life. If private industry will do the bidding of the political elite,

---

[178] Carl R. Trueman, *The Rise and Triumph of the Modern Self*, (Wheaton, IL: Crossway, 2020), 172-73.

then the non-compliant will be denied freedom of travel and entrance into restaurants and department stores—a despot's dream.

The futility of such efforts is obvious to those who have a reason to seek the truth. Reality has a voice of its own. Leaders can lie, but human experience is more powerful than the most convincing ideology. That leads us to my final point. What finally convinces a person they need redemption?

Lesslie Newbigin said it well. "It is the word made flesh that is the gospel. The deed without the word is dumb, and the word without the deed is empty."[179] Man has not progressed morally because morality is a spiritual issue, and man has a fixed nature that has existed ever since the first man Adam. "When Adam sinned, sin entered the world. Adam's sin brought death, so death spread to everyone, for everyone sinned." Paul goes on to say, "Yes, Adam's one sin brings condemnation for everyone, but Christ's one act of righteousness brings a right relationship with God and new life for everyone" (Rom 5:12, 18).

Redemption is a concept that declares that someone owes a debt to another. Who, therefore, owes what to whom? As Newbigin said, "Incarnation without explanation is 'dumb,'" meaning it remains unspoken and not understood. For God to say, "I care for you. You have a problem I want to solve" and not do anything about it is not convincing. The only way that God could speak to people and help them at the same time was to voluntarily become human. That was the ultimate "word." Embodied truth is the most powerful way to convey truth.

---

[179] https://www.goodreads.com/author/quotes/110888.Lesslie_Newbigin.

Ever since the fall of the human race and sin's entrance into the human experience, a gap of alienation has existed between God and his creation.[180] God has slowly but consistently closed that gap by revealing himself more fully through history.

God's redemptive action began in earnest with a specific people and land with his choice of Abraham and his lineage. His relationship to Abraham, Moses, the Ten Commandments, subsequent law, and the nation of Israel continued the thread of redemptive work.[181] The capstone, so to speak, was the incarnation of Christ—the promised Messiah and savior of the world.[182] In God's economy, our sin is a debt that must be paid for. The apostle John, a seasoned follower and original disciple of Jesus, wrote the following words near the end of his life:

> My dear children, I am writing this to you so that you will not sin. But if anyone does sin, we have an advocate who pleads our case before the Father. He is Jesus Christ, the one who is truly righteous. He himself is the sacrifice that atones for our sins—and not only our sins but the sins of all the world.[183]

The bad news is that we have sinned. We have missed the mark of righteousness that qualifies to be reconciled to God. The solution requires a qualified representative. The good news is there is one who satisfies the requirements that God set.[184] Jesus came to give his life as a ransom for many.[185] Jesus alone is righteous and

---

[180] Isa 59:2.
[181] Matt 5:17-20.
[182] Isa 53:3-5.
[183] 1 John 2:1-2.
[184] 2 Cor 5:21.
[185] Matt 20:28.

qualified to be sacrificed as atonement for our sin debt. To atone means to pay for.

Most spiritual leaders do not sacrifice. They ask their followers to do all the sacrificing. Mohammad and many popes have recommended and sometimes insisted on sacrifices from their followers. Jesus is different. He leads the way. He gives himself up and releases us from our debt and frees us to live a new life.[186]

To accept this idea, the skeptic must eventually accept Jesus' action as the proof that this is true and required. He or she may not access this level of spiritual knowledge through argument or pure intellect. It requires humility and honesty to admit, "I have sinned. I know down deep inside that I want everything to go my way. I want to be king of my kingdom. I realize that Jesus displayed a quality of life that compels me to confess my sin and to follow him."

If that is where you are, you are in. You are on your way. If not—if you are holding out for more evidence that you are broken and need help—then you will not find help. But your redemption awaits you. You are not far from the kingdom of God (Mark 12:34).

---

[186] Rom 6; Col 2:13-14.

What Kind of Disciples Do We Need?

Christians, especially conservative evangelical Christians, do not take the power of culture seriously. Culture is something that is cultivated. It is what we as people tend to and create. If you enter a museum, you might run into the curator. Curators tend to the art. They display it, explain it, and find ways to improve the exhibits in order to effectively promote the art's importance. There are many ways to define culture: the water we swim in; the institutions we establish; the things we do without thinking. It is probably best to call it our way of life.

I think it was Peter Drucker who first said, "Culture eats strategy for lunch every day." For example, if a pastor calls on the congregation to love one another while two of its elders are at each other's throats, the church's culture defeats the exhortation to love. If leaders call the congregation to reach out to rescue people from living unfulfilled lives and being banished in spiritual darkness forever separated from God, but a tolerant, sentimental culture has programmed all the hell out of hell leaving no sense of urgency to act, culture wins again.

Slowly, but with certainty, we have watched our culture change our theology and our churches. We have largely been bystanders. We stand and lament how the powerful and ruling elite have taken control of the universities, school districts, local governments, sports leagues, and the most powerful tool of all, the media.[187] Add to that the corporate and very "woke" Twitter, Facebook, Amazon, Apple, Google and old boring Microsoft, the national narrative has changed dramatically in the last fifty years. It is a post-Christian story of moral confusion and permissiveness. Religion moved from mainstream and important in the 1950s-60s to something worthy of rejection and scorn in the 1970s-80s to now largely being ignored and considered irrelevant in the early twenty-first century. Of course, I generalize, but I will not take time or space to say all the things that I do not mean to say or list exceptions to the above summary.

We are in a fight to tell the truth. Christians do not seem to understand this. We cannot continue to be passive. That would be continuing a mistake of the past fifty years. We do want to render to Caesar what belongs to Caesar and to God what belongs to God.[188] The answer is not political, but politics are important and cannot be left out. Politics reflect the culture, which in turn is driven by religion and worldview.

I started *The Bonhoeffer Show,* a show about religion, culture, and politics, in order to help serious Christians think and act in a way that would influence culture.[189] I believe with A.W. Tozer, " . . . that whatever comes into my mind when I think about God is the most important thing about me."[190] Those thoughts about God determine my worldview and the personal culture I create

---

[187] Media includes television, theater, music, museums, film, and the most potent tool of all, the thirty-second commercial.

[188] Mark 12:17.

[189] You can access *The Bonhoeffer Show* on any podcast platform or at thebonhoefferproject.com. Choose "The Bonhoeffer Show" on the menu.

[190] A.W. Tozer, *The Knowledge of the Holy*, (New York: Harper & Row, 1961), 9.

in my own life, the life of my family, my workspace, and other settings. A wonderfully freeing thought is that 99% of Christians can engage the culture on the job—job discipleship, if you like. Christ uses and forms us in our jobs, not around, under, or over them, but through them. It is an entirely different matter to support religious professionals in their work. Religious activity per se should not be promoted as special, better, or more holy than simply doing every kind of work as Christ's disciple.

My political views are a product of my worldview and my culture. I fight for my views in my community, state, and nation. I choose the candidates who best represent the world in which I would like to live. At the same time, my worldview says that this life is temporal, but I am a steward for future generations, particularly for my own children, grandchildren, and those who will come after them.

This is the reason so many are concerned about everything from public education to the environment. This is why Donald Trump is such a great object lesson. He is a cultural creation who emerged from reality television cosmic ooze, dripping with irony, all things horrible, and much good as well. He is controversial. Much theory, core beliefs, and propaganda swirl around him. He gives everyone a focal point for presentation of beliefs.

Most of the ardent Christians against Trump erupt with outrage and protest that any Christian who takes the Bible seriously cannot possibly be anything other than a hypocrite if they support him. They tend to lean left of center in their political affiliation. In the past, many of these more moderate theological conservatives voted Republican, but they have been caught up in the pathological personality of Trump, which caused them to reject him. They like to shame their fellow Christians for supporting Trump and use the Scriptures that talk about being nice, passive, and even pacifistic. They pick up that stick and beat Trump supporters about the head and shoulders: "Look at you with all that Trump filth all over you."[191] At the same time, they support politicians who call for abortion on demand even through all nine months of a pregnancy. They do not seem to mind that the Trump Impeachment scandal was actually about a real threat to liberty—the Obama administration spying on Donald Trump via the FBI for political reasons.[192] They support many other policies that are terrible for our country and would destroy the family, religious liberty, and other cherished institutions.

Donald Trump never refused to respond to a court order. He worked through the system. He only has done what is his right to do—challenge subpoenas or court decisions by appealing to higher courts. None of that is illegal. If Trump were a fascist, as it is popular to say, then why are all his enemies not dead or in jail? Why did he not provide a fleet of buses after the Oscar ceremony for all his enemies and have them bused to detention camps and executed? The reason is that he is not a fascist. He has done more to protect the unborn, religious liberty, and to put people back

---

[191] Eric Metaxas and David French debated at John Brown University whether a Christian should vote for Trump. David French's position essentially was the unholy unsuitability of Donald Trump for office from a biblical position. He accused Metaxas of ignoring his own biblical standards in supporting Trump. Catherine Nolte, "Metaxes and French Discuss 'Should Christians Vote for Trump." *The Threefold Advocate*, 8 September 2020. http://advocate.jbu.edu/2020/09/08/metaxas-and-french-discuss-should-christians-vote-for-trump/.

[192] Georgetown University Law Professor Jonathan Turley is a widely respected, non-partisan voice. Jonathan Turley, "More Willful Blindness by the Media on Spying by Obama Administration." *The Hill*, 25 July 2020. https://thehill.com/opinion/white-house/509002-more-willful-blindness-by-the-media-on-spying-by-obama-

to work, particularly minorities, than any president in modern times.[193]

To be clear, I do not admire very much about Donald Trump. I have no desire to be his friend, nor do I want to know most of his friends. I would not point to him and say to my children or grandchildren, "Be like him." But no leader on the left would inspire my allegiance either. They are a feckless bunch, changing their minds and selling their souls to get some votes, but, more importantly, to get fortunate and fame. I would give Bernie Sanders a tip of the hat for being consistent and a man of conviction even though socialism/communism (Bernie is both) has never worked and never will work. The millions of bodies left in its wake after the twentieth century demonstrate that it does not work even if you execute all the people who said so.

Here is what I do respect about Trump. Even though he was as careless with the facts as a carnival barker, almost always exaggerating his accomplishments, he seemed to be realistic about who was trying to destroy him. He understood that the barbarians were at the gate, and he would not let up. His enemies were not only the Democrats but also the press. (One could argue the Democrats and mainstream press are the same thing). Unlike President George W. Bush, he decided to call them out, call them names, and beat them to a bloody pulp. Trump

---

[193] Without providing an unreadable pile of data from the United States Treasury and economic reports, the claims made about Trump's accomplishments are a matter of public record. They are undisputed facts. There is great disagreement about whether they are all good and about the means used to accomplish them. One can disagree about his tax cuts, the building of the wall on the southern border, or his picks for the Supreme Court, but the fact that he did them is not in dispute.

has the stomach for the battle, something that causes most of us benign evangelicals to wrench.

I admire Trump's toughness. He speaks his mind, has convictions, and follows through with action on what he promises regarding abortion, religious liberty, personal freedom, job creation, prison reform, and stimulating the economy through tax cuts and the removal of harmful restrictions. Of course the rich get tax cuts, but they also create the wealth that makes it possible for minorities to get new jobs, buy homes, and take care of family needs.

The left protests that this does not work for everyone. What does work for everyone? No matter what the government does, there will still be poverty. There will always be people left behind, regardless of who occupies the White House. People have a variety of goals in life. There is an array of motivations with differing financial compensations. A social worker is energized by helping those who struggle while a captain of industry is driven to succeed financially. Furthermore, most people on earth do not live freely in democracies. For generations, they have been dominated and thus acquired habits of systemic cultural pathology.

Just as there are differences in opportunity, there are differences in effort and result. The smartest most conscientious people will generally get the best results and, therefore, the lion's share of reward. We now live and always will live in a hierarchal society. There are no exceptions. Christian, Muslim, Hindu, secular—it does not matter. There is always a top and a bottom.

In America, the question is will we keep our liberty or give it to the government? Trump, despite what his opponents say, is further away from a monarch or king than his predecessor, Barak Obama. If one drops all the vitriol and looks at the facts regarding presidential decrees, it is apparent that President Obama attacked his opponents with the IRS and spied on political campaigns, among other things.

Reality has its own voice, and a growing number of Americans can hear it. It is saying what Trump did leads to a country where people are free to speak their mind, worship their God, work at a good-paying job, and keep the government at bay. That is a powerful message. For those who repudiate Trump, cannot stand him, and violently disagree with me, that is fine. I am not angry with you. If I am wrong, I will admit it. But in a few more years, Trump will be gone, and I would like to be as free then as I am today—actually more free. I want to use a plastic straw again when I go out to lunch.

Politics are Sport

The conversation and depth of feeling around politics exist because politics is tribal and competitive. People used to kill each other over theology, but people no longer care enough about theology to even get exercised about it, let alone kill over it. The playing field is political. It is a sport where people can divide up into teams and compete, watch on television, and have favorite players and favorite commentators. It appeals to the need to compete for what we all care about: the culture and where our money goes. That is why religious or theological friends can be affiliated but have differences and give each other a pass. But when those same friends enter into political discussion, they get angry, even hostile, and break fellowship over political theory.

When I was in Rwanda around 2000, I kept asking Hutu pastors how things got so bad that the Hutus were killing millions of Tutsi Christians. The answer was that ancient tribalism ran thicker than the blood of Christ. This is the present danger we face. The culture matters. In many ways, it affects us more deeply than religious belief. This is why we not only need to make many more disciples but a certain kind of disciple: less fearful, less feckless, and more courageous, willing to both take and deliver a punch.

What Jesus Never Taught

"Do you think I have come to bring peace to the earth? No, I have come to divide people against each other!" (Luke 12:51)

Jesus never taught his disciples to retreat from conflicts in front of them. He never instilled in them a belief that they should not dirty themselves with battles that were not directly religious. He did not teach them to retire from the cultural or political battles that they would find themselves in because of preaching the Gospel.

You might say, "Who says that anyone says that?" I say that the conventional advice in church right now is, "We need to all calm down, retreat from the cultural wars, and pray for revival, peace, and unity." If Jesus had actually lived that way and his disciples followed him in that way, there would be no church at all.

"Blessed are the peacemakers" does not mean passivity. Some of the greatest peacemakers in history were the great generals that made peace possible through war: Dwight Eisenhower, George Patton, Douglas MacArthur, Matthew Ridgeway, and Norman Schwarzkopf, Jr. Patton, nicknamed "ole blood and guts," was profane, temperamental, and grandiose. He was just what was needed to bring peace to the earth during the Second World War.

After Jesus offered the olive branch to Israel, he was rejected by his own and his ways were rejected by much of the world.[194] In the final analysis, the Prince of Peace himself will use violence to bring peace to the earth. He will destroy the armies of the world.

---

[194] John 1:11.

He will kill millions and throw the fiery angel Lucifer into a pit along with all his cohorts and those who refuse God's love and mercy. [195]

It is hard to tell the truth. I wish it were not so. But if this is not true, why should we care about any of this? Sell the church building, divide the cash, and have a nice day.

If we believe the world will like Jesus more if they like Christians more, we are ignoring history and current reality. Just how does Christians acting nicer and being more compliant work? I read a comment by a Christian leader who proposed that the problem is Christian celebrity leaders failing morally because they discredit the church. Yes, they do. They always have and always will. The author also equated Christians leaders who believed in Donald Trump with those who had fallen morally. Proof of a twisted mind is to first believe that a political difference is a moral failure, and, secondly, to proclaim that the difference of opinion is a major barrier to evangelism. Then, of course, the writer called for evangelicals to come together and practice peace and humility. That is only possible if you accept the premise that you are morally flawed for holding the wrong opinion. If you confess your sin of wrong opinions, then we can come together and show a unity to the world that will cause them to fall on their knees and ask, "What must we do be saved?" The whole idea is ridiculous.

The more cultural decline we experience, the more of it we will produce. I suppose that the answer is for the Christian culture to stop making celebrities, but that is akin to proposing that men stop looking at women because it creates problems. If men did not like to look at women, it would create bigger problems. People become celebrities because some people are more talented than others.

---

[195] Rev 19-20.

The rarer a talent is, the more famous the person with that ability will become. It is as fundamental to humanity as is the reality of hierarchy in every society, from orangutangs to Harvard professors.

Our country has a newly crowned royalty that controls the culture—at least it seems they do. We can briefly describe that royalty as big tech, big media, big money, big corporation, big entertainment, and big government. They are led by smart and somewhat lucky leaders who either by singular strokes of genius or by genetic blessings, such as good looks, great athletic ability, and extraordinary ambition and networking capabilities, have been able to claw their way to the top of the heap. They have developed what I call MacTruth—truth that is fast served to the public with the nuance strained out. Its wisdom is not wise, and its truth is a diminution of the First Amendment. In other words, what they deliver is not the truth, the whole truth and nothing but the truth. An obvious current example is the government considering as a non-crisis the open southern border with over one million people crossing into our country illegally. They have attempted to hide the truth of it by censoring the media from covering it. Whether it is blaming the police for increased violence or claiming that rapid inflation is not actually inflation, there is a concerted effort by those in power to censor the truth and create their own "news."

This is no way to run a country, democracy, or a republic, nor is it a way to create a well-informed free-thinking society. Big tech giants Google, Facebook, Twitter, and YouTube determine what truth they want you to hear by censoring truth they do not like. Big media—major television networks and the majority of cable news—is in full alignment with big tech. Big money supplements this through grants to think tanks, political PACs, and advertisement. Big corporations like the NFL, NBA, Coca-Cola, Nike, and American Airlines supplement the narrative, and big government makes policy and law that codifies MacTruth and installs it as the new order. They will tell their lies, but the population will not have it forced down their throats. No. It will be assimilated through their pores via a mental and emotional osmosis that will feel good, be pleasant to the eye, and even seem like an elevation of humanity. But it is doomed to fail because it is not true.

Reality has its own voice. Women and men are different. Women cannot actually be men, and men cannot actually be women. Men are stronger than women. They can run faster, jump higher, and are generally rougher and tougher. It is immoral for a man to pretend he is a woman and then take a trophy from a woman because he beat her in a race. Children should not be able to identify as the other sex or some new form of being just because the culture around them lies to them daily and tells them they can.

The idea that equality is more than an opportunity to be disciplined and to work hard to achieve is now considered a lie. Equality of opportunity is a God given right; so is living with the result. Equality of result cannot be achieved without tyranny—a prison to put away violators and punish high performers who will not share. Soviet history alone teaches this reality.[196] Socialism violates every human impulse to improve and to voluntarily help society around you by choice. Equality of result is a scourge on humanity. Real liberty is the opportunity to freely make your own choices, work as hard or as little as you like, and then live with the results. Hate speech is protected speech. The most heinous statements a person can make are constitutional and must be

---

[196] The treatment of dissentients, the restrictions on movement of citizens, the lack of personal freedom, the long lines outside of stores, the empty shelves inside the stores: everyone knew it was not working and finally the dam broke and the game was up for communism.

allowed in order to protect liberty and human flourishing. The Big Lie Industrial Complex is upon us. What are we Christians supposed to do?

Jesus taught us that telling the truth is hard. It has never been harder for Christians than it is right now. Jesus told the truth, and he was executed. His disciples told the truth, and they were killed.

We must make different disciples for this difficult age. We are called to tell the truth to those around us because truth sets people free. As Jesus told those who believed in him, "You are truly my disciples if you remain faithful to my teachings. And you will know the truth and the truth will set you free" (John 8:31-32).

Some of us have a large megaphone and are positioned to speak directly into the ruling class and elite. With that comes great opportunity, great impact, and great risk. To see this, one only needs to survey what has befallen celebrities who have been attacked and cancelled for promoting biblical worldviews on issues such as abortion, the family, and traditional values, especially in the realm of sexual purity and responsibility.[197]

Jesus taught us to step up and speak up. But what did he speak up about? There is no evidence that Jesus attempted to join the

[197] Kalhan Rosenblatt, "J.K. Rowling Doubles Down in What Some Critics Call a 'Transphobic Manifesto.'" *nbcnews.com*, 10 June 2020. https://www.nbcnews.com/feature/nbc-out/j-k-rowling-doubles-down-what-some-critics-call-transphobic-n1229351; Jenna Ryu, "Rupert Grint on Why He Criticized J.K. Rowling's Transphobic Comments: 'Silence is Even Louder.'" *USA Today*, 22 March 2021. https://www.usatoday.com/story/entertainment/celebrities/2021/03/22/rupert-grint-why-he-criticized-j-k-rowling-trans-comments/4796412001/; Madeline Holcombe and Joe Sutton, "Kevin Hart Says He Won't Host Oscars After Furor Over Homophobic Tweets." *cnn.com*, 7 December 2018. https://www.cnn.com/2018/12/07/entertainment/kevin-hart-oscars-step-down/index.html

Pharisees, Herodians, or Zealots or that he looked for a hiding place with the Essenes. Paul did not run for office. He was already positioned among the elite as a leading Pharisee prior to his encounter with Christ on his Damascus journey.[198] Why did they both find themselves in trouble and have politicians try to get rid of them? Because they told the truth, and truth challenges authority. While they did not aspire to political power, their messages threatened political power, and they were thus thrown right into the middle of politics.

There was no separation between church and state in ancient Israel. It was a blend of state and religion in a former but still desired theocracy. During Jesus' day, Israel was ruled by the most powerful nation state on earth at the time, the Roman Empire. Jesus and Paul were a threat to the religious structure of Israel and to the Roman Empire, particularly its local leaders. Local Roman officials' positions and advancement were threatened by unrest or riots in the streets. This was why Pilate was concerned about Jesus and attempted to wash his hands of the matter.[199] But how does this inform twenty-first century Christians in the United States?

When biblical morality collides with the prevailing cultural narrative championed by big media, big tech, big money, big corporations and big government, the fur will fly. You will find yourself tangled up with one of these forces who are selling MacTruth. The only thing to remember is to tell the truth.[200] It will be hard, sometimes so hard you may not be able to do it. You may fade away or melt down but be of good courage. God will reshape you and give you grace to tell the truth the next time.[201]

---

[198] Acts 9:1-9; Phil 3:4-9.
[199] Matt 27:24.
[200] Eph 4:15.
[201] Luke 12:11-12.

The Disciple Making Preacher

"I believe I am not mistaken in saying that Christianity is a demanding and serious religion. When it is delivered as easy and amusing, it is another kind of religion altogether."[202]

Neil Postman

A disciple-making pastor is a disciple-making preacher because the first and most important step in making disciples in the church is the sermon. When the two are disconnected, the disciple-making cause is debilitated because the pastor, the preacher, is to be a leader of a disciple-making movement.

What this looks like has much to do with context and times. Church growth experts tend to look at numbers while historians look at overall cultural impact. There is both ignorance and argument as to what constitutes a disciple-making movement. Those who claim to have experienced them quantify movements to fit their work. Those who do not experience movement-type results tend to discount them.

A movement defined by a professional missiologist is normally something like four generations of reproduction of churches or Christian generations multiplied by a certain number of units.

---

[202] Neil Postman, *Amusing Ourselves to Death*, 147.

For example, let's say fifty churches have each started four new churches in four years. That would be eight hundred new churches in four years. In some settings, particularly in the developing world, this would mean eight hundred Bible studies. The premium is on reproduction and multiplication. The missionary generally presents this to Western churches as an example of what could happen if the churches in the United States would follow the methods being used in some other place.

By these standards, it is common to assert that there are no disciple-making movements in the United States. However, individual churches can, as a congregation, function like a disciple-making movement. This may all be leadership balderdash and probably is. My point is that one preacher is in one church, and it is in that one church where he or she begins.

The media celebrity culture in which we work creates preaching specialists who have been trained to think of big crowds as success. Great preaching excuses the big-number preacher from the accountability to lead a disciple-making movement. The congregation normally plays along because everyone is now off the hook to do the hard stuff. This is an example of the statement nothing fails like success. Disembodied sermons separated from a connection to the body life of the congregation will create disciples who do not believe in discipleship. That is why so many preaching pastors are looking for disciple-makers for hire— people who will take less money and prestige in order to take what the pastor says and make it work in the church.

This is not always the case, but one of the hardest lists to make is the one of lead pastors who are great preachers that also know something about making disciples. (We are talking now about product and process.) Most of them think it means to organize people into small groups so they can talk about the sermons, but this would be to confuse form with function. The function is to make disciples. The form could include small groups, but they are not the same. This is ambiguous at best. Ambiguity is our enemy, specificity our friend. If a pastor does not know with specificity what the product is, he will have no clue as to whether he is doing it right.

A sermon can be included in making disciples. Whether or not a sermon actually helps to make disciples depends on what the preacher has in mind when he pictures a disciple and whether he possess personal convictions about the discipleship process. What are preachers modeling in their personal lives and have they acquired habits and a schedule that reflect their spoken priorities? Too often preachers think of themselves as a cheerleader for the staff or lay leadership who do the work of ministry.

The present environment creates a major challenge to how the Gospel is preached to the congregations we face. As Neil Postman's statement says, "I believe I am not mistaken in saying that Christianity is a demanding and serious religion. When it is delivered as easy and amusing, it is another kind of religion altogether."[203] When the call to follow Christ is turned into a convenient transaction, the Gospel is being delivered as easy and amusing. It ceases to be the Ggospel and the message that Jesus commissioned us to spread through the entire earth.

Contemporary sermon makers seem to closely follow a series of commandments.

1. Thou shalt have no prerequisites
No previous knowledge is needed. Learning is not hierarchical. You can enter at any point without prejudice. In television, every program stands alone. Sequence and continuity are out. This

---
[203] Ibid., 121.

means you can walk in off the street and the sermon is packaged for a "drop in" listener.

2. Thou shalt induce no perplexity
Nothing has to be studied, remembered, or applied.

3. Thou shalt avoid exposition like the ten plagues visited upon Egypt.
Television is a poor place for serious arguments, hypotheses, discussions, reasons, and cross-examination. Television is all storytelling conducted through dynamic images supported by music. It is entertainment. Some call it infotainment. Sermons become second rate television shows, sound bites, and clichés. The television commercial is the single most powerful mode of communication in present society.

4. Thou shall not be allowed to talk about anything that you have not at least attempted yourself.

5. Thou shall not recommend anything that you have not provided the training and learning infrastructure to make reachable to your congregation.

Different Disciples for a Dystopian Age

The late great statesman, diplomat, scholar, and Christian Dr. Charles Malik both warned of and described the present cultural situation in his 1982 address at Wheaton College. "The problem is not only to win souls, but to save minds. If you win the whole world and lose the mind of the world, you will soon discover you have not won the world. Indeed, it may turn out you have actually lost the world."[204]

---

[204] Charles Malik, *The Two* Tasks, (Wheaton: InterVarsity Press, 1980), 32.

In the book Malik published on this theme, *Two Tasks,* he argued that the first task is to evangelize souls and the second to evangelize minds. He warned of the left's long walk through our universities. [205] He claimed that failure to produce Christian scholars to populate university faculties would produce future generations of leaders who would be cut off from their nation's history and first principles. Now, forty years on, Malik's warning has become our reality.

The American Revolution was about equality of opportunity and required liberty and morality to flourish. The French Revolution was about equality of result and required tyranny and the guillotine. The present revolutionaries running through the streets of America do not know the difference. Marxist socialist theory as taught in most of our universities has been dumbed down to burn it down, tear it down, shout it down, shut them up, and get a utopia of freedom and equality as a result.

The word utopia means an imaginary world. It really means no place because utopia does not exist. What does exist is dystopia, a society that is dehumanizing and unpleasant. It is a tyrannical stew, a brew of Huxley's *Brave New World*, Orwell's *1984*, and Ray

---

[205] By "left," I am talking not about the Democrat Party per se. Politics are downstream from religion or worldview. Culture is at midstream. Politics merely reflect culture. Political correctness and cancel culture are examples of downstream results of upstream beliefs. By "left," I refer to Marxist-socialist Critical Theory that is rooted in Lucifer's words to Eve, "Hath God said?"—something that questions the authority and veracity of God. Its more modern manifestations have been the Frankfort School, the Critical Principle, Hegel's thesis, antithesis, synthesis dialectic, and truth becoming a work product of logic and reason alone outside of divine revelation. The left's philosophy is more prevalent in the Democratic party right now, but hopefully that can change. All hope is not lost. It also exists among Republicans in popular forms but is not baked into its principles.

Bradbury's *Fahrenheit 451*. Huxley feared that no one would read or be informed because we would amuse ourselves to death.[206] Orwell warned of Big Brother controlling individuals' thoughts and words and punishing those who violate the codes. An idea that cannot be stated cannot be refined, articulated or even thought. Vonnegut portrayed a society of betrayal and distrust, a world of censorship and denial of liberty.[207]

For those who care enough to be alarmed, it is alarming that our present revolutionaries do not know the difference between Martin Luther King, Jr. and Black Lives Matter. King's protests were peaceful, principled, and built on the Christian narrative reflected in the Declaration of Independence—what he called America's promissory note. Of course, King was a sinner as we all are, but that does not invalidate his life any more than the sins of the church cancel out its ideals and message. One day, every knee shall bow and every tongue will confess that Jesus Christ is Lord. We live to please God, and to worship him only.[208]

Black Lives Matter, the organization that is, holds to a very different creed. They deceive the public by marching through our culture for the sake of destroying it, not improving it. They aim to redefine the family, break down the heterosexual dominance, as they put it, and to validate any configuration of people self-identifying as a family.

If there is one thing that must be done to address the problem of the Black underclass, gang violence, bad schools, and

---

[206] The same main idea is also found in Neil Postman's *Amusing Ourselves to Death*. Great book.
[207] Kurt Vonnegut was a novelist who was most famous for his depiction of a dystopian society in *Fahrenheit 451*.
[208] Phil 2:10-11; Deut 6:13; Luke 4:8.

fatherless families, it is to strengthen the Black family. A major change will be needed for the government to end its patronage system. *Wall Street Journal* columnist Jason L. Riley recently wrote *Please Stop Helping Us: How Liberals Make It Harder for Blacks to Succeed.*[209] In the book, Riley pointed out that well-intentioned efforts to assist Blacks have lost their positive impact. Riley mentions such problems as young Black men largely being fatherless, the Black family becoming less disciplined, and the integrity of Black achievement being threatened because it was provided by a motivation of white guilt. Is Black achievement really Black if the way was paved by whites? *Stop Helping Us* is a plea to the establishment to stop intervening and to leave Blacks alone because they are free and able to achieve on their own.

We are at war! It is a cultural war, but, more profoundly, it is a war of ideas. Behind those ideas are persons and ultimately only two persons, God and Lucifer. We are in what writer Michael Walsh so eloquently calls The Devil's Pleasure Palace. In his high culture exposition, *The Devil's Pleasure Palace: The Cult of Critical Theory and the Subversion of the West*, he describes it this way:

---

[209] "The sober truth is that the most important civil rights battles were fought and won four decades before the Obama presidency. The Black underclass continues to face many challenges, but they have to do with values and habits, not oppression from a manifestly unjust society. Blacks have become their own worst enemy, and liberal leaders do not help matters by blaming self-inflicted wounds on whites or "society." The notion that racism is holding back Blacks as a group, or that better Black outcomes cannot be expected until racism has been vanquished, is a dodge. Encouraging Blacks to look to politicians to solve their problems does them a disservice. As the next chapter explains, one lesson of the Obama presidency—maybe the most important one forBblacks—is that having a Black man in the Oval Office is less important than having one in the home." Jason L Riley, *Please Stop Helping Us: How Liberals Make It Harder for Blacks to Succeed* (New York: Encounter Books, 2014).

... a modern Devil's Pleasure Palace, a Potemkin village built on promises of "social justice" and equality for all, on visions of a world at last divorced from toil and sweat, where every man and woman is guaranteed a living, a world without hunger or want or cold or fear or racism or sexism . . . The corpses of untold millions have died in the attempts of the literally Unholy Left to found the Kingdom of Heaven here on earth . . . something wicked this way has come, and we are in the fight of our lives. How, or even whether, we choose to fight it is not the subject of this book. The subject is why we must."[210]

Why would we the church dirty our hands and join the fight? Why not just stick to the business of souls? Because our disciples have failed. Because we have lost the culture. We have been making our kind of disciples for the past fifty years and look what we have accomplished. The disciples we have produced allowed the culture to be taken over by leftist ideology that is clearly anti-Christian, anti-Gospel, and has cut off at least two generations from the biblical, literary, social, and cultural foundations of a working society. Those young people tearing down statues are our disciples. We must make different disciples to get different results. The church must take some responsibility as to why our members have not created our own Amazons, Googles, Facebooks, movie studios, and television networks—all means by which the cultural elite run our society.

So where do we begin? Let me suggest one place as a starting point that has not changed in two thousand years:

---

[210] Michael Walsh, *The Devil's Pleasure Palace*, (New York: Encounter Books, 2017), 15-16.

We are human, but we don't wage war as humans do. We use God's mighty weapons, not worldly weapons to knock down the strongholds of human reasoning and to destroy false arguments. We destroy every proud obstacle that keeps people from knowing God. We capture their rebellious thoughts and teach them to obey Christ" (2 Cor 10:3-5).

Deconstructing the Empire of Lies

"To do evil, a human being must first of all believe that what he is doing is good or else that there it is a well-considered act in conformity with natural law."[211]

Alexander Solzhenitsyn, *The Gulag Archipelago*

The general malaise and moral confusion of the culture being what it is reminds me of Saint Francis' claim, according to early church legend, that he would need to go to the city center in Assisi and stand on his head to see the world aright. The early Christians were given credit for turning the world upside down.[212] The Christian worldview required everyone outside of the Christian faith to stand on their heads to make sense of things. But now, the world is back where Christians found it in the early days of the church and they find themselves, along with Saint Francis, standing on their heads to see it aright. Light has been declared darkness and darkness declared light. Right is wrong; wrong is right. Up is down, and down is up. The old greeting, "What's up?" requires the answer, "Who knows?"

---

[211] https://www.goodreads.com/quotes/9700887.

[212] Typically, the expression "Turned the world upside down" is a pejorative and part of the accusation made by those in authority. The Greek text speaks more literally of them being troublemakers and agitators—those motivated by insurrection. Acts 17:6 KJV.

I do not find myself standing on my head as much as simply scratching my head, befuddled as to how so many have gotten it so wrong. But as Solzhenitsyn said apparently the world has construed its actions as "good."

When you watch elected leaders attempt to prosecute people who use legally held firearms to defend themselves against protestors who threaten to burn down their home, but hundreds of looters are freed with no bail, you scratch your head. When a mayor of a world-class city allows anarchists to take over a part of the city and the mayor refers to it as a street festival or a summer of love, you scratch your head.[213] When leaders decide to keep schools closed during a pandemic and simultaneously decide that a Marxist-socialist movement has a right to protest, tear down statues, attack police and destroy public property because their right to protest cannot be denied, you start scratching with both hands.[214] When marijuana dispensaries remain open along with liquor stores because people cannot live without them, but churches are considered non-essential, you just put your head into your hands and moan.[215] The irony is almost laughable.

---

[213] "Goodbye, Summer of Love," *The Wall Street Journal*, 13 December 2020. https://www.wsj.com/articles/goodbye-summer-of-love-11607898398.

[214] Andrew Restuccia and Paul Kiernan, "Toppling of Statues Triggers Reckoning Over Nation's History." *The Wall Street Journal*, 23 June 2020. "https://www.wsj.com/articles/trump-seeks-to-protect-monuments-from-vandals-with-tougher-sentences-11592922449.

[215] Isabella Redjai, "Coronavirus: Churches Are Essential. If Protestors Can Assemble, So Should People of Faith." *USA Today*, 20 Augusts 2020. https://www.usatoday.com/story/opinion/voices/2020/08/08/coronavirus-pandemic-churches-essential-businesses-open-religious-freedom-column/3323082001/.

In previous articles, I have quoted Charles Malik's important words that our challenge is to both win souls and save minds.[216] If we lose the minds, we have lost the souls, and, as a result, the culture, the battle, and the war. If a person's Christian faith is not intellectually plausible, it will not penetrate the whole person or the soul. So what is our defense? Even better, what is our offense?

I learned early on in basketball that defense must be played but putting the ball in the basket is what we count. This is where the apostle Paul's words to the Corinthian Christian community come into play:

> We are human, but we don't wage war as humans do. We use God's mighty weapons, not worldly weapons, to knock down the strongholds of human reasoning and to destroy false arguments. We destroy every proud obstacle that keeps people from knowing God. We capture their rebellious thoughts and teach them to obey Christ (2 Cor. 10:3-5).

The Corinthian church was new, small, and culturally unimportant, but it was located in a large and important city. Rebuilt in 44 BCE by Julius Caesar after the desolation of war, Corinth was located on a small isthmus that saved sailors weeks of sailing since they could move goods and services much more quickly through Corinth. That made it a busy cosmopolitan seaport that brought the best and worst to the tiny strip of land. The rebuilt Corinth had some of the staples of the old Corinth. The Temple of Aphrodite along with the Roman gods of Mithras and Isis returned. The church was primarily composed of Gentiles who had been trained to glorify wisdom, ecstatic utterance, eating meat sacrificed to local gods,

---

[216] Malik, "The Two Tasks," *JETS*.

promiscuity, and prostitution.[217] The Temple of Aphrodite provided one-stop shopping with its hundreds of prostitutes, juicy steaks, and Viking Cruise level lectures on pop philosophy and travel.

If anything, the church had less to hold on to culturally and historically than we do today. They had no unified Christian worldview culture to stand on and compare to what they were experiencing. The Bible was in the process of being written, and orthodoxy would not come for another three hundred years. All they had were Paul's words and their lived experience. They learned as they went along. Paul, his rivals, and leaders of other religions or philosophies were their only lifelines to making it in a culture that worked against them in every part of life. That is why Paul encouraged them to keep perspective, to reject his rivals' philosophies, and to adhere to the gospel. "The message of the cross is foolish to those who are headed for destruction! But we who are being saved know it is the very power of God. As the Scriptures say, 'I will destroy the wisdom of the wise and discard the intelligence of the intelligent.'" (1 Cor 1:18-19).

However, Paul did not tell them to hide in the castle and pull up the drawbridge. He said in a later letter to them, "Let's go on offense." He made it clear: "We are human, but we don't wage war as humans do."[218]

We are at war! I think this means that we must take a cold hard look at what confronts us in the twenty-first century. Our opponent, Satan, is not interested in truth. He has no interest in a national conversation on race, justice, poverty, capitalism, socialism,

---

[217] Paul addressed all these ills in his Corinthian correspondence: philosophy and acquiring the mind of Christ in 1 Cor 1-2; the cult of celebrity 1 Cor 4; decadent living in 1 Cor 5; promiscuity in 1 Cor. 6; and ecstatic utterance in 1 Cor 12-14.

[218] 2 Cor 10:3.

abortion, school choice, or even what is right and wrong and why it is right or wrong. Truth does not matter to our enemy. Satan is a liar. He is the father of lies.[219] He is only interested in winning, winning, winning. He has come to lie, to kill, and to destroy.[220] He lied and tempted Christ in the wilderness.[221] He is after one thing: to destroy what God loves most, his creation. Even though he knows that he cannot win, he will fight to the death knowing that even if he loses, at least he can take millions of dead corpses with him and that hurts God. Paul understands this and stands a bit straighter and sticks out his chest and says, "We are going to take down Lucifer's Empire of Lies."

Most of Lucifer's disciples do not know they are his disciples.[222] In fact, he is the great deceiver and has convinced them, through an elaborate system of lies, images, and emotions, that they are doing good.[223] In fact, they believe they are morally superior to Christians, and they call on Christians to repent, to confess, to shut up and listen, and to cancel, deny, and remove all that we and our ancestors have done wrong. Christians are accused of hate, but we actually love. Christians are called intolerant, but we are open-minded. Christians are said to repress the true glory of humanity. However, we want everyone to flourish and express their full potential. We too believe that Black lives matter along with all other lives, including the thousands of pre-born innocents that are killed year after year, decade after decade, in their mothers' wombs. Of course, those who rationalize the taking of pre-born life do so in the name of helping women. The reality, though, is that there is money to be made in harvesting fetal tissue, and

---

[219] John 8:44.
[220] John 10:10.
[221] Luke 4:1-13.
[222] 2 Cor 4:3-4
[223] Isa 5:20; John 16:2; Acts 26:9.

abortion on demand gives women and their male partners the "freedom" to live their lives without taking responsibility for their actions. The battle is on, and the battlefield already has two dead corpses—truth and reason. Now what?

We must use our own special weapons that the enemy does not possess which will

"knock down and destroy their strongholds of human reasoning and destroy their arguments."[224]

What weapons is Paul referring to? His words have been used to launch apologetic ministries. They have inspired our greatest minds to write books to engage the enemy's best and brightest. Is this what Charles Malik refers to when he says that if we lose the mind, we have lost the soul?

It is true you cannot bypass the mind if you want a whole person who understands the reasons for their own actions. Lucifer has done a spectacular job of getting vast throngs to watch five hundred episodes of the *Simpsons*, *Seinfeld*, *Friends*, or some other repeatable series that will cause one to bypass the mind and program the emotions to be cynical about a life without meaning, and to believe, in that cynicism, that people can have sex with anyone they want and then get an abortion to avoid consequences of an unwanted pregnancy, such as being overlooked for a promotion at work due to maternity leave.

Paul's immediate context is his authority with the Corinthian church.[225] His words indicate that his opponents' lies will be exposed by the truthfulness of his own life, his belief in prayer,

---

[224] 2 Cor. 10:4.
[225] 2 Cor 10:1.

and the full armor of God as detailed to the Ephesians in 6:10-18. He believed that when he arrived, his personal presence, his anointing from God, and the power of God working through him would destroy all their arguments. This is the underlying assumption of his words. He is speaking of the intangible—of spiritual authority and presence. In that immediate context, this issue for Paul was of first importance. This is of equal importance now as we interact with those we meet personally because they must sense that we speak with authority. That authority is rooted in our calling and in our lived experience. [226]

There is a broader context that leaps off the page and across the generations as well that speaks to Malik's words and warning. Malik was concerned in his 1982 speech that we had lost the culture.[227] I think we have lost the culture. The train has left the station, and we find ourselves standing on the platform asking what happened and what can we do about it.

The 90-10 Rule

My take is that 90% of protestors, and people in general, are thinking normally and are operating from a moral foundation provided by Christian-based Western civilization. If you combine the image of God in every person along with a moral base of the Ten Commandments and the teachings of Jesus, you get a platform from which to relate to one another. When everyone

---

[226] Matt 28:19. Jesus said he had all authority, and he issued to us the charge to make disciples based on that authority. His authority is now vested in every Christian. As we live our lives in that authority and stick to God's word, then we know that God is with us and working through us. He also promised in Matt 28:20 that he would be with us until the end of the age or the end of this project to make disciples of all peoples.
[227] Malik, "Two Tasks," *JETS* , 293.

agrees, it is clear with whom and where authority lies, and people do not waste time fighting about it.

Since 90% percent of people fall into this category, that means 90% of the people are not in favor of insurrection. When they chant or agree with "Black lives matter" as a motto, they simply mean that Blacks have had a tough go and we need to take a hard look at ourselves and improve race relations. Those people are open to normal human interaction. They will discuss issues and listen. In that sense, being loving, kind, and interested in them will often break down some of their arguments against God.

The 10% who are the protagonists of the elite culture—the media, the academy, the entertainment community, the loony left and right who are determined to marshal an aggressive intellectual and cultural campaign to win over the American public to their side—want to remake America. They want to tear it down and rebuild a new Tower of Babel for the purpose of holding both political and cultural power. They are generally angry and hostile toward their opponents and are ungoverned by moral principles. This is where Christians are at a disadvantage. Christians are limited in tactics and are constrained by divine revelation. We must fight fair: no lying, stealing, cheating, slandering, and murder. This removes many useful tools from our arsenal. If Christians played by the enemies' rules, such as Saul Alinsky's *Rules for Radicals*, the church could score many cultural points through slandering and cheating its enemy, but in the long run we would lose.[228]

---

[228] The rules are divide and conquer, create scapegoats, create chaos, make it a movement, political trash talk, disinformation, the thing is never the thing, and seize power. Saul Alinksky, *Rules For Radicals: A Pragmatic Primer for Realistic Radicals*, (New York: Vintage, 2010).

What is our goal?

"We destroy every proud obstacle that keeps people from knowing God."[229]

To put it like the commonly used motto, our mission is to know Christ and to make him known. That is the focus of all this warfare and the activity we engage in. In order to do that, we need to destroy these proud obstacles by exposing them and teaching God's worldview for the world. In fact, much of this information is inherent to the Gospel.

When you say you know God, people are immediately suspicious. The wisdom of God seems like foolishness to them. When you show them a Jesus turning over tables and screaming at the Pharisees, they are baffled at how a peacemaker becomes so confrontational. The idea that the meek and mild Jesus would one day return in the world's last battle with King of Kings and Lord of Lords tattooed on his thighs and slay the nations with a word from his mouth, blasts all their categories into smithereens.[230] But first, before the Apocalypse, we must live in this age of argumentation and disagreement, debate and conflict.

What are some of the lies that have been constructed that keep people from knowing God? What is the content of the Empire of Lies? That is the subject of the next essay.

---

[229] 2 Cor 10:5.
[230] Matt 21:12-13; Mark 11:15-18; Rev 19:15-16.

Calling Out The Idols

"But God shows his anger from heaven against all sinful, wicked people who suppress the truth by their wickedness."

Romans 1:18

*"We destroy every proud obstacle that **keeps people from knowing God**."*

2 Corinthians 10:5a

The Christian's responsibility is to call out idols that keep people from knowing God. This is not a pleasant duty, but it is part of the battle plan. It is not quite as simple as tearing down a statue alongside a chariot path in 700 BCE Israel. These days idols are ideas. They pop up here and then there. They move fast and are hard to get a hold on. They are arguments that have memorable catch phrases like "if it feels good, do it;" "anything is okay if no one gets hurt;" "all we need is love;" and "a woman's right to choose." These statements separate freedom from authority, morality, self-denial, and the discipline and perseverance necessary to have real freedom to overcome human weakness and destruction.[231] There are many idols (ideologies) that need to be identified, captured, put on trial, and sentenced to the fiery pit from whence they came.

---

[231] In the natural realm, the freedom to play Chopin or Beethoven on the piano with abandon is a joy reserved only for those whose discipline and practice have freed them to achieve such heights.

The suppression of truth

In general, we begin by identifying and calling out anyone and everyone who suppresses the truth. In Romans 1:18, God appears to be angry. The Greek word οργη or "wrath" means a rightly directed anger to destroy evil. The goal of nearly everyone from the far-left anti-war protestor to the Navy Seal with a knife in his teeth and a gun in his hand is to get rid of evil. God's anger is not lurking as much as it is going to be revealed.

Religious skeptics do not think God will let the hammer of justice down or bring this moral drama to an end. They do not believe that the Lord's second coming, judgment, and eternal reign will happen. They suppress the truth. That suppression is what God intends to destroy, and he calls on us to participate.

Those who suppress the truth do so with what is called wickedness. Wickedness is a seldom-used word that means a willful decision to sin or do evil. God's anger is directed at those who willfully choose to suppress the revealed truth from God about himself, humans, and the state of the world.

Suppression, or the pushing down of the truth, is fundamental to Lucifer's global strategy. I am reminded of this watching cable news. Something as simple as the evening news can be infuriating to watch. Networks routinely suppress storylines they do not agree with. The press used to be the referee and hold each political party accountable. You can now watch what is being covered by CNN and Fox News and conclude that they are reporting on two different universes. Their power lies not only in what is covered but also in what is not covered. A network's guests and the comments of its on-air talent reveal the agendas and biases inherent in the network's philosophy. Down-the-middle hard news coverage is difficult to find.

Depending on your political views, you can find yourself murmuring to yourself, shouting at the TV, or simply shutting it off and leaving the room. This is the kind of disgust that God experiences when he sees his opponents suppressing the truth because it keeps people from knowing the truth about him. He is angry about this.

This is not about politics

Everything is political except God. Politics involve arguing about what is true, and, frankly, people rarely find a place of agreement in such discussions. The result is compromise due to the limits of human reasoning and capacity. Human communities find synthesis, a blending of opinion into a livable accommodation of what is acceptable truth. God, however, is the source of all truth. He is the truth, and our very lives depend on knowing and living by that truth.[232] Ignorance of the truth is deadly. It separates humans from their creator and evil flourishes. It rips the world apart into tribes who war against each other.

The facts are obvious

"They know the truth about God because he has made it obvious to them. For ever since the world was created, people have seen the earth and sky. Through everything God made, they can clearly see his invisible qualities—his eternal power and divine nature. So they have no excuse for not knowing God" (Rom 1:19-20).

To qualify as a willful suppressor of God's truth, it makes sense that the people would have ready access to that truth. God is not

---

[232] John 17:17.

indiscreetly ready to take out every ignorant human. All humans, outside of God revealing himself, have been and are ignorant of God and his ways. Those people are not his wrathful target. It is those who know the truth, suppress it, and keep the knowledge of God from those who need it. Who then is in danger?

I have special animas for proud pseudo-intellectuals, some with degrees and some who have just read a couple of books and deny the obvious reality of God. The history of contemporary philosophy and its stepchild, progressive theology, states that you cannot really know anything. From Kant's assertion that you cannot trust your own eyes to Hegel's infamous dialectic, thesis, antithesis, and synthesis which says truth is a blend of opposing ideas synced together, human reason's shortcomings leave you scratching your head.[233] As Dallas Willard once quipped, "If you laid every philosopher in the world end to end, they couldn't reach a conclusion."[234]

Human reason is a wonderful tool that makes science possible. However, it has not and never will scratch the surface of the true nature of reality. Human reason is limited in ability. It lacks the capacity to process the ways of creation, the person of God, and the mysteries of the universe. This is the reason most people grab their heads and say, "Those thoughts are too big for my head." Human logic, though somewhat similar to the mind of God, runs aground in every important category. The definitions of good, evil, the universe, supernatural events, and beings are all outside its purview. It does not grasp why the world exists, what is best

---

[233] These are well known teachings of both Kant and Hegel. For further information, see Imannuel Kant's *Critique of Pure Reason* (1781, 1787) and G.W.F. Hegel *Phenomenlogy of Spirit* (1807). https://plato.stanford. edu/entries/kant/ https://plato.stanford.edu/entries/hegel-dialectics/.
[234] This is not in written form, but I have personally heard Dallas Willard use this statement as joke many times.

for it now, how it all will end, and how it should end. Revealed truth from holy Scripture is the doorway to reality and that is what God is upset about. "Don't suppress my message. Don't reject your visitation in Jesus the Christ. Let the light of the world shine through. Don't suppress it."

The fundamental platform on which suppression of truth stands is a sinister motive to oppose God. Paul mentions this in his penetrating phrases, "They know the truth about God. It is obvious to them . . . through creation he has made the invisible clearly visible." Obvious, clear, and visible. If they do not know God, it because they have a very deep-seated reason not to. Paul goes on to tell us why: "Yes, they knew God, but they wouldn't worship him as God or even give him thanks. They began to think up foolish ideas of what God was like. As a result, their minds became dark and confused" (Rom 1:21).

To know God in this case means they had ample evidence for his existence, divine nature, and eternal power. The appropriate response would be to worship and thank him. They chose instead to suppress him and to invent silly ideas about him. Why? They—those who suppress the truth—are motivated to control their own lives and not submit to a higher power.

Some might point out they suppress the truth because they are not elect. That is too simple, quite unsatisfying, and reveals a desire to dismiss the problem. There is present in every human heart the desire to control one's life and to resist any authority who threatens individual sovereignty. Some submit to God's redemptive reach; some resist and then submit; others, for mysterious reasons, do not submit, and it is this group that is in danger.

Cultural revolutions, the sexual revolution, and other such movements were all preceded by the death of God revolution.

The death of God movement began on the European continent in the mid to late nineteenth century and continues in a niche sort of way in the United States today. Nietzsche famously said, "God is dead. God remains dead. And we have killed him . . . all that the world has yet owned has bled to death under our knives: who will wipe this blood off us?"[235] There is only one answer as to why people became wicked. Their leader Lucifer is wicked, and his goal is to destroy everything that God created and loves. He is determined to kill what God loves the most, his creation.[236]

People do not become wicked; they are born wicked.[237] From our viewpoint, we choose wickedness. But why do we choose it? We don't quite know. However, we know that when we choose it, we have done something wrong or nonsensical.

The atheist does not really live with a clear conscience. He lives with a seared conscience or in a state of suspension of all his innate knowledge. He is mad that God does not exist and is also mad at God for not doing a better job with the world.

The first idol to be identified and laughed off the stage is that God either does not exist or is some manufactured being too weak to control his world, too cold to care for it, or too occupied with his other worlds and projects to care about the people on planet Earth. These inventions are about as plausible as the Dancing Jesus bobblehead doll that my son gave me for Christmas. It came with instructions. It made me laugh. But I have never once surrounded it with fruit & flowers, bowed before it, or prayed to it. It is just a stupid doll that I should probably put in the garage.

---

[235] https://www.goodreads.com/quotes/22827-god-is-dead-god-remains-dead-and-we-have-killed.
[236] John 10:10.
[237] Rom 5:12; Eph 2:1-2.

Calling Out
The Idols Part 2

*"First you must **say**, black is white. Then you must **believe** black is white, then you come to **know** that black is white and finally, you **deny** that there was ever a difference between black and white."*[238]

George Orwell, *1984*

Once a society denies what is obviously true, it slips and falls. It becomes a victim of its own foolishness. Such was the dystopia *1984*'s main character Winston Smith experienced. He lived in a world made of lies, but he rebelled because reality has its own voice. The dystopian world he lived in was harsh, dark, dirty, and not free. His own inner voice told him that this bleak life was his reality, not the bright and lovely utopia that Big Brother told him it was.

When you are hoping for a utopia, first you hear only the whispers of reality. After many disappointments, that same voice speaks clearly. Finally, in your own agony, it shouts at the top of its lungs. We could call it Reality's Revenge. It is a process that seems gradual and slow, but, as it gains momentum, you notice the change and suddenly it is an avalanche. What Winston Smith experienced in the Orwellian novel *1984* is similar to what suppression of the truth creates in modern society.

---

[238] Emily Temple, "All of the Passages in *1984* That Relate To You Right Now." *Literary Hub*, 27 January 2017. https://lithub.com/all-of-the-passages-in-1984-that-relate-to-you-right-now/.

The idols of skepticism, agnosticism, and atheism, exemplified in the myth of religious evolution and moral progress, lead to a denial of what is obvious, and humans choose to worship other humans, avatars, and creation itself. They reject revelation. They reason without revelation which always leads to foolishness; so God does what he does:

> "So God abandoned them to do whatever shameful things their hearts desired" (Rom 1:24).

In large part, this has already happened in America. Our society has chosen to live for desire rather than in obedience to God's laws and principles. It is often said, "Follow your heart." This is terrible advice particularly because "the human heart is the most deceitful of all things, and desperately wicked. Who really knows how bad it is? But I the Lord, search all hearts and examine secret motives. I give all people their due rewards, according to what their actions deserve" (Jer 17:9-10). God has not forsaken us; however, he has given us our head and said, "Okay. Have it your way."

God puts good desires in us. Paul tells us in Philippians 2:13 that God works in us to give us the desire and power to do what pleases him. But when left to our own devices, when we decide to not listen to God, he lifts his hand from our shoulder and the decline begins. The idol of human desire is an abyss of decadence that is degrading to the soul. "As a result, they did vile and degrading things with each other's bodies" (Rom 1:24). This could be called the sexual revolution.

In Orwell's *1984*, The Ministry of Truth building was an enormous pyramidal structure of glittering white concrete soaring up, terrace after terrace, three hundred meters into the air. The Party had three slogans: war is peace; freedom is slavery; and ignorance is strength. It is easy to say, "That is nonsense! It is upside down and backward. Have they have lost their minds?" Everyone knew it was nonsense until they didn't. At first, society rejects bad ideas. Then as people hear them repeatedly, they become accustomed to hearing the bad ideas until they eventually do not hear any more. Those nonsensical ideas become cultural artifacts. Then younger generations think those artifacts are normal because they have always been present in their lives. If history is pushed down the memory hole and then rewritten, you develop citizens who believe the absurd to be true.

When you see a riot on television and the commentator tells you it is peaceful, you shout, "What?" But if you we are told that often enough, you finally say, "Maybe there is some truth in that." That is how revolutions begin and that is how Lucifer changed society's mind about sexual behavior.

I did not go to Woodstock, but that was my generation.[239] The 1960s were tumultuous. It was a decade of sexual permissiveness, "free love," unabated public nudity, increased violence in movies, and increased popularity of LSD and other mood-altering drugs. Music and literature challenged traditional morality. Society regularly witnessed mass protests on college campuses and demonstrations in the streets. Rebellion was in the air as organized groups of student protestors, Students for a Democratic Society, the Black Panthers, Martin Luther King, Jr. and other civil rights activists all protested issues ranging from the Vietnam War to inequities in education, housing and voting rights.[240] The decade closed with the assassinations of

---

[239] Woodstock was a music festival held in upstate New York August 15-18, 1969. It was attended by four hundred thousand people.

[240] Legislative changes, including The Civil rights Act, The Voting Rights Act, and The Fair Housing Act, came as a result of ongoing nationwide protests. The legislation that came from the peaceful protests led by Martin Luther King were constitutional and yielded good results.

King and presidential candidate Robert Kennedy and also with riots at the 1968 Democratic National Convention in Chicago. The tumult of the 60s spilled into the 1970s as the very unpopular Vietnam War remained in full swing and President Richard Nixon resigned from office in the wake of the Watergate scandal.

From my perch as a high school student, then a college student, and then as a newly married young man, I was a bystander to all of this. I became a Christian in 1967 at a private Christian university and then joined an evangelical student organization. The sexual revolution happened all around me but not to me. The church was clearly a bystander and was not penetrated in any noticeable way by these events until the mid-1970s.

In 1969, I was given a Bible with a cover that proclaimed, "Revolution Now!" Our goal was to fulfill the Great Commission by 1976 in the United States and in the world by 1980. We, the one thousand staff members of Campus Crusade for Christ, went about this mission with all our beings and with complete sincerity. Much good was done, great numbers heard an abridged Gospel, and millions worldwide prayed the "sinner's prayer." Only God knows what really happened. If the Great Commission was fulfilled, the result did not include societal change or a culture of higher moral values.

Since then, society has become more morally confused, its institutions more corrupt, and its leaders more feckless. Presently the national character is collapsing. Truth as a serious category has collapsed. The only place people want the truth is when they walk into their bank. A society built on desire is like a house built on the sand. It has become like Isaiah's lament: "What sorrow for those who say that evil is good and good is evil, that dark is light and light is dark, that bitter is sweet and sweet is bitter" (Isa 5:20).

Karl Marx's "false consciousness" applied today might go something like this. "You may think you're happy in your home with your little family, singing in the shower, mowing the grass, going to work every day, having dinner at 6:00 every night, but you're really not. Someone has just taught you that. Actually, you are unhappy. Your life should be better. It is false consciousness. It is a form of mental illness. You may think only women can have babies, but that is just a social construct. Men who pretend to be women can beat actual women in a foot race, boxing, arm wrestling, and hairy chests, but the glorious thing is that it's all fair and people don't think these confused men are cheating. It is all so glorious. The welfare state is not a trillion-dollar con. It has worked, so we need more of it. If you appease rioters, don't arrest them. Let them go with no bail. They will stop on their own because down deep they just want what's best for humanity. They won't take it as weakness and do it again. When you exercise your constitutional right as a woman to terminate a pregnancy, that goblet of flesh inside of you is not a helpless, innocent human being. It is a potential life that would have hindered or threatened your freedom. Don't worry. It is not a person who would have called you 'Mommy' and brought great joy to your life. It would not have grabbed you around your neck and said, 'I love you, Mommy! I love you!' It wasn't a loving son or daughter who would have taken care of you in your old age and given you grandchildren. That is just false consciousness."

We are living in a world from which, to some significant degree, God has lifted his hand of guidance and protection. He has abandoned us to the shameful things our hearts have desired, including shameful things we do with each other's bodies. We have traded the truth of God for a lie. Truth is temporarily set aside. Let us see where it leads us.

Calling Out Still
More Idols

"Nearly all that we call human history...
[is] the long terrible story of man trying to find
Something other than God which will make him happy."[241]

C. S. Lewis, *Mere Christianity*

New Testament scholar Scot McKnight has made reading Romans backward fashionable.[242] I'm still working on reading it forward. We have established thus far that idols make God angry. Rome was a city crawling with idols. Like zombies, they were ubiquitous throughout homes, public buildings, and infrastructure, dominating the architecture of the era.

Many idols today are also inanimate objects that the human mind animates: business successes or images brought to life by the right automobile, clothes, vacation home, or travel experience. Twenty-first century idealists who fancy themselves as revolutionaries tear down statues of dead Confederate generals, displaying their ignorance of history. Confident that they would have made different choices if they had grown up on a nineteenth century plantation in Georgia, they merely repeat the

---

[241] C.S. Lewis *Mere Christianity*, (Nashville: Harper One) 2009, 53.
[242] Scot McKnight, *Reading Romans Backwards: A Gospel of Peace in the Midst of Empire*, (Waco, TX: Baylor University Press) 2019.

history they repudiate with their own morally superior prejudice, outrage, and destruction. Using their own brand of hate, they repeat the sins of the people they hate. They compound their ignorance when they tear down statues of people like Abraham Lincoln, the champion of freedom who signed the Emancipation Proclamation. It is easy to destroy someone else's property, especially when feckless political leaders have told authorities to stand down and do nothing, but it violates all semblance of moral order, established law, and anything having to do with righteousness, justice, or the will of God.[243]

Thus far in our reading of Romans Chapter 1, we have learned that God gives societies over and abandons them to do whatever their hearts desire. When they insist on rejecting God's revelation of himself, he gives them over to their foolish and darkened minds.[244] What is the result? It could be called a sexual revolution—the destruction of human sexuality as God intended. There is no doubt America is a prime example of that, particularly from the 1960s – present day, circa 2000.

But it can get worse. Romans 1 shows that culture goes further prompting God to abandon people to their shameful ways.[245]

The Fateful Plunge: Confusion of the Sexes

Even women turned against the natural way to have sex and instead indulged in sex with each other. And the men, instead of having normal sexual relations with women, burned with lust for each other. Men did shameful things with other men, and, as a result of this

---

[243] Rom 1:24.

[244] Rom 1:21.

[245] Rom 1:26.

sin, they suffered within themselves the penalty they deserved (Rom 1:26-27).

I am amused by the growing number of very astute "woke" exegetes who pensively ask, "I wonder what Paul meant here?" If there is a passage in Romans that does not require a commentary, this is it. God once again lifted his hand and said, "Okay. It's all yours. Have it your way."

I have read the articles and the thick commentaries. I can read the Greek New Testament. I have listened to the debates and am aware of all the "new" discoveries that have been unearthed after two thousand years. It is amazing how so many serious students find exactly what they are looking for—alleged truths hidden for many years but discovered just at the time society insists they be found. We are told about homosexual "love" versus homosexual lust and are told that the apostle Paul was not bothered by the homosexual practices of loving couples but only the abuse of young boys.[246] Even though no such claims can be found anywhere in the New Testament, we can increasingly read reconfigured narratives written by modern scholars who try to fill

---

[246] E.P. Sanders points out that acceptable behavior in the Roman world was for men to have sex with women, but they could have sex with other males if those males were at least eleven years old. It was acceptable as long as the person being penetrated was below you in status. If a man allowed some male of lower class to penetrate him, he was despised. Even though there is great nuance in the Greek words used, a point that Sanders makes at length, Paul continues to hold his ground on the sin of homosexuality. Clearly Paul was bothered by abuse of boys and would condemn present society's increasing acceptance of pedophilia. He certainly would not sign on to any effort to remove it from APA's official directory of psychological disorders. E. P Sanders, *Paul: The Apostle's Life, Letters, and Thought* (Minneapolis: Fortress Press, 2015), 346-47.

in "missing data" and provide "cultural expertise" and modern wisdom to read the "real story" back into ancient documents.[247]

It is painfully obvious that Paul was calling homosexual practice a sin in Romans 1. He made no allowance for it. It is equally obvious that the phrase "as a result of this sin, they suffered within themselves the penalty they deserved" is about venereal disease. I am not even sure how this is debatable. The fact that the penalty is applied to their bodies demonstrates that it is a physical malady. Paul did not say in this passage that homosexuals go to hell. He did not say that homosexuals cannot be Christians. You do not go to hell for being homosexual, and you do not go to heaven for being heterosexual. The bottom line in the larger context of God's anger, God's turning them over to sexual decadence, is that they rejected God's ways and made idols of their own freedom and choices leaving society unprotected from its own destruction. This gets us to the C.S. Lewis quote at the article's start:

Nearly all that we call human history...
[is] the long terrible story of man trying to find
Something other than God which will make him happy.[248]

Lewis knew the struggle from atheist to theist to Christian. For him, it was a long, painful journey that began in the blood-soaked trenches of the Maginot line in World War I and ended in the sidecar of his brother Warne's motorcycle. His life then began to make sense.[249] Nancy Pearcy put it this way, "If you do not start

---

[247] This is evident in reading most progressive or liberal commentaries, articles, or classroom teaching in progressive seminaries. The more leftist interpretation of the sexual behavior passages in the New Testament is trending and seeping into more mainstream thought.
[248] Lewis, *Mere Christianity*, 53.
[249] Lewis told his story in his autobiography *Surprised by Joy: The Shape of My Early Life*, (New York: Harcourt Brace, 1955).

with God, you must start somewhere else. You must propose something else as the ultimate, eternal, uncreated reality that is the cause and source of everything else."[250]

That something else is looking grimmer every day. Moral confusion is "gay." "Freedom" is federal funding to abort innocent children. Chaos, looting, and violence in the streets is "the right of peaceful assembly." "Intellectual honesty" is the erasure of history in order to rewrite a more palatable version. "Freedom of speech" is freedom to say what the thought police—media and the intellectual elite—think should be said. Failure to define freedom of speech in this way results in cancellation, marginalization, job loss, and being kicked to the curb. We must find the biggest megaphones we can, climb to the highest hills, and shout at the top of our lungs, "God visited us in the person of Jesus the Christ. Listen to him, do what he says, and you will live."

---

[250] Nancy Pearcey, *Finding Truth, 5 Principles for Unmasking Atheism, Secularism and Other God Substitutes* (Colorado Springs, CO: 2015), 61.

Your Best Argument with God

I don't know if it could be called an argument, but I find myself wondering how much longer I will be living in my present manifestation on earth. God seems to be involved in this, and he made the decision a long time ago. Before there was time, there was God. He not only knew everything actual and potential but has worked it out in the larger scheme of things. [251] But the answer to my question has something to do with my assignment and when it will be finished.

I know the more romantic side of human nature likes the idea that God loves us for ourselves just like we are to love him for himself, but this seems to ignore that God has done a great deal for us that makes us grateful to him. He does not ask us to love, obey, and follow him for no reason but for actions he has taken on our behalf.[252] In the same way, my assignment—what we label a calling—is something I do for him in return. The length of my days has something to do with the completion of this assignment.[253] This may be the reason some of us do not want to retire and stop working. It makes us feel that our lives are over. There are many counterpoints to what I have just said that could balance the relational scale with God, but I will set them aside for my more immediate point.

---

[251] Ps 139:1-16.

[252] 1 John 4:4.

[253] Ps 139:16.

Sometimes God allows you to know that something in the future will take place and gives you confidence that you will be alive at least until it happens. Here is one that may have faded from your memory. It is the story about Paul's shipwreck on his journey to Rome. After the first part of the voyage began and the ship had struggled to make progress, they came into a port. Paul warned the ship's officers that danger would be ahead if they continued.

> "Men," he said, "I believe there is trouble ahead if we go on—shipwreck, loss of cargo, and danger in our lives as well." But the officer in charge of the prisoners listened more to the ship's captain and the owner than to Paul (Acts 27:10-12).

The officers decided to not winter in Fair Havens. They preferred to attempt to make it to Phoenix, a more protected harbor.[254] Very soon they lost control of the ship. They were caught in a typhoon and were blown out to sea. They could not turn the ship into the wind and had to let the gale force winds take the ship where it would. Then conditions grew worse. They not only threw cargo overboard, but the sailors threw their own gear overboard. This went on for several days. No one ate or slept. All hope was gone. [255] It was in this moment that Paul stood up and was a bit of an "I told you so."

> Men, you should have listened to me in the first place and not left Crete. You would have avoided all this damage and loss. But take courage! None of you will lose your lives, even though the ship will go down. For last night an angel of the God to whom I belong and whom I serve stood beside me, and he said, "Do not be afraid, Paul, for you

---

[254] Fair Havens and Phoenix were cities in the nation of Crete.
[255] Acts 27:14-20.

will surely stand trial before Caesar! What's more, God in his goodness has granted safety to everyone sailing with you." So take courage! For I believe God. It will be just as he said. But we will be shipwrecked on an island. (Acts 27:24-26)

The pessimistic sailors would have locked up on the simple declaration "the ship will go down." The optimists would have focused on "none of you will lose your lives." The pragmatists, who liked to know the situation, would have centered on, "We will be shipwrecked on an island." There was something for everybody. However, Paul hung onto the simple promise that he would have his day in court. He would live long enough to stand before Caesar's court.

This story shows us that when the voyage began, Paul was sailing with the officers and crew of over 250, but it becomes clear at this stage that 250 men were sailing with Paul.[256] It presents an example of how God sometimes spares many lives in order to save one life that will accomplish his purpose. Not always. It is dangerous to be presumptuous. But for the follower of Jesus, it is a possibility, and there is nothing wrong with praying for it when in a tight spot.

I really like the detail in the story—the navigational details that provide authenticity and the combination of man's effort, failure, and frustration with the way God controls all of it to spare their lives. "About midnight on the fourteenth night of the storm, as we were being driven across the Sea of Adria . . ." He goes on to describe how the sailors dropped a weighted line measuring the water at 120 feet deep, then 90 feet. Paul reminded the panic-stricken crew who wanted to abandon the ship that only

---

[256] Acts 27:37.

those who stayed on board would live. [257] This combination of human action, common sense, belief, courage, and tenacity through people is how God works. I find it all so fascinating and encouraging. The reality of God, his knowledge of the details of our lives, how humans act and react, and what we need and do not need is brilliantly on display.

Paul then led them in a prayer, and they ate. After the toughest two weeks of their lives, they were somewhat at peace, and they knew it had something to do with the strange man Paul and his God.[258] Finally the ship did wreck. Most of the crew swam to shore while others floated on debris.[259] They were safe on the island of Malta. This is where Paul was bitten by a poisonous snake and shook it off, no harm, no foul. The island natives decided he was a god.[260] This was not the first time Paul was mistaken for a god.[261] This is a hazard when you are close to God.

Paul healed a few people in Malta, became quite popular, and, by the time they sailed, the locals provided the sailors with everything they needed. Paul and his now disciples and companions sailed on to Rome.[262]

So What?

Our lives as disciples and our purpose as a church have some similarities with Paul's situation. I sit here at more than seventy years of age as a writer and ministry leader. What is my argument

---

[257] Acts 27:27-31.
[258] Acts 27:33-37.
[259] Acts 27:41-44.
[260] Acts 28:1-6.
[261] Acts 14:11-13.
[262] Acts 28:7-14.

to God for keeping me around, in my right mind, and on target? I would like to stipulate that in the end, I do not know if any argument on my part as to my importance to redemptive history has any merit. I think my best shot is, "Lord, I really like this, and I want to get in on as much of it as possible, so be gracious to me, a sinner and adopted son. Give me a bit more, please." But there is something else. Charles Finney used to say, "Make your calling your argument." His meaning was to make your assignment the basis of your petition. Paul thought this way. He spoke of finishing his race, keeping the faith, and making sure his work was done.[263]

The United States of America is going through stormy conditions, but the church is still on board. The United States of America plays a crucial role in the world economically and geopolitically. What holds back Communist China, Russia, tyrants, and socialists from gobbling up weaker nations and enslaving them? How about terrorist states like Iran and other bad actors? What accounts for the 50% reduction of poverty in the world in the last fifteen years? It is the creative power and good will of the United States.

We are a flawed country. One only needs to watch the news to see that. We are politically divided, morally degraded, and our national consciousness regarding the recognition of evil is seared. It looks grim from a biblical point of view. We are a country that has sinned, but we also have repented and have strived to get better as this struggle continues.[264] God has given us power because we are largely a force for good over evil. That is why we require borders and have rules about who can enter our country. People want to come here because of freedom and opportunity. What makes America great is slipping through our fingers, and

---

[263] 2 Tim 4:7.

[264] Civil rights is the most obvious way in which our nation has repented and gotten better.

that is why we, the church, are on board the ship that carries the message of Christ. That is our argument to God to keep us afloat—so that we can make disciples of Christ until the entire world hears and understands.

I like what Lance Wallnau says about this. The call to "go into all the world" is no longer simply geographic. We must go into all the systems of the world. He calls them the seven mountains or seven molders of culture: religion, family, education, government, news media, entertainment, and business/economics. [265]

This goes far beyond politics. The church's role is to throw our entire energy and weight into this project of making disciples. It begins in the church, but it actually begins with me. My argument for a continued assignment is about my faithfulness to the assignment God has given me as a disciple maker. This entire matter keeps driving me back to the parting words of Dallas Willard in his book *The Great Omission*:

What do I do now! Convert the world? No. Convert the church? "Judgment," it is famously said, "begins at the house of God." It has the divine light and divine provisions, and because of that is most responsible to guide humankind. But "No" again. Do not "convert the church." Your first move "as you go" is in a manner of speaking: Convert me" . . . Jesus said to his disciples "Make disciples." We have no other God appointed business but this, and we must allow all else to fall away if it will."[266]

---

[265] Lance Wallnau, *God's Chaos Candidate: Donald J. Trump and The American Unraveling*, (Roanoke, TX: Killer Sheep Media Inc., 2016), Table of Contents.
[266] Dallas Willard, *The Great Omission*, (San Francisco: Harper and Row, 2005), 225.

Don't Shut Up - Show Up

*"And so dear brothers and sisters, I plead with you to **give your bodies to God** because of all he has done for you. Let them be a **living and holy sacrifice**—the kind he will find acceptable. **This is truly the way to worship him.** Don't **copy the behavior** and customs of this world, but let **God transform you into a new person** by changing the way you think. Then you will learn to know God's will for you, which is good and pleasing and perfect."*

Romans 12:2

*"...the beautiful young things of the reformed renaissance have a hard choice to make in the next decade. You really do kid only yourselves if you think you can be an orthodox Christian and be at the same time cool enough and hip enough to cut it in the wider world. Frankly, in a couple of years it will not matter how much urban ink you sport, how much fair trade coffee you drink, how many craft brews you can name, how much urban gibberish you spout, how many art house movies you can find that redeemer figure in, and how much money you divert from gospel preaching to social justice: **maintaining biblical sexual ethics will be the equivalent in our culture of being a white supremacist.**"* [emphasis added]

Carl Trueman

Carl Trueman's prophetic claim is now open to examination. The ten years are up. Was he right or wrong about the Christian impulse to identify and assimilate into the secular culture? Have those who tried it stayed orthodox? Have they remained on course? Have you become more likeable or acceptable to the general culture? Or has staying true to your orthodox views on homosexuality, abortion, gender, and race made you persona non grata? Have you been declared a racist, a homophobe, an anti-science, climate-change-denying Philistine?

Only a very tiny percentage of you really know the answer because the vast majority of Christians have not spoken up or stood up. They are unable to answer those questions. That might be okay. Not all of us have been called to be on the front lines, but all of us have a lot on the line. There are a minority who have spoken up and stood their ground. They have ventured into conversations, written articles, submitted to interviews, authored books, spoken out on social media, and they can answer the above questions clearly. Yes, they have been called these names.

The big surprise is not that secular culture has spit them back out like used gum. The surprise is who has chewed them up first. Would it be a surprise if I told you it was probably members of BigEva? BigEva is shorthand for the new "woke" elite of neo-evangelicalism. What makes them seem less threatening is they are true Christians who have adopted a leftist worldview, such as Christianity Today, Inc. and their magazine. They decided that Donald Trump was immoral and to vote for him would be immoral. They seriously question the minds and critical thinking capacity of Christian Trump supporters. They do not come right out and call Trump supporters bad names. That is below their station. They have compassion on their weaker friends. If only those friends could be enlightened in the halls of the academy. If only they could see some of the new research and the great strides in social justice. If they could just adopt our more integrated and compassionate worldview, they would see how giving up the fight and allowing the secular left to run our country unabated would create greater harmony, peace, and civil conversation in the long run.

BigEva reminds me of the dreamy utopians of the 1930s who thought the social experiment in the Soviet Union would bring equality and harmony to the world. For those who think equality of result is utopia, I would recommend Malcolm Muggeridge's *Winter in Moscow*, a marvelous expose of a malevolent and evil force.

Let's follow Paul's line of thought through the book of Romans for a moment. Walking through the cultural sludge is difficult, but Paul's document provides clarity. The root of the problem facing society is its refusal to worship God as he is. This is what God is angry about, and eventually he will unleash his wrath upon it and destroy all who oppose him. He is angry because of the damage that failure to worship has done and continues to do to what he loves the most—his creation. His anger is what a parent feels when his child is being attacked. When danger lurks, his natural impulse is to protect. There are some telling phrases in the Roman letter's introductory thesis:

> "Yes, they knew God, but they wouldn't worship him as God or even give him thanks."
> "As a result, their minds became dark and confused."
> "And instead of worshiping the glorious, ever-living God, they worshiped idols."
> "As a result, they did vile and degrading things with each other's bodies."[267]

Paul pivots in Chapter 12 and begins to explain the practical everyday response:

---

[267] Selected from Rom 1:21-24.

And so, dear brothers and sisters, I plead with you to **give your bodies to God** because of all he has done for you. Let them be a **living and holy sacrifice**—the kind he will find acceptable. **This is truly the way to worship him.** Don't **copy the behavior** and customs of this world, but let **God transform you into a new person** by changing the way you think. Then you will learn to know God's will for you, which is good and pleasing and perfect" (Romans 12:1-2, emphasis added).

Worship and bodies are connected throughout the extended argument Paul makes. He says that unbelievers refused to worship God and, therefore, abused their bodies. People who refuse to worship God with their bodies will use their bodies for self-gratification. They will invariably separate their spiritual life from their body. The antidote, the countercultural action now, is to worship God with your body.

Your body is your personal delivery system to the world. When it comes down to it, worship is living practically every day for the purpose of Christ. All other forms or functions named worship by Christians through the ages are worship accoutrements. The entire complex of the human personality and body work together to form behaviors that reveal either abuse of the body or the body flourishing.

It used to be that if you wanted to confront the culture, you would need to make a sign and march in a protest. This is no longer necessary. All you need to do is worship God. Do not conform to the world around you but know that you will be confronted. To extract a phrase from the aforementioned Carl Truemann statement: "maintaining biblical sexual ethics will be the equivalent in our culture of being a white supremacist."

If you choose to conform to the present culture, to become "woke," to lament and confess your "white privilege," and to work not only to *not* be the racist you are but to fully becoming anti-racist, then you will be accepted into the new church of the enlightened ones who will craft your future for you. They will let you know what your future sins will be.

You might recall somewhere that you were taught that Christ died for all your sins, past, present, and future. I know you thought you knew what your sins were: breaking the Ten Commandments, not following the Sermon on the Mount—you know, the routine. But now, at the first church of "Woke Theology," you will be introduced to a new set of sins that begin with your ancestry, or your past and present sins of being white and privileged, and your future sins concerning reparations to aggrieved groups of oppressed peoples. They will teach you to loathe yourself, your country, and your church. Their teachers will disciple the young in our society to reject the church. They will tell you they don't want to be associated with the church because it is racist, homophobic, and misogynistic.

I do not share the cynicism in the above paragraph, I would rather take a more reasoned approach. Anyone who attempts to be honest about the matter would admit that there is racism in society and in the church. Yes, there is homophobia as well, but the fear of homosexuality, or even prejudice against it, is a separate issue from what the Bible teaches concerning its practice.

It is important to understand that I can believe that homosexual practice is a sin which hurts the people involved in it and at the same time respect gay individuals and believe that as a matter of public policy they deserve the same rights as any citizen of the United States. I can care for them, live next to them, do business with them, be a friend. This is not only possible. It is what I normally experience among Christians in churches today.

"Misogynistic" is a term that smears anyone who happens to believe that there is a divine order in the family and the church. By divine order I mean that the husband is the leader of the family and that elders should be exclusively men.[268] There is not wide agreement on this issue in the church. It continues to be a matter of debate. But misogynistic means to hate women, which I believe is extremely rare in the church. Ever since the birth of the church, one of its great appeals has been its elevated treatment of women. Women are loved, honored, and fully active in churches around the world. There is disagreement, but to use the word misogynistic is horribly slanderous.

Love God with Your Body

The most obvious way you can be all in with God is to put your body on the altar. The altar is a religious metaphor that carries the idea of sacrifice. By offering your life as a living sacrifice, it means your entire person is his to use for his purpose. Your body carries you and presents you to the world. Everyone can

---

[268] Male leadership in the church is based on both cultural custom and God's instructions. The qualifications for leadership in the church are focused on men. That is most evident in the lists for characteristics for elders found in Titus 3 and 1Timothy 3. It is presented from a male point of view. Paul also mentioned in 1 Timothy 2:11-14 that a woman is not to exercise authority over a man in the church. First Corinthians 11:2-16 mentions a hierarchy that puts God as head of Christ, Christ as the head of man, and man as the head of woman. The Corinthian text seems to interweave custom and authoritative edict. There is wide disagreement among the orthodox believers on this matter.

see it, touch it, and tell an awful lot about you by observing it. It makes seen what is unseen. Your spirit—the condition of your soul—emit from your body via your posture, facial expressions, the sound of your voice, and the look in your eyes. God does not divide you into spiritual and physical. This is proven by the way he asks so much of our body.

Christ demonstrated the same commitment in his body via the crucifixion. The resurrection would have been superfluous without a physical body with wounds still intact. For those who regard the physical world as crude and unspiritual C.S. Lewis said, "There is no good trying to be more spiritual than God. God never meant man to be a purely spiritual creature . . . He likes matter. He invented it." [269]

Your body is the ultimate in personal presence and in what we call "showing up." Showing up is contemporary slang for stepping into situations that require all of you and your commitment. Showing up will cost you! It will cost you friends, make you enemies, and could threaten your career. But be of good cheer. You will find yourself filled with satisfaction and a sense of well-being, knowing that you are a transformed being in sync with your God.

---

[269] Lewis, *Mere Christianity*, 64.

The Reckoning

Are Evangelicals responsible to now have a reckoning? Reckoning means a calculation. It can also mean estimation or computation. It sounds sort of mathematical. I ask the question because I just read "The Evangelical Reckoning Begins" by Emma Green in *The Atlantic*. It is an interview with one of our own, the lovable and properly sensitive Andy Stanley.[270]

When I hear the word reckoning these days, the word has morphed into something much more than Jethro Bodine's "cyphering" on the 1960s sitcom *The Beverly Hillbillies*. Jethro, the country bumpkin, would take out a scrap of paper and scratch a few simple figures on it and come up with his sum. Reckoning now means something much more threatening, like someone is going to get what is coming to them. After reading the article and making some notes, my fundamental question is "Who is going to do the reckoning? Who might be qualified?"

Usually those who insist on a reckoning are those blinded by the luminous glow of temporary victory. There are many volunteers: the media; possibly the white ruling class represented by the elite print media, such as *The Atlantic*, *Vanity Fair*, *The New Yorker Magazine*, and *The New York Times*; and progressive religion professors from left-wing seminaries (please feel free to name any Ivy league university). I would venture to say if reckonings are

---

[270] Emma Green, "The Evangelical Reckoning Begins." *The Atlantic*, 15 November 2020. https://www.theatlantic.com/politics/archive/2020/11/andy-stanley-evangelicals-trump/617103/.

done, and I am sure they will be, they should be ignored. But then again, the winners write history. What did they win? They think by winning an election that they have defeated a regressive strain in the American character, and this is another serious body blow to premodern religion. It may have been a blow but nothing that would make a serious dent.

I suppose the church could do with a self-examination, but which part of the body of Christ will examine another part of the corpus Christi. Jim Wallis and the progressive left wing could pick apart the religious right fools who attached themselves to the "Donald of Orange" (Donald Trump).[271] Let's face it. Whenever a body of any kind examines itself, the result promises to be dubious. Surgeons cannot perform procedures on themselves. It is illegal. Evangelicals are divided over the candidates, and, frankly, have differing worldviews. And what determines a person's placement of evidence or opinion into a mind slot or category is worldview.

Both the progressive left and the reserved conservative right of evangelicalism will claim a worldview based on the Bible. The left would drive a stake in the ground around a correctly contextualized, non-literal, reimagined hermeneutic geared to modern sensibilities. Its concept of public and personal morality would lean toward Reinhold Niebuhr's concept of systemic societal sin as being more dangerous to nations than personal sin. It throws back and forth ideas like whether one is born a racist or becomes one in a racist society. Is the problem the human heart or society? If the answer is society, then systemic racism is the more serious condition.

---

[271] Not to be confused with William of Orange, the Dutch leader who fought France and became King of England and was assassinated by a Catholic fanatic on July 10, 1584.

A more conservative hermeneutic would see biblical authority as absolute. It would claim that people and their natures have not changed. People are not more enlightened. They have not made moral progress. We are east of Eden and there is no going back by that route. Indeed, the opposite is true. We have become morally confused, and it shows in our declining moral standards. Individuals cannot repent for a nation or for a society. They can feel bad about it. They can lament concerning it. However, an individual does not make a society, and a society cannot repent or find redemption for individual persons.

I just do not see evangelicals bringing a reckoning to themselves. Each segment, and there are several, could examine themselves and ask God for insight. That would probably be the most productive and the least divisive way to proceed. Inquisitions are messy. The church could lock itself away in councils, commissions, and conversations for years, in search of some formal document signaling unity. But in the end, Satan laughs. He laughs because they are doing everything he wants them to do and very little of what Jesus commissioned us to do, namely make disciples.

We must remember that it is the politically minded who call for such a reckoning. How many progressive pastors will now find their way to the new resident of the White House, take their own selfies, and make the same mistakes the conservatives have made? I turn to my favorite twentieth century psychiatrist Karl Bonhoeffer, the one-time Director of Neurology at The University of Berlin. When speaking of a focus on introspection, "he dismissed it as the bad fruit of people who like to 'busy themselves' with themselves."[272]

---

[272] Marsh, *Strange Glory*, 384.

This takes me back to the people's choice for administration of the reckoning, Andy Stanley, the evangelical who *The Atlantic* tells us is easy to like and acceptable to Oprah Winfrey. Andy does seem approachable. He has—forgive me, Andy—an "Andy of Mayberry" sensibility to him. Stanley made some good points and spoke in measured tones. He was fair and put on the breaks when necessary. The entire idea, however, that more conservative Christians who voted for Trump—around 75% of them—did serious damage to the Great Commission is simply fiction. The only people who seemed to be worried about it are those evangelicals and others who did not vote for Trump. Their hands are clean and now they stand on the high ground of inquisitors. When will we start believing what the Bible teaches us about this?

Jesus taught us to love the world, but he also told us the world would not love us back, and if it does, watch out. You may have changed teams without knowing it.[273] It is very much like a political figure wounded by his own party being used by the opposition as a witness against his former friends. Jesus' own life and death teach us something very important. A perfect man, God himself, lived among us and most of the world rejected, hated, and ultimately killed him. He told us that if we openly obeyed and followed him, the world would hate us.[274] So pardon me if I do not pay much attention to what the world system or its disciples think of the way I or we conduct ourselves. Didn't we just go through about forty years of the church trying to figure out what our "customers" wanted with results of losing the culture, declining numbers, and increasing moral compromise?

---

[273] Luke 6:26.

[274] Matt 5:11-13; John 16:31-33; 1 Cor 1:18-2:16.

These results did not happen because 75% of us voted for Trump but for other reasons, such as our personal moral behavior or misbehavior. The Jerry Falwell Juniors, Bill Hybels, and James MacDonalds of our generation are products of the wider cultural decline rather than the result of a change in biblical teachings.[275] A greater acceptance of sexual choices and perversions are the real culprit. Considering biblical truth to be an unenlightened, antiquated, regressive truth that holds people back from moral progress is the problem.

Is it really credible to blame contemporary Christians for this decline? Why do we not blame the Corinthian Church for the Temple of Diana? How about, as Edward Gibbon believed, Rome fell because of the Christian doctrine of returning good for evil, turning the other cheek? He claimed that Christians took away Roman society's will to fight.[276] Have we considered that the critical comments and judgment that has fallen on evangelicals

---

[275] Each of these men lost their dignity and their jobs because of either leadership failure or moral failure: Kate Shellnutt, "Harvest Settles Multi-Million Dollars Agreement with James MacDonald." *Christianity Today*, 16 October 16 2020. https://www.christianitytoday.com/news/2020/october/james-macdonald-harvest-walk-word-million-arbitration.html; Emily McFarlan Miller, "Misconduct Allegations Against Willow Creek Founder Bill Hybels, Independent Report Finds." *The Washington Post*, 1 March 2019. https://www.washingtonpost.com/religion/2019/03/01/independent-report-finds-allegations-against-willow-creek-founder-bill-hybels-are-credible/; Andrew Prokop, "The Jerry Falwell, Jr. Scandal Explained." *Vox*, 25 August 25 2020. https://www.vox.com/2020/8/25/21399954/jerry-falwell-jr-resigns-scandal-liberty
[276] Historian S. P. Foster says that Gibbon blamed the other worldly preoccupations of Christianity that helped the Roman people become passive and weak. Edward Gibbon, *The History of the Decline and Fall of the Roman Empire*, Vol. 3 (New York: Fred De Fau & Company, 1906). https://oll.libertyfund.org/title/gibbon-the-history-of-the-decline-and-fall-of-the-roman-empire-vol-3.

have been done largely for political reasons? Someone is looking for their pound of flesh.

One needs to be careful and precise before we evangelicals accept the blame for voting for a president that the press claims did or said something that he did not actually say or do. *The Atlantic* article suggests that evangelicals remained silent about "the deadly 2017 white-supremacists rally in Charlottesville and on the blame for family separation" on the Mexican border.[277] The truth is that Trump did, if you listen to his entire statement, condemn the Ku Klux Klan and white supremacy. In the context of his statement he said, "There were good people on both sides" referring to the argument about the Confederate flag controversy. Yet this has been inaccurately reported thousands of times and has become pulp fiction. The family separation was another misrepresentation of the actual facts on the ground. It left out a glut of facts that set the story in context. Those who have misrepresented the facts in context are now the ones who say, as Green does in the article, "Before they can reach anyone with a message of faith over politics, they'll have to contend with the political baggage their fellow Christian leaders created."[278] Says who? Says big media who misrepresented the facts in the first place for their political purposes.

I don't know that evangelicals can have a faith over politics message or a faith without politics message because a faith or Gospel that ignores or denies the actual lives people live leads to a form of denial that is deadly to the Gospel. Good news is not very good if it ignores the realities of one's daily life. This has been at the root of the problem for over fifty years now. We have made disciples who are equipped to serve as church workers

---

[277] Green, "Reckoning," *Atlantic Monthly,* n.p.
[278] Ibid.

but ill-equipped to engage the culture and penetrate the walls that separate faith from life. Leslie Newbigin, one of the great Christian thinkers of the twentieth century helps us here:

> A preaching of the gospel that calls men and women to accept Jesus as Savior but does not make it clear that discipleship means commitment to a vision of society radically different from that which controls our public life today must be condemned as false.[279]

That radical message does not mean we must extol the stereotypical benign holy person who people admire for their kindness alone. It does not refer to the Christian who refrains from arguing, protesting, fighting, and who stays out of the fray. It does mean honest and fierce dedication to the truth. It means disciples who stand up, step up and won't shut up. It means Christians who challenge the norms and myths of the secular city. It means disciples who believe what they see and hear and proclaim it. That is true for presidents and for other public leaders.

Right now, some evangelicals have moved away from their conservative roots because of Trump and have gone over to the progressive side. I question whether they will they return to their more conservative theological roots when the side they have chosen denies the basic truths of Scripture. Is abortion on demand enough to bring them back? Is the fight for freedom of speech and religion enough to bring them back? Is the leftist propaganda presented and protected by big tech, big media, and big money, along with censorship of Orwellian proportions enough to bring them back? Is the fight for liberty in life and equality of opportunity rather than equality of results enough

---

[279] Lesslie Newbigin, *Foolishness to the Greeks: The Gospel and Western Culture* (Grand Rapids: Eerdmans, 1988), 132.

to bring them back? An inquisitive woman once asked Benjamin Franklin, "Mr. Franklin, what do we have?" He replied, "A republic if we can keep it."[280] The price of keeping it is now upon us.

There is more to say here. In her article, Green questioned Stanley about Trump's non-Christlike behavior. Stanley stated that he believed that the greatest damage had been done by Trump's mocking people with disabilities or calling people from Mexico criminals and rapists. Stanley also believed that the president's attack on journalists was a "terrible move."[281] I agree about his mocking of individual citizens or even people trying to get into America illegally. But he did not call all of them criminals and rapists. He said some of them were, which has proven to be true.[282]

Yes, Trump often speaks with the accuracy of a carnival barker and presidents should do better. However, I take issue with Stanley's concern about journalists. Even before Trump was inaugurated, his legitimacy was being questioned by "journalists."[283] They never gave Trump a chance. They had it in for him from the very beginning. The Russia probe was illegitimate. It was created from a false dossier, and the previous administration illegally used the FBI to spy on Trump and his campaign. All of this is now a matter

---

[280] Eric Metaxas, "Introduction," *If We Can Keep It* (New York: Penguin Books), 2016.

[281] Green, "Reckoning," *Atlantic Monthly*.

[282] Adrienne Dunn, "Fact Check: Meme on Trump 'Very Fine People' Quote Contains Inaccuracies." *USA Today*, 17 October 2020. https://www.usatoday.com/story/news/factcheck/2020/10/17/fact-check-trump-quote-very-fine-people-charlottesville/5943239002/.

[283] Brian Naylor, "Impeachment Timeline: From Early Calls to a Full House Vote." *NPR*, 17 December 2019. https://www.npr.org/2019/12/17/788397365/impeachment-timeline-from-early-calls-to-a-full-house-vote.

of the public record.[284] These "journalists" have lost credibility because real journalism is now practiced by only a tiny remnant in major media markets. No President has given greater access to the press than Trump. He has answered more questions than any I can remember, and 95% of the questions were hard and hostile. They were peppered with accusations. The press has to be skeptical, and I am okay with that. Trump said some stupid stuff starting with his claim about the size of his inaugural crowd.

The hardest thing to accept from our press is their duplicity and being in the tank for one party or the other. This has been and continues to be on daily display. The most egregious manifestation of this has been the protection of President Joe Biden. The press failed the American people. They failed to play their role in protecting the American people's right to hear from both candidates prior to voting.

Biden's lack of access to the entire press and to being scrutinized by the American people was a terrible disservice to our democratic process. A representative democracy cannot function this way. People must be informed in order to exercise their power to hire a new president. The president and Congress work for the people. Joe Biden was asked some hard questions during the primaries when it seemed he would not get his party's nomination, but once he secured it, he was bunkered in his basement. When he did come out, the questions were an embarrassment to the American people and the democratic process. He was asked how he felt about things or what was his favorite ice cream. This was dishonest and reminded me of third-world banana republic type

---

[284] James S. Robbins, "Spygate: Did American Intelligence Agencies Spy On Donald Trump? Barr Says We'll Find Out," *USA Today*, 11 April 2019. https://www.usatoday.com/story/opinion/2019/04/11/spygate-william-barr-spying-donald-trump-campaign-column/3434458002/.

stuff. If he would have played eighteen holes of golf, it would have probably been reported that he scored eighteen holes in one just like North Korea's tyrannic leader.

Then there was the story about Hunter Biden and his grifting off his father's name and power for personal gain. Fox News was the only media outlet that covered the story. The rest of the press did not cover it. This is dereliction of duty and a disgusting display of partisanship by the press. If you watched CNN or MSNBC, which I have done, switching back and forth to see what is and is not covered, you would think the reporters live on different planets

My point is simple. Trump did not run against Joe Biden. He ran against a corrupt media that lives in a house of mirrors. They only see their own reflection and their dishonesty is staggering. They report a church service as a virus super-spreader event but a peaceful protest of thousands as necessary and inspiring. How dumb do they think Americans are? The press is not free. The First Amendment is under siege, and this is a serious threat to our way of life. If Trump was right about one thing, that thing was that the press is corrupt and cannot be trusted. If they would have been as hard on Biden as they were on Trump and Biden still won, I would have no problem with that. It would be evidence that our democratic republic is healthy. But that is not what happened.

I think the best approach for the church is not to hold meetings, conversations, and councils where we beat our breasts and rend our garments. Just read Romans 3:9-20 and get on with it. The ruling class and popular culture would prescribe confession of systemic sin—ours, not theirs—insisting that we admit we are bigots and haters plagued with as many phobias as they can create and that we make amends by giving the victims what we owe them, and then serve them until they need more and we can do it all over again. We have entered a topsy turvy world where darkness has been declared light and light declared darkness. "What sorrow for those who say that evil is good and good evil, that dark is light and light is dark, that bitter is sweet and sweet is bitter" (Isa 5:20).

Go forward, church! Do what the apostle Paul did. He kept the mission of spreading the Gospel moving forward. He merely represented the entire spirit of the early church. He was run out of several cities, but he kept going to the next place and preaching the Gospel. He kept on making new disciples. I see this happening all over the world. The church is getting outside of itself and making many new disciples who create a new and fresh crop of Jesus followers who hold the same values as their Lord. The longer we stay in church doing church stuff, the more dangerous it is for the mission of the church. Keep moving fast, church. Leave a cloud of dust. Every generation must build a new burgeoning infrastructure that penetrates the culture. Inquisition is no answer; neither are truth commissions, lists, nor formal laments laid at the feet of self-appointed cultural masters. Replace what our society has with what God promises, a replacement culture, or at least an alternative one that makes Ringo Starr's "peace and love" and John Lennon's "Imagine" seem like the cliches they are.

The Medium is the Message

"If the church could have solved their problem on their own, they would have"[285]

Daniel Grissom

Canadian communication theorist Marshall McLuhan coined the phrase "the medium is the message" in *The Extensions of Man* in 1964. It has now become part of communications folklore. His original meaning had to do whether a message was delivered in print, visually, musically, or through some other art form. The medium would determine how the message would be perceived. For example, Christmas music playing in stores while people are Christmas shopping puts most in a good mood. It creates an emotion of joy and a desire to spend money on loved ones. But if "Joy to the World' was played in your favorite department store during July, more than likely, shoppers would be repulsed. The calendar or context is an important part of the medium. A poem about love can reach a person in a powerful way that a logical explanation or clinical approach could not. The medium as the message is also a valid observation when it comes to the Gospel and its spread to the world.

One could even say McLuhan's statement could be stripped of its adroitness and rewritten to say, "The method is the

---

[285] Daniel Grissom, telephone conversation.

message." My interest in this matter goes to another highly respected writer and thought leader, Dr. Robert Coleman, and his little masterpiece, *The Masterplan of Evangelism*. The book to date has sold over seven million copies since its publication in 1963. On page 21 of the book, under the chapter title "Selection," a little phrase was used that reveals the secret sauce Jesus used to spread his message. That jewel of a phrase is, "men were his method."[286] An updated adjustment would be, "People were his method." I would adjust it a bit more and say, "People were his medium and therefore his message." Now before I distort this phrase any more than I have from McLuhan, Coleman and, of course Jesus, let me get to it.

I read an article this morning in the *Wall Street Journal* about the growth of Netflix, Amazon Prime, Hulu, Apple TV and other media companies during the 2020 pandemic. There was an explosion in the industry created by a nation stuck at home. The rich have gotten richer while the poor have become poorer, but at least they have been entertained. The message is that the new and most widespread medium is on-demand movies and entertainment. The temptation is to conclude, "If we want to reach the world, then we must invest more time and energy in media over the internet." This conclusion, even though superficial, has merit at some level.

Religion via media over the last fifty years has been a net loss. For every good program, there have been many bad ones. It has been dominated by either the most bland, poorly produced, and cliché-ridden presentations or the pathological and bizarre

---

[286] Robert Coleman, *The Masterplan of Evangelism*, (Old Tappan, NJ: Revell, 1964), 21.

displays of religious hubris that turned the Christian faith into a circus without a tent. Yes, millions can be "reached" but reached with what and for what purpose?

Recent research by the Barna Group has cited a steep decline in the American population identifying as Christian. They report that in the last decade those so identifying has declined from 50% of the population to 25%.[287] That is a serious and alarming fall from grace for America. Competing pollsters may discover reasons to be critical of the finding, but in a general sense, this should tell us something quite clearly. If the medium is the message and that medium is primarily the media itself, the campaign has been an abysmal failure.

Christians should not leave the media. In fact, we should endeavor to engage in a divine conspiracy to infiltrate and influence it. But if we are to obey what Jesus told us to do, make disciples of all nations, then there is no substitute for the human being in the flesh—in other words, the gospel incarnated in the lives of Jesus' followers in direct contact with other humans.

Part of getting that message is the reality that people are Jesus' method, which is itself a message. The good news is that Jesus became a person, lived among other persons, taught them, loved them, rebuked them, challenged them, and suffered by their hand. In the end he said, "Father forgive them. They don't know what they are doing."[288] As a resurrected king, he left them with instructions and his example. The Acts of the Apostles tells us how they followed his example and how personal it all was

---

[287] "Signs of Decline & Hope Among Key Metrics of Faith." *Barna.com*, 4 March 2020. https://www.barna.com/research/changing-state-of-the-church/.
[288] Luke 23:34.

through their lives. This leads me to the quote from my friend Daniel Grissom at the top of this column. "If the church could have solved their problem on their own, they would have."

Daniel's statement struck me as a clarion call for those of us who have been or are leaders in the church to be honest about our failures, particularly about our chosen methods and the message our methods have sent to the general population. That church problem can be stated in so many ways but let me be brief.

We keep trying to reach the world without making disciples. I do not mean that no person or church is attempting to make disciples. In fact, every church makes disciples. But often those disciples are inept, spiritually sterile, fearful, untrained, or simply trained to be good church members. By that I mean they can do "Christian chores" assigned by the clergy. They end up in 95% of cases getting stuck with a stopped up ecclesial system that backs up on them and behold how it stinks. You may have heard the axiom "Your system is set up to get the exact results you are getting." Many have said it in a variety of contexts. It means that if a system is taking in input but has no healthy way to get output, then the system is clogged. This in general means that churches are infamous for an insular populace who desire programs to service the perceived needs. Very often the needs do not include the discomfort of outreach.

There is a way out, but most need three things. 1) A theological/ Gospel reform that reasserts the why of what they do. 2) A clear understanding for "what." What is the church's product? What kind of disciples are we to deploy into the world? This deployment experiences conflict as they create coverts. 3). How will we get there? Most leaders need a guide to lead them through this process.

In the end, that process of examining why, what, and how is about transformed people. Those people are the method, and they are the message in that when people ask, "Where is God?" the answer can be, "He is sitting beside you in the form of a person who is his disciple."

APPLICATION

Work Matters: Exploring the Integration of Spirituality in Work

Works have fallen on hard times in the Christian world. One of the nastiest accusations that can be made toward another Christian is that they are a legalist. If you want to get down and dirty, you say, "I bet you believe in works salvation." In fact, the clarion call of the Reformation was the five *solas: sola Scriptura* (Scripture alone), *sola fide* (faith alone), *sola gratia* (grace alone), *solus Christus* (Christ alone), and *soli Deo gloria* (to God be the glory alone). The five *solas* declare the separation of God saving us from any effort or ability inherent in man. I have spent a great deal of time in my books talking about how even a slight corruption of what Luther actually taught has led to a disastrous discounting of the role of works and effort.

I do not think it is an overstatement to assert that many people erroneously believe that work, particularly frustrating imperfect work, is part of the curse.[289] Humankind yearns to work, and that erroneous belief pollutes our understanding of grace and spiritual salvation. I suppose it has and does come into play that the divorce of faith from the good works James requires to demonstrate proof of new life has been devastating to the witness of the church.[290] But I would like to take a different angle with regard to the issue of work.

---

[289] Gen 3:1-19.

[290] Jas 2:14-26

Work has trouble being integrated into the spiritual life because in the minds of some people, it violates grace. For example, many hold to the idea that work is part of the curse upon humankind, and if that curse were lifted, we would all be sauntering in the South of France consuming banana daiquiris—that heaven, or something close to it such as an all-expense vacation to a Sandals Resort, is the kind of pleasure that could go on forever. The problem with this is that we are Jesus' disciples. We are called to be like him, and he went to work six days a week from the time he was old enough to help his father until he was thirty years old.[291]

There are some very thick theology books that have sections called, "The Work of Christ," but let me be even more fundamental about this. God was the first person to work. He worked for six days. This is the Genesis narrative. It was not only good; it was very good.[292] Then to confuse our minds even more, the God who never sleeps or tires rested on the seventh day.[293] From what did he rest? Work. Yes, work. God was no sinner, and he worked.

Christians often say, "God is at work. God is working." Work matters, and without it, we would be lost. We would not know what to do. Leisure is like a warm bucket of spit if it is a way of life rather than merely a break from work. Rest is only sweet when one is tired. It is also meaningful when work is accomplished. There is satisfaction in a vacation if you sense it has been earned. Otherwise, it is not valued. In fact, too much rest ruins people. It creates harmful habits. It damages a natural sense of personal value, and it numbs the mind and spirit that creates a defeatist

---

[291] It is assumed that Jesus apprenticed with his father Joseph in the carpenter trade and worked a six-day week. That was Jewish custom and culture.
[292] Gen 1:31.
[293] Gen 2:2-3.

passiveness. God loves workers. He needs many workers for his harvest[294]

Almost everyone works. Life starts as a child with chores, then homework, and finally one enters the adult work world. But many Christian workers are not successful in integrating their faith into their work. They have been taught that their work is not holy like religious activity, Bible study, or church work are. Therefore, they believe they spend the majority of their time outside the holy category and in the secular or profane realm.

Can you imagine what kind of work we will do in eternity? Possibly you have never thought heaven would include work, labor, or anything to do. Since we will live in a new heaven and new earth, someone will need to manage it, cultivate it, and enjoy it. That would be all the people who like God and want to be with him forever. Yes, there will be work. It will not be hard work as in unproductive or frustrating work, but there is no reason to believe that God will not give us something to do besides sing, float around, and admire Him.[295] Start figuring out now how to integrate the life of God into your work because you will be doing so forever.

---

[294] Matt 9:37.
[295] 2 Tim 2:12; Rev. 7:15, 22:3.

Taking Lies Prisoner

"It's not enough to deploy Good Samaritans;
we must also guard the road."[296]

Lesslie Newbigin

Before a soldier charges up a hill to destroy a fortress, that warrior had better know the enemy. Our enemies are systems of thought that have established high ground—false arguments that are set up to keep people from knowing God.[297] What are the systems of thought that presently qualify?

There are so many that the analysis would fill quite a tome. Allow me to rely on Martin Luther's guidance to narrow my field.

If I profess with the loudest voice and clearest exposition every portion of the Word of God except precisely that little point which the world and the devil are at that moment attacking, I am not confessing Christ, however boldly I may be professing Him. Where the battle rages, there the loyalty of the soldier is proved; and to be steady on all the battle front besides is mere flight and disgrace if he flinches at that point. [298]

---

[296] https://twitter.com/LesslieNewbigin.

[297] 2 Cor 10:4-5.

[298] Martin Luther, *Luther's Works. Weimar Edition. Briefwechsel [Correspondence]*, Vol. 3 (Minneapolis: Fortress Press, 1999), 81.

In other words, if you and I only preach, teach, write, or speak in the safe lanes of culture, ones that are not relevant, we will be left alone. You can argue various schools of end times doctrine, Reformed versus Arminian theology, the finer points of kingdom theology, or schools of spiritual formation and discipleship, but, frankly, it is all "inside baseball" to our enemy. It occupies the church's time and keeps it sidelined from meaningful activity, such as mobilization of trained disciples who are to make new disciples.

Here are the issues that threaten the plausibility required to believe the Christian message in the surrounding world.

1. **Abortion**: The secular argument which has taken much ground and millions of lives is that the unborn child is not a person. It does not have viability on its own outside its mother's womb. This is the secular starting point because it frames the issue so that abortion becomes morally defensible. Because everyone is born in the image of God, even abortion advocates and the unborn themselves, they must believe that somehow it is moral, or they could not give themselves permission to fight for it. The argument also plays on the sympathy of a moral people who can see how a woman might need to choose to abort a child for personal or financial reasons. Science is on the side of the pro-life movement. The arguments are clear and well known. Primarily, the advancements in science show that human characteristics such as sensitivity to sound and pain and a natural will to survive are present in the very early stages of pregnancy. This particular battle is almost 100% a matter of bias, power, money, and Lucifer's lust for blood. Speaking up and working against the abortion industry is not safe and to do so will confirm you are in a battle.

2. **Human sexuality**: For starters, much of what gives humans identity, dignity, and meaning is the simple statement, "So God created human beings in his own image. In the image of God he created them; male and female he created them" (Gen 1:17). This separates humans from animals, and, along with Genesis 2:7 in the creation narrative, establishes humans as living souls with an immaterial reality that has a transcendent and eternal quality. Additionally, they are either 100% male or 100% female meant to complement each other in a union that is fruitful and multiplies so that the earth is populated, cultivated, and advanced.[299] Anything contrary to this is a human or social construct propagated by those with a competing agenda. The contemporary assertion that you can proclaim a sexual identity that belies your genetic code is an assault on one's body that is inherently damaging to body and soul. That is what the word abnormal means. There are a few exceptions, but that is what they are—exceptions or flaws in human genetics. A sliding scale of morality, aberrations, exceptions, and choices create the destruction of God's creative order. This is no more evident than in destruction of the family. When the family disintegrates, everything from respect for authority to the value of discipline and achievement along with the power of love dissipates into the declining culture.

3. **Race**: In 2020, race relations became an issue for the far left to exploit and use as a Trojan Horse to destroy liberty and freedom. This is not merely a political attack. It runs much deeper into reworking the First Amendment to say, "You are free to speak your mind as long as the

---

[299] Gen 1:28.

most powerful agree with your statement. You are free to worship your god as long as it does not challenge society's dominant orthodoxy." In practice, it means that if you do not tow the line, you will be punished. You will not be able to work in certain fields or hold positions of influence. You can look at Orwell's *1984* or Huxley's *Brave New World* for hypothetical portrayals of dystopia. There are also real examples such as the abysmal failure of the Soviet Union, the tyranny and bloodshed by Mao Tse Tung, Pol Pot, and even the contemporary examples of China, Venezuela, and Cuba. One is not permitted to say, for example, "All lives matter" or "Black lives matter too," and certainly not to say, "Asian lives matter" or "Yellow lives matter" or "White lives matter." This is all considered racist or hate speech. It is twisted and tortured logic that causes anyone to attack a well-meaning statement and make it hate speech "worthy" of censorship and punishment.

But as an aside, I want to put in a good word for hate. It is clear from Scripture that God hates a number of things. Since God alone is perfectly good and holy, to hate certain things is good and holy. God hates sin, divorce, haughty eyes, lying tongues, hands that shed innocent blood, a heart that devises wicked schemes, feet that are quick to rush to evil, a false witness, and a person who stirs up conflict in the community.[300] I hate child abuse, bullies, and oppression. I hate racism. I hate poverty. I hate war, hunger, starvation, and disease. There is much I hate, and I feel very good about hating them.

A somewhat overused term that defines the enemy of God's truth is Marxism. Karl Marx himself was Jewish but

---

[300] Prov 6:16-19; Mal 2:16.

raised Catholic. He even did a bit in seminary like Joseph Stalin. He finally ended up a practical atheist and wrote *The Communist Manifesto*, which would be considered unreadable trash by any objective literary critic except for a few passages that survived critical analysis.[301] It is built on the false theory that imperfect fallen souls can build a utopia where everyone will share all they have regardless of who created the wealth. It is the ignorant idea that a world without God could operate as though everyone were God. The irony is they intend to destroy the Christian faith, but their only hope for anything close to their goals would be the Christian faith because only inner transformation would cause a normal human to share what they earned with a person who had not worked as hard or as well. I also hate Marxism and socialism for the pain, anguish, and death they have brought to millions.

4. **The Rule of Law:** It is estimated that 1% of police officers break the law themselves. That is 8,800 police officers out of the 888,000 officers in the United States.[302] The 1% who bring disrespect to the profession can create a lot of bad press for the 99% who do their jobs well. They can create a perception for an entire nation, particularly when the offense of the 1% is played repeatedly in the national media. The desired scenario for those who

---

[301] Marx presented a utopian society where everyone could share equally in ownership, goods, and services. He believed society was an economic construct and living in a shared community or collective was the best possible life. Karl Marx and Fredrich Engles, "Manifesto of The Communist Party," 1848. https://www.marxists.org/archive/marx/works/1848/communist-manifesto/.

[302] "Law Enforcement Misconduct," The United States Department of Justice. https://www.justice.gov/crt/law-enforcement-misconduct.

want to attack the police is to use the police narrative to undermine law itself and the underlying authority that stands behind it. This is Satan's model: to shut people up, to tear down statues, burn buildings, demonize authorities, and create instability. Out of that chaos can come revolution supposedly enabling the utopian dream to be constructed—a new Tower of Babel.[303] However, it is only a matter of time until God breaks it all up, confuses them, and sets it all back a few decades. What the Christian enemies presently want is more than a few fallen crosses, broken steeples, and discredited clergy. They want the church to heel, shut up, and go back to their private meetings, memorizing Bible verses and whimpering a few verses of an eighteenth-century hymn. The beauty of this for Christians is that we do not need to organize outreach events to engage. All we need to do is keep moving forward into life as we know it and we will run smack into it. When we do, we are to speak and live the truth which will lead to conflict and gladly to converts. [304]

5. **Human Reasoning:** We are to take every thought captive to the obedience of Christ.[305] This happens when we take down false arguments that keep people from knowing God. Human reasoning is not all bad. In fact, most of it is good and works to society's benefit. But it does not take

---

[303] Led by Nimrod, people attempted to build a tower to heaven to demonstrate they could do great things and to secure their future. God confused their language so they could not understand one another thus halting the construction of the city and tower. That is why the location is referred to as Babel. Gen 11:1-9.

[304] A good example of this is Paul's experience in Athens as recorded in Acts 17.

[305] 2 Cor 10:3-5.

too much bad reasoning to corrupt a great deal, such as when a person who stands for an objective moral order is called a hater or bigot. The cultural high ground of human reasoning has been and continues to be the academy—the major universities that continue to produce most of our political leaders like Wall Street executives, writers, journalists, and people of the literary elite.

The National Basketball Association player roster is 86% African American. As I write, the sport's pandemic reboot is about to start in the Orlando bubble where the teams are quarantined. The recent national crisis regarding race and the death of George Floyd has put these young African American players in the national spotlight as never before.[306] They have been given the freedom to use slogans on their jerseys. Some plan to display George Floyd's last words, "I can't breathe." Others may say, "How many more?" referring to the number of Black men killed at the hands of white police officers. Apparently, the playing floor will be adorned with "Black Lives Matter." The question then becomes, how are Christians who endeavor to be the salt and light in the world

---

[306] The George Floyd killing was and remains a difficult matter to discuss due to the different angles from which it can be viewed. The most common narrative is that an evil white police officer killed a Black man. It was unnecessary but indictive of the racist ideology of white cops. Floyd became a symbol of black victimhood by police violence, and he became a hero with his own statue in downtown Minneapolis. Another way to see it is that it was a personal tragedy. The police officer was wrong and was duly convicted of murder. However, George Floyd was a convicted felon with the drug fentanyl in his system, which contributed to his death. Additionally, making Floyd a victim and hero is not good because he is not a good role model and is of no real help to African Americans. The African American grievance industry is taking advantage of the situation to raise funds and to grab political power. The reader will need to reach their own conclusion.

supposed to take this situation captive to the obedience of Christ and keep it from preventing people from knowing God?

- First, empathize with the Black community by acknowledging their history with the police, the justice system, and with the racism they have experienced.
- Second, understand that the 90% of Americans who believe that "Black Lives Matter" is not offensive considering the context we are in and that they are different from the Black Lives Matter Marxist-socialist organization funded and organized by those whose intend to destroy America. That organization's desire is to rebuild America into a utopia that will end up as a dystopia requiring tyranny to maintain.
- As a Christian, I suggest cutting the NBA a little slack on this partisan display while pointing out to them that there is a difference between the Black Lives Matter organization and others who believe the slogan "Black lives matter." I do not believe that most of the Black players in the NBA would support the overthrow of the United States government, the destruction of our cities, the end of capitalism, free speech, freedom of religion, and most of our human rights.
- Many players in the NBA claim to be devout Christians. Do not forget that God is at work in and through the lives of these young men who influence many others. God has a witness there, but it does not mean that those witnesses are political conservatives.
- Consider how the current opportunity to give Blacks more attention in society might help the cause of Christ. The special care that the government has given to them for the last fifty years has created a Black underclass and is the biggest contributor to broken Black families, high crime rates, murders, and gang violence. That is

not the type of help Black people need. Government throwing more money at the problems just makes them worse. That philosophy is built on white guilt and a white patronage system that keeps Black people down and beholding to the powerful.

- Recognize that what will keep people from believing in God are Christians who refuse to love with concrete actions for the benefit of others. The most powerful truth is the Christ gave himself for others. Will Christians give themselves for the benefit of Blacks they know and care about? This is not about guilt or blame. It is about "God so loved the world that he gave."[307] The greatest gift we can give to the cause of Blacks is equality of opportunity and friendship.

---

[307] John 3:16.

An Empire of Lies

Daily I am reminded how the Judeo-Christian foundation of our culture is crumbling beneath our feet. The law, the Ten Commandments, and the worldview that "in the beginning God created the heavens and the earth" are under attack. [308] The Declaration of Independence itself says, "We hold these truths to be self-evident, that all men are created equal, that they are endowed by their Creator with certain unalienable Rights, that among them are Life, Liberty and the pursuit of Happiness."[309]

From this declaration came the most successful experiment in human history—the idea that a people can govern themselves. But this is dependent on a certain level of piety. Virtue is essential for self-government to succeed. It inherently requires participants to want to obey and enforce the law.

In 2020, this appears to be falling apart. Why? Because of secularism and its false idea that we have evolved beyond the mythology of religion allowing real progress to be made. These secular ideas are not common among the common people but are believed and practiced by the cultural elite who control 90% of the media and therefore the national narrative.[310] What is self-

---

[308] Gen. 1:1, NIV.

[309] United States Declaration of Independence.

[310] Alison Durkee, "More Americans Now Socially Liberal Than Conservative for First Time, Poll Finds." *Forbes*, 24 June 2021. https://www.forbes.com/sites/alisondurkee/2021/06/24/more-americans-now-socially-liberal-than-conservative-for-first-time-poll-finds/?sh=da163f548d87.

evident is that when you abandon the idea that our rights are God given and that equality is necessary because every person is made in the image of God, then you lose your reasons to support the First Amendment, freedom of speech, and the freedom of religion. Society becomes untethered from its moral base and begins to abandon its moral compass, the very moral compass that is the foundation of the Bill of Rights.

This is seen most vividly in two ways, one political and the other in general society. Some politicians are attempting to abandon common sense, dismiss basic mathematics, and sell their souls for power. They promise people free health care, and they claim that they will pay for it by taxing the top 1% of income earners.[311] They want open borders and expect that we can absorb the extra expense of unlimited numbers of immigrants without raising taxes on the middle class. They want no limits on abortion. They want to take your guns. They want to redirect your charitable giving as in the case of an IRS review of a Christian foundation's choices. This was seen with the recent Chick-fil-A dust up. Progressives will never be happy until every last chicken leg that is served is a gay or transsexual chicken. [312]

The other way to understand the crumbling of the foundation is to examine the product of this untethered philosophy.

---

[311] Raising taxes on the top 1% of United States taxpayers will not be able to pay for the additional costs being proposed with regard to lower cost health care. "The Effect of Rising Health Care Costs on U.S. Tax Rates," *Bulletin on Aging and Health*, No. 1, (March 2011). https://www.nber.org/bah/2011no1/effect-rising-health-care-costs-us-tax-rates.

[312] Kate Taylor, "Chick-fil-A Is Under Attack Over Its CEO's Ties to A Christian Charity Accused of Trying to Squash Proposed LGBTQ Protections. Here's What We Know About the Chain's Donations." *Business Insider*, 4 June 2021. https://www.businessinsider.com/chick-fil-a-ties-to-anti-equality-act-efforts-explained-2021-6.

Attorney William Barr said this in a 2019 speech at Norte Dame University Law School:

> I think we all recognize that over the past 50 years religion has been under increasing attack. On the one hand, we have seen the steady erosion of our traditional Judeo-Christian moral system and a comprehensive effort to drive it from the public square. On the other hand, we see the growing ascendancy of secularism and the doctrine of moral relativism. By any honest assessment, the consequences of this moral upheaval have been grim.
>
> Virtually every measure of social pathology continues to gain ground. In 1965, the illegitimacy rate was eight percent. In 1992 . . . it was 25 percent. Today it is over 40 percent. In many of our large, urban areas, it is around 70 percent. Along with the wreckage of the family, we are seeing record levels of depression and mental illness . . . [and] soaring suicide rates.
>
> As you all know, over 70,000 people die a year from drug overdoses . . . *And yet, the forces of secularism, ignoring these tragic results, press on with even greater militancy.* Among these militant secularists are many so-called progressives. *But where is the progress?* We are told we are living in a *post-Christian era. But what has replaced the Judeo-Christian moral system? What is it that can fill the spiritual void?* What we call values today are really nothing more than mere sentimentality, *still drawing on the vapor trails of Christianity.*[313] [Emphasis added]

---

[313] Attorney General William P. Barr Delivers Remarks to the Law School and the de Nicola Center for Ethics and Culture at the University of Notre Dame, South Bend, IN, October 11, 2019, *The United States Department of Justice.* https://www.justice.gov/opa/speech/attorney-general-william-p-barr-delivers-remarks-law-school-and-de-nicola-center-ethics.

Barr goes on to talk about the theory and expectation that the pendulum will swing back. However, he claimed something is different about this assault, meaning that this pendulum swing may not happen. This attack is organized destruction. Secularists and their allies have marshaled all the forces of mass communication, popular culture, the entertainment industry, and academia in an unremitting assault on religion and traditional values. These instruments are used not only to promote secular orthodoxy but also to drown out and silence opposing voices and to viciously attack and hold up to ridicule any dissidence.

> So the reaction to growing illegitimacy is not sexual responsibility, but abortion. The reaction to drug addiction is safe injection sites. The solution to the breakdown of the family is for the state to set itself up as ersatz husband for single mothers and the ersatz father to their children. The call comes for more and more social programs to deal with the wreckage[314]

Progressivism grows like a cancer. It will never be satisfied. Can you imagine the grievance industry ever saying, "Okay, call off the dogs. Discrimination is no longer a problem. Now we're even, and we no longer need advocacy groups." The grievance industry thrives on its fascist crusade to destroy all that has made the United States the most free, liberal, fair, and successful society that has ever been formed. America has faults and has engaged in some bad behavior, but that has been the exception, not the rule. The only reason they can get away with all this is that the people they hate and disparage have died for them, such as American soldiers. Because of that sacrifice, they can throw a rock at you because someone took a bullet for them. They can be free to be ridiculous and shame themselves. We are becoming that upside

---

[314] Ibid.

down kingdom, the one that Saint Francis quipped, "I will need to go to the city square and stand on my head to see the world aright."[315] At least for the 6% of people who compose the cultural elite, light has been declared darkness and darkness declared light. It is a kingdom turned upside down.

"We are human, but we don't wage war as humans do. We use God's mighty weapons, not worldly weapons, to knock down the strongholds of human reasoning and to destroy false arguments. We destroy every proud obstacle that keeps people from knowing God. We capture their rebellious thoughts and teach them to obey Christ" (2 Cor 10:3-5).

---

[315] This public domain quote may be folklore. Like many sayings from the middle centuries CE, it may not be reliable regarding accuracy. Father Paschal Robinson, *The Writings of Saint Francis of Assisi* (Philadelphia: The Dolphin Press, 1906). https://oll.libertyfund.org/title/assisi-the-writings-of-saint-francis-of-assisi .

Thank God for Bill Maher

If I really want to get upset or listen to some really misguided people, I watch *Real Time with Bill Maher*. My wife cannot even be in the same room when it is on. I feel her pain as she retreats to a Hallmark movie. But there is something salvific about it. That means it has a redemptive quality.

I am very curious as to how the world has gone mad and why people can believe such dangerous propaganda which does not match reality. They believe in an evolutionary based progress of human beings into enlightened souls who will eventually end war, famine, pestilence, and stop people like Bill Clinton, Prince Andrew, and Jeffery Epstein from flying to private islands with underage girls on the *Lolita Express*. They seem to believe there are a different set of rules for the elite and powerful than for the rest of us. That is the reason they cover up for each other, while at the same time preach that no one is above the law.

Bill Maher is very smart, articulate, well informed, and at the same time twisted and closed off. He lives in his leftist bubble determined to convert others to his cause. Of course, he is a hypocrite. We all are. It is part of being human. Bill is on a crusade against global climate change, too much meat in one's diet, soda pop, and desserts, while simultaneously being an advocate of smoking and legalizing marijuana. He claims the substance does no real harm. He does not believe it will contribute to America, which he already believes is dumb, becoming even dumber. You can see how he is inconsistent. Watching his show is not the way to get smarter, but it does help you learn to think sometimes.

Bill has trouble getting smart, articulate conservatives on his show because they know it will not be a fair fight. There will be three and sometimes four plus the studio audience against one. Dennis Prager, Ben Shapiro, and some other quality conservatives sometimes appear, but mostly it is retired or back benchers who go on. The best and the brightest stay away.

Additionally, there is mockery and ridicule. This is not only the condescending heritage of the left. They have permission to do all the things they accuse the right of doing but with impunity. It is all very Freudian, projecting onto others what they do themselves. They accuse Donald Trump of being racist and at the same time they show themselves to be naïve Western imperialists by arguing that people of color in other nations who have politically incorrect ideology would come around if only we could reason with them. For example, Islam was founded on the sword. Violence and oppression against women and gays are part of their teachings. They really do hold these views. Democracy is not in sync with their teachings. Islam calls for a worldwide caliphate which includes a theocracy-run government. This is the same racist arrogance that led to colonialism.

I think Bill Maher truly believes he is smarter than most and fair in his political assessment. I would tell him he is fair just like Sean Hannity is fair. Sean Hannity is a conservative commentor on Fox News who claims to be fair but is exceedingly partisan. Maher is somewhat of an atheist. It seems he has hedged his bet on this a time or two in keeping open to the idea that there might be something out there. I do not blame him. He, like any human, would like to live forever, not as a pothead but in a perfect environment with a perfect body and a perfect society. I would love to see Bernie Sanders in heaven because finally he would have to shut up about the environment and everything will be free, but he might miss his comrades, Trotsky, Stalin, Lenin, Marx, and the Marque de Sade. Maybe Larry David would be a good replacement since his SNL impersonation of Bernie is so spot on. He he would not even need to curb his enthusiasm.

Ok, what was this column about? Oh yeah, now I remember: hypocrisy. We evangelicals are hypocrites too. I think a good quote from my book *The Cost of Cheap Grace*, written with Brandon Cook, could be good here. It is always fun to quote our friend Friedrich Nietzsche who went mad at the end of his life. But he had a few things sort of right. Here is one of them:

> "The Christians have never practiced the actions Jesus prescribed to them; and the impudent garrulous talk about 'justification by faith' and its supreme and sole significance is only the consequence of the Church's lack of courage and will to profess the works Jesus demanded.[316]

It is a bit like the Grand Inquisitor said to Jesus in the story from Dostoevsky's famous novel, *The Brothers Karamazov*. He had arrested Jesus and went to his cell to give Jesus some advice. "The church is no longer yours to run. It has taken us fifteen hundred years to reduce the burdensome and unrealistic demands you left behind. We can't have you coming back and undoing all that good work . . . Go now and do not come back . . . ever. You must never, never come again!"

Jesus will come again, and I hope he touches down in Bill Maher's studio during a live session of *Real Time with Bill Maher*. Even my wife might watch that. That studio audience would finally be quiet though I still think Bill might try to finish his bit.

---

[316] Hull and Cook, *Cost of Cheap Grace*, 7.

Want to Ruin the World?
Start with White Guilt

"What I wanted most for America was an end to white guilt, or at least an ebbing of this guilt into insignificance—white guilt is the terror of being seen as a racist—a terror that has caused whites to act guiltily toward minorities even when they feel no actual guilt."[317]

African American Writer Shelby Steele

There was a time when I was quite creative in the kitchen. I invented what my wife calls "Billy Food." Every recipe begins the same: "Fill the bowl with a bed of chips." After that it was either plop on some cottage cheese or real cheese which required the extra step of 30 seconds in the microwave before topping it with fresh salsa.

I have recently discovered the recipe for the post-Christian "woke" religious revolution playing out in the streets of America as presented on cable television. This revolution is anti-family, anti-church, anti-capitalism, anti-truth, and anti-Christ. The recipe begins, "Start with a foundation of white guilt." The entire enterprise of deconstructing America begins with destroying the basic biblical narrative that Western morality has been built on.

---

[317] Steele, *Shame*,1.

I took some pretty good notes the other night listening to John Zmirak on *The Eric Metaxas Show*.[318] I am not that familiar with Zmirak but thought his summation of the reasoning on this topic worthy of my time. It goes something like this. Whites are uniquely evil and guilty in the evil they have done in the name of America. They brought the slaves to our land in 1619. They took the land away from the Native Americans. They created a constitution for themselves but not for slaves and the native people. They purloined the natural resources of the land and set up institutions to enrich themselves and oppress minorities and those who were not born to the manor. Beneath all this was their white religion, with a white blue-eyed Jesus whose blessings were bestowed upon their members. Americans need to be awakened, to be "woke," to these evils. When statues are being torn down and courthouses and public buildings are destroyed and looted, it is symbolic of the revolution meant to tear it all down and to start over with a new religion, one created by man, made for man, and sustained by man.

The premise is partially true, but in context and on the whole, it is a tub of rot. Whiteness is allegedly the original sin. There is nothing you can do about it. One wonders why and how whites created wealth and power that led to this dubious distinction. Why not Blacks, Asians, or Latinos? This creates some real philosophical problems for the thesis, but let us continue. If you were born white, you must admit your sin, repent, and confess to the "woke" god, then redemption can be yours.

In 303 CE, the Roman Emperor Diocletian issued at edict that rescinded Christian rights and demanded that they comply with traditional religious practices. They were required to make sacrifice to the gods. Diocletian created a golden statue of his

---

[318] https://www.youtube.com/watch?v=e2KGaJnResl.

image. The head of the statue can now be viewed in the Istanbul Archaeological Museum—the kind of place you can find most former gods. All the Christians needed do in order to stave off any persecution from Roman officials was to pay ceremonial homage to the Caesar and recite a statement.

Right now in America, if you want to avoid being punished by the cancel culture movement, this new religion has a simple repentance and confession that will bring redemption to your soul. All your need say is, Black Lives Matter." Do not say more. Do not say, "All Lives Matter." That is *verboten*. Do not say "Black Lives Matter Too," or anything that includes Cambodians, Chinese, or the people of India.

You see, your whiteness can only be forgiven if you repent, confess, and make affirmation to being different. This is your affirmation of faith just like at baptism you say, "I believe in God the Father, God the Son, and God the Holy Spirit, and that Jesus the Christ is my savior and leader." This is the post-Christian religious cult's rite of passage.

The culture knows that something has gone wrong, but instead of taking personal responsibility, the white oppressors must pay for the sins of the world. Whiteness becomes the scapegoat that takes away the sins of the oppressors. Of course, they may institute their own Day of Atonement, so it must be done annually. Whites confess their sins and nail themselves to the cross of political redemption. The problem this religion has is quite common. It doesn't have a resurrection and a sovereign loving God who gives a damn.

What does this all mean? This new post-Christian "woke" religion is a part of pop culture. Granted, the current pop culture is meaner and more destructive than the hula-hoops and saddle shoes of the 1950s, but it remains temporary and will pass away. There are two reasons for this. First, there is no pot of gold at the end of its rainbow, only a big bowl of tasteless wrong that humans will not eat for long. Second, the prophet Isaiah declared:

> What sorrow for those who drag their sins behind them with ropes made of lies, who drag wickedness behind them like a cart! They even mock God and say,
> 'Hurry up and do something! We want to see what you can do. Let the Holy One of Israel carry out his plan, for we want to know what it is.'
> What sorrow [woe to those] who say that evil is good and good is evil, that dark is light and light is dark, that bitter is sweet and sweet is bitter. What sorrow for those who are wise in their own eyes and think themselves so clever (Isa 5:18-21).

In John Milton's *Paradise Lost*, Lucifer lay chained on the floor of hell, and he reasons that being in hell is not so bad. Losing is not the end of all things because, after all, it is all a state of mind. He has the ability to make hell seem like heaven and for heaven to seem like hell. He is an expert at convincing those not protected by God that light is darkness and darkness is light, that right is wrong and that wrong is right.[319] God says through his prophet "woe to those" who fall for it.[320]

Excuse me for being the master of the obvious, but yesterday I heard elected representatives in Congress declaring lawless, brick throwing, laser pointing, fire starting, chainsaw hacking criminals peaceful and then shaming the Attorney General of the

---

[319] https://www.sparknotes.com/poetry/paradiselost/section2/.
[320] Isa 5:20.

United States for trying to stop them.[321] On national television, they denied the reality that everyone could see. They did not denounce it and would not allow the Attorney General to answer their questions. But these were not real questions. They were accusations. They should have just sat a cardboard cutout of their guest in the chair and yelled at it. It would have saved everyone a lot of time and money.

Americans watch cities burn and it seems like hell. Lucifer is at work. He is saying through his representatives that hell is actually heaven. "This is the utopia we promised. We are just a few more burned buildings, a few less cops, a few more closed churches, a few more shamed white people, and one election away from heaven. Just wait. You will see. We will all be like God. Everyone will be white; everyone will have privilege. Everyone can go to Harvard and Yale, and everyone can vacation like Jay-Z and Beyonce. We know they aren't white, but they live white. And as soon as you give us the power, all this mayhem will stop because we will order them to stop. We will stop cutting them checks. Trust us. Antifa will all go away. They belong to us."

Oh yes, I told you there was a second reason this pop-up cultural phenomena would go away, and it is conditional. If we Christians fight instead of cowering and running for cover, then it will be exposed. We live under the protection of the First Amendment until we don't. I am not sure what it will take to awaken the lethargic, self-indulgent, self-protecting church, but we are called to "knock down the strongholds of human reasoning and to destroy false arguments. We destroy every proud obstacle that

[321] "Attorney General Barr Testifies on Justice Department Mission and Programs," *C-Span*, 28 July 2020. https://www.c-span.org/video/?473384-1/attorney-general-barr-testifies-justice-department-mission-programs.

keeps people from knowing God. We capture rebellious thoughts and teach them to obey Christ" (2 Cor 10:4-5).

Elisabeth Noelle-Neumann gave us her masterpiece on forming public opinion in her 1984 work *The Spiral of Silence*. Her research presented a not-surprising thesis that powerful entities like governments, titans of industry, and despots use intimidation to quelch free speech.[322] They find ways to punish you, in modern parlance "cancel you," and then you shut up. Fifty percent of humans won't speak up. However, the other 50% are in play and using various forms of intimidation. You can use the spiral of silence until the last hold outs can be jailed or reeducated. [323]

May I remind you of what legendary missiologist Lesslie Newbigin taught in his great work *Foolishness to the Greeks* in the 1980s? The weapons that the church uses in this battle are God's mighty weapons, not worldly weapons. Newbigin names three primary characteristics of what it means to establish what he calls a missionary encounter with the culture. First, however, he gives three things a missionary encounter is not:[324]

1. Not a withdrawal. This has been tried, and it never worked.
2. Not accommodation. This is the "what harm could it do to back up another step" approach. Also well tried and never worked.
3. Not a takeover: attempted coup via political action.

---

[322] Neumann here develops her thesis of the factors that cause people to remain silent. Fear and isolation are the primary reasons. Elisabeth Noelle-Neumann, *The Spiral of Silence: Public Opinion-Our Social Skin* (Chicago: University of Chicago Press, 1984), 37.

[323] Ibid, 8-36.

[324] Newbigin, *Foolishness to the Greeks*, Chapter 6.

What is a missionary encounter?

1. Confrontation. Speaking up and speaking out will get you confrontation.
2. Converts. Create push-back and conflict. You will get converts
3. Identification of cultural idols and false arguments that keep people from knowing God.

White Guilt Part Two

In 2008, African American Shelby Steele stood before a largely white liberal audience at the Aspen Institute during a symposium on social justice and presented what he wanted for America. He stated without apology that he wanted to see the end of white guilt. He defined white guilt as "the terror of being seen as racist—a terror that has caused whites to act guiltily toward minorities even when they feel no actual guilt."[325] If that was not shocking enough, this veteran of the civil rights movement, once a young man of the left, stood before this room of liberal elites as a rebuke of their white guilt and paternalistic attitudes toward Blacks.[326] Steele was what some would call an Uncle Tom—a traitor to the Black grievance industry's narrative that racism is everywhere.[327] He stands as a living rebuke to the victim narrative that seeks to keep Black people upset and angry. His life, along with those of other successful African Americans, is a clarion call to Blacks that they are free in the United States of America—a fact that Al Sharpton and his kind work to hide from the African American community because they have badly botched freedom

---

[325] Steele, *Shame*, 1.

[326] Shelby Steele, "The Decline of the Civil rights Establishment." *The Wall Street Journal*, 21 July 2013. https://www.wsj.com/articles/SB100 01424127887324448104578618681599902640.

[327] Uncle Tom is the main character in Harriet Beecher Stowe's 1852 novel *Uncle Tom's Cabin*. "Uncle Tom" is a pejorative term used today to describe a Black man considered to be excessively obedient or servile to white people.

and helped develop a greater level of Black dependance.[328] Yes, there is a Black underclass, around 25%, but more on that later.

Steele went on to say that white guilt has spawned a new white paternalism toward minorities since the 1960s and that, among other things, it has damaged the Black family more profoundly than segregation ever did. Steele should know. He speaks with great moral authority. The first chapter of his book *Shame* presents a story from Steele's adolescence concerning racism that is quite moving.[329]

What does white guilt have to do with Christian discipleship? The very question reveals a long-standing separation of Christian activity from what actually happens in our lives. The separation of Christian discipleship from social justice and racial reconciliation has been a great mistake on the part of the disciple-making movement. The first mistake was the impulse to simply disciple those in our own congregations, shutting ourselves off from the variety of kinds of people that intersected our daily lives. This set up a system that kept white Christians busy with themselves. Efforts to work with churches of color were simply not done because no one really knew what to do. Therefore, it was a sin of omission because the obligation was present, but the will was not. I would say that congregation to congregation, racial reconciliation has gained momentum in the last twenty years, but the tendency of churches to gather around their own kind is very natural regardless of race. Today, the disciple-making movement seems largely white, but mixed politically. I see larger and larger

---

[328] Al Sharpton is the most obvious example right now of the Black Grievance cabal who utilize various forms of hyperbole and demagoguery to stir up resentment in the Black community. It is largely about power, ego and money.
[329] Steele, *Shame*, Chapter 1.

numbers of woman and minorities participating, which is very encouraging. The political environment is highly charged right now, and a lot of grace must be extended on every side. I do not, however, sense a strong resistance to it, but it continues to fall by the wayside because of the preoccupation with church success. Often the best way is to work together on common ground and become friends.

There is no more powerful force at work in the white American evangelical church right now than white guilt. What is happening in the streets—the peaceful protestors, the angry protestors who confront and curse the police, the organized agitators, and the criminals who tear down statues and deface public buildings—all of it has roots in white guilt. Again, white guilt means the fear white people feel of being labeled racist. White people will do almost anything to avoid being stigmatized. Whites are saying as they march in the streets, as they take a knee and recite an oath written by someone for them, "I'm innocent. I'm not racist. Please don't ruin me. Don't judge me. Don't censor my work and cancel my job." I do believe that a great majority of white protesters are ashamed of our country and upset with our past, and they do feel bad about it. This guilt is a major motivation. They want to make things right and that is a good trait.

Therefore, when you see a group of young rioters tearing down a statue of George Washington, Abraham Lincoln, or Andrew Jackson on television, and you yell at the TV, "Where are the police? Why isn't anyone doing something about this?" you will know where they are—standing on the sidelines where their chiefs, mayors, or governors have told them to stand. Their elected bosses are paralyzed by white guilt. Even Black leaders have white guilt. Appeasement and accommodation do not work when it comes to crime. If you allow it, you invite more of it. Every parent knows this is true.

White Guilt and the Creation of a Black Uunderclass

A little history would help here. After the Civil War, America entered what was called Reconstruction. This is when free Blacks began to flourish. Numerous Blacks were elected to high office, with many in the U.S. Congress and state legislatures. At the turn of the twentieth century, primarily in the South, Jim Crow laws were established to curtail integration into schools, public bathrooms, churches, restaurants, hotels, and other retail establishments. In spite of these odious practices, African Americans continued to flourish. What is forgotten is that Black Americans made the greatest gains and cleared the highest hurdles in a shorter span of time that any other racial group in history because they lived in a better land than most people in the world. The late Water Williams, a Black Professor of Economics at George Mason University, stated that if you totaled the earnings and spending of Black Americans and considered them a separate country with their own gross national product, they would rank in the top twenty richest nations.

In 1940, the Black illegitimacy rate was 11%; today it is 75%.[330] Most of the problem has been fatherless homes. The poverty rate among husband-and-wife Black families has been in the single digits for more than two decades.[331] From the late 1800s until 1950, some Black schools were model academic learning centers. Often, they outscored white students. Then came America's finest moment regarding race. In the 1954 *Brown v. Board of Education of Topeka* decision by the United States Supreme Court, the justices declared in a 9-0 decision, that schools should

---

[330] "In Depth: Walter Williams," *C-Span*, 1 November 2015. https://www.c-span.org/video/?326444-1/depth-walter-williams.
[331] Ibid.

be available to all races. Then came the Civil Rights Act of 1964 and the Voting Rights Act of 1965.

If the government would have stopped then, Black America would be a very different place today. But white guilt could not resist. This is when the government, well-meaning I'm sure—I am not criticizing hearts or motivation—pulled the rug out from beneath the African American community and helped create a Black underclass by setting up the Great Society and the welfare state that still exists in 2021.

Martin Luther King's dream that all people would be judged not by the color of their skin but by the content of their character was often quoted but slowly abandoned by his successors. A Black grievance society was created alongside President Lyndon Johnson's Great Society. The Black grievance society had tributaries like the NAACP led by Ralph Abernathy, Jesse Jackson, and other well-known figures, such as Roy Wilkins and Andrew Young. It is also worth mentioning the more radical elements of the followers of Malcolm X and the Black Muslims led by Louis Farrakhan. Malcolm X and Farrakhan were more radical and separatist. Only the NAACP enjoys societal sanction in today's world. This topic is worthy of being its own book but let me boil it down to a paragraph.[332]

The Great Society was white society's guilt offering to the Black community. It set up another patronage system between the whites who had stuff and Blacks who did not. The deal is simple:

---

[332] For further information, see also Jemar Tisby, *The Color of Compromise: The Truth About the American Church's Complicity in Racism* (Grand Rapids: Zondervan, 2019) and Shelby Steele, "Is White Guilt Destroying the Promise of Civil Rights?" https://www.youtube.com/watch?v=HF3VaJdConY&t=4132s, posted November 25, 2014. *The Color of Compromise* presents a younger and different point of view.

"You won't call us racist, and we will give you stuff. Okay?"[333] I cannot think of anything more demeaning to Black Americans than such a Faustian deal.[334] Nothing describes it better than welfare. Yes, there are some people who are so disabled or helpless that tax dollars should temporarily help them to get them back on their feet. People of many races qualify for such help. But the basic tenants of welfare violate the human condition.

1. Many will take a payment, even a small amount, that, together with food stamps, not paying taxes, and community programs for children, allows them to have an income for which they do not need to work or qualify.
2. If they are paid per child, they are not required to marry. In fact, they receive less if married. Having more children out of wedlock boosts income.
3. This takes away dignity. It says, "You cannot make it on your own. You need the white- run power structure to assist you."

The New Society has been a disaster for African Americans. The Black underclass would be much smaller without it. It has weakened the entire Black culture, and the entire nation needs to look at itself on this issue. The Black grievance community needs to look in the mirror and ask themselves, "Why won't we dismount this dead horse?" The answer for them is the same

---

[333] For more information see "Lyndon Johnson's 'Great Society,'" at https://www.ushistory.org/us/56e.asp.

[334] A Faustian bargain is an agreement where someone trades personal moral or spiritual values for worldly knowledge or material benefit. Faust is the protagonist of a classical German legend who, despite being successful, is dissatisfied with life and trades his soul to the Devil for knowledge and worldly pleasures. The legendary Faust is based on the historical Johann Georg Faust.

answer for many of us white Americans: because we have a vested interest in the way things are. What if Black leaders said to the African American community, bullhorn in hand, "White supremacy in America is dead. It has lost all its moral authority. You are free. Let's learn to thrive in freedom." No government program created the civil rights movement, and freedom is not a land. Freedom is just freedom—freedom to succeed and freedom to fail.

I wish this whole thing would disappear. I am tired of talking about it. I am no expert, but I cannot stop thinking, praying, and researching it because I believe that *different disciples must be made for difficult days*. If we continue to lead in making disciples around the world, but they are not different disciples—ones who can step into this breach into our society—then we have failed.

Paradise Lost: the Search for Justice Concept

John Milton's famous poem *Paradise Lost* is a difficult read. Most guess that the poem's plot is about Adam and Eve being thrown out of the Garden of Eden. But the story is about what Lucifer, the fallen angel, has lost. He has lost his paradise. The opening scene has him lying on the floor of hell wondering how he got there and why he has been defeated. He decides to take his revenge on this new creation of God's called humans that he loves more than the angels. Satan decides, along with his angelic army, to get his revenge on God through the destruction of the human race. He will conquer, seduce, and destroy man. As Satan observes in Book One:

> The mind is its own place, and in itself
> Can make a Heav'n of Hell, a Hell of Heav'n.
> What matter where, if I be still the same...
> To reign is worth ambition through in Hell:
> Better to reign in Hell than serve in Heav'n[335]

Right now, I must conclude that confusion and chaos, like a storm front, has covered the American mind, and people are asking, "What is going on and how did we get here?" This runs much

---

[335] John Milton, *Paradise Lost*, 1667. https://poets.org/poem/paradise-lost-book-i-lines-221-270.

deeper than race, the police, or political arguments. Lucifer is having a great run right now in the destruction of those whom God has made, loves, and to whom he has fully given himself.

The need for justice is deeply embedded in the human soul.[336] That is why I have been sitting around recently with my head in my hands. Like Lesslie Newbigin said, "All great thinking begins with a pain in the mind." I am searching for some great thought, and I have experienced some significant mental anguish in my quest to understand what is going on around me. It seems that the protesters in the streets, the heated debates on the cable channels, and the young Blacks' expressions of anger all seem to be a common cry of great pain, a world suffering from injustice. People of my generation have seen this many times over the years going back to the 1960s. We lived through the civil rights movement. I have clear memories of the 1963 March on Washington, the speeches of Dr. Martin Luther King, Black Americans being denied access to schools and universities, and the use of dogs and fire hoses to punish Black protesters in our southern cities. I also remember the radical, violent element, such as the Black Panthers, seeking justice.

Americans largely agreed that racism written into the law was morally wrong. We had already decided that slavery was wrong. We killed each other in large numbers in the Civil War to officially stop slavery. In 1964, Congress passed the Civil Rights Act, and President Lyndon Johnson signed it into law, making it illegal to discriminate based on race. America has made great strides in race relations. America is the most-free, least racist nation in the world. We are the least tribal or even prejudiced people in the world. In principle, we are free to have our say, and we are free to express ourselves, to worship our God, or not to worship any god.

---

[336] Mal 6:8.

It is also true that while racial injustice is illegal, it still exists. More than one thing can be true at the same time. We are not racist by law, but in practice we still clearly see many cases of racial injustice. There are studies that demonstrate that white applicants for jobs get hired at twice the rate of minorities, even when candidates of both races have the same qualifications.[337] It is also true that one in seven churchgoers believe that interracial marriage is morally wrong. Holding that belief is not illegal, and some members of white and minority races adhere to it.[338]

Have many of the people currently marching in the streets experienced racism? Yes, they have! Are they fed up? Of course they are! Will marching in the streets change opinions? No! Will the marches and protesting communicate that there is a problem? Yes indeed!

This is a both/and situation. We can be the least racist nation on earth and at the same time have a good amount of racism in our culture. Yes, there are some changes that need to be made in law enforcement, but there are also many long-term issues to be addressed, which are problems of the heart. Most of the conversation about race that should take place will need to be in private conversations among Christians and non-Christians alike. But none of this can happen until everyone respects the rule of law and everyone's voice can be heard. If white males are not allowed to express their opinions because they are the oppressor and, therefore, whatever they say is dismissed as a mere attempt to protect their power, then meaningful conversation is impossible. Assigning motives to every person based on what

[337] Dina Gerdeman, "Minorities Who Whiten Resumes Get More Interviews." Harvard Business School, 17 May 2017. https://hbswk.hbs.edu/item/minorities-who-whiten-job-resumes-get-more-interviews.
[338] "Racial Divides in Spiritual Practice," barna.com, 12 January 2017. https://www.barna.com/research/racial-divides-spiritual-practice/.

oppressed or oppressor group they allegedly belong to based on skin color alone is a losing proposition and will go nowhere. It is similar to the accusation that if you don't have a vagina, you cannot have an opinion about the morality of abortion. The white male is apt to claim that while racism does exist, they would need to sort out through dialogue where they might be culpable.

So here I sit, hoping and praying that all of us will realize that justice is essential, and that God put the need for it in us. God created us, but we have all sinned and need redemption as a result. A starting point for me is that God created all of us in his image. Every living soul is equally loved and valued by God. To look down upon or abuse another human because of skin color is a sin. It is a sin against God and against that person. God has promised justice in the end for every living being.

He showed us this most clearly in how he invested in us by becoming a human, suffering with us, and, finally, in sacrificing himself in what has become the defining moment of our world. He died on the cross for us. That was the most unjust event in human history. "For God made Christ, who never sinned, to be the offering for our sin, so that we could be made right with God through Christ" (2 Cor 5:21). One thing is true of every person marching, looting, policing, or sitting at home sipping coffee watching it all on television: we have sinned and have fallen short of the glory of God.[339] We are to work now for as much justice as humans can provide for one another. It will not be perfect or unanimous, but it could be the dominant characteristic of my life, your life, and the lives of those we touch.

Pulitzer Prize winning author Jack Miles writes in his book *Christ: A Crisis in the Life of God*:

---

[339] Rom 3:23.

All mankind is forgiven, but the Lord must die. This is the revolutionary import of the epilogue that, two thousand years ago, a group of radical Jewish writers appended to the sacred scripture of their religion. Because they did so, millions in the West today worship before the image of a deity executed as a criminal and—no less important— other millions who never worship at all carry within their cultural DNA a religiously derived suspicion that somehow, someday, "the last will be first, and the first last."[340]

I think this is what everyone wants, but not everyone who wants it even understands that they want it or how to get there. Pray, my friends. Pray.

---

[340] Miles' comment "the first will be last, and the last will be first" is derived from Matthew 10:16. Jack Miles, *Christ: A Crisis in the Life of God* (Visalia, CA: Vintage Press, 2011).

Critical Theory

"Men won't be free until the last King is strangled with the entrails of the last Priest"[341]

French Philosopher Denis Diderot 1713-1784

"The deepest motive for mission is simply the desire to be with Jesus where he is, on the frontier between the reign of God and the usurped dominion of the devil."[342]

Lesslie Newbigin

My first memory of Critical Theory was Lesslie Newbigin's lecture on nihilism.[343] The context was that nihilism posited in a strict sense means that there is nothing. This is nonsense, of course. It seems superfluous to say that attached to nihilism is the belief that there is no absolute truth. This is not a good beginning for a philosophy that portends to give people a helpful answer to life's mystery. The "Critical Principle," as Newbigin called it, is deeply rooted in philosophy, and its essential purpose is to criticize or take apart anything whole or biblical, particularly in the context of Western civilization.

---

[341] https://www.brainyquote.com/quotes/denis_diderot_105429.

[342] https://twitter.com/lesslienewbigin/status/1081780063169843200?lang=en.

[343] Lesslie Newbigin, "Lecture on Nihilism," https://www.youtube.com/watch?v=5WyrC7JVd5Q, posted July 28, 2012.

This puts humans in a dilemma articulated by Friedrich Nietzsche: we are not able to say that anything is true or false, good or bad. The only thing left is the will to power. However, Nietzsche was skeptical that the secular community would be capable of finding an able replacement for Judeo-Christian based morality. [344] He was right.

The Critical Principle then is that all truth claims must be subjected to critical examination. This, Newbigin said, " . . . has been the crown jewel of western modern scientific civilization." It is the same idea Hegel presented: truth is a product of the dialectic—a critical back and forth between thesis and antithesis which blends together in synthesis, a new truth. Truth then moves forward on philosophy's escalator as humans evolve and become wiser, smarter, and more advanced toward some sort of utopia which, according to this line of thinking, means nowhere, and, based on nihilism, means nothing.

Why spend time talking about this useless and morally bankrupt philosophy? Because it is slowly taking over Western civilization, threatening to destroy the Christian faith, domesticate the church, and realign society into a dystopic nightmare. We cannot pretend to be engaged with the spiritual battle and not lock in on the battle for the minds and souls of the global community. Taking every thought captive to the obedience of Christ requires it.

The Basics of the Critical Theory

On the surface, you may have heard of this in its more popular forms such as Critical Race Theory, political correctness, and

---

[344] Omar Bin Salamah, "Nietzsche's Critique of Morality and Revaluation of Values" (Honors Thesis, University of Iowa, 2018). https://ir.uiowa.edu/cgi/viewcontent.cgi?article=1383&context=honors_theses.

cancel culture. You may recognize it as people trying to solve problems that are not really problems like gender confusion, Hollywood not being diverse enough, a downturn in yacht sales, or point guards under five feet being underrepresented in the NBA. But it is in the deeper ideas where the real battle resides. The basic tenets of the Critical Principle are:

1. God is dead; everything is power
2. Separate people by race, age, and class
    i. Oppressor vs Oppressed
    ii. Superior vs Subordinate
    iii. Majority vs Minority
    iv. Strong vs Weak
3. Breakdown the status quo and rebuild society. Divide, conquer, and win.
    i. Critical Theory rejects divine revelation as pre-modern and pre-scientific. Once we learned that the sun was the center of the universe and that we are on a subservient planet in orbit, then all enchanting mythologies were ferociously destroyed. This is particularly evident in biblical criticism and the Hegelian dialectic process that led European theologians to deconstruct the biblical text. This traveled to the United States via American graduate students studying for advanced degrees in Europe, reading the works of liberal theologians Paul Tillich, Rudolf Bultmann, and Emil Brunner, and then becoming faculty members of American seminaries. We might call them tenured radicals.
    ii. Society is hierarchical. The oppressors must confess their sins and provide the oppressed with what they need to be equal. If they will not confess and provide such goods and services, it

should be taken from them. Just yesterday I heard some "serious" people recommending a Truth and Reconciliation Commission. Let the twenty-first century Inquisition begin.[345] Revenge is on its way.

iii. Freedom is not only equality of opportunity. It is also equality of result. The government must enforce equality of result regardless of the cost.

iv. The ideas of equality of results advocates are so grand and virtuous that they claim insurrection, military actions, imprisonment, and related penalties should be employed. [This tyranny in the name of tolerance and social engineering has been most graphically attempted in the former Soviet Union, life behind the Iron Curtain, Cambodia, Venezuela, Cuba, North Korea and China.] It begins idealistically with grandiose humanistic theories of human life that, in the end, do not square with the human experience. Humans have not changed since we were expelled from Eden. Equality of result will never work until God changes the human being in fundamental ways.

v. Critical Theory is anti-God, according to as Solzhenitsyn who said, "At the heart of Marxism is a militant hate of God."[346] It depends on Lucifer to accuse oppressors and their descendants that they are racists to the core, and regardless of what

[345] Sarah Souli, "Does America Need a Truth Commission and Reconciliation Commission?" *Politico*, 16 August 2020. https://www.politico.com/news/magazine/2020/08/16/does-america-need-a-truth-and-reconciliation-commission-395332.

[346] "Acceptance Address by Mr. Aleksandr Solzhenitsyn,: *Templeton Prize*, 10 May 1983. https://www.templetonprize.org/laureate-sub/solzhenitsyn-acceptance-speech/.

they do they will always be racists. It refuses to celebrate progress or reward reformation.

The Christian Response

Let it be stipulated by every Christian that injustice, cruelty, suffering, and inequity are present in life and sometimes in abundance. This is what we call the fall. The story of God and humans is that innocence was lost when sin entered the human race, and with that came all the evils previously named.[347] But then came the promise of deliverance as early as Genesis 3:15. Satan's head would be crushed by a savior, and, over time, God would gradually unveil his plan to redeem and reclaim his creation. The apex of this plan came when God visited us in the person of Jesus the Christ. Rather than an imperfect capricious god requiring people to sacrifice themselves for him, God turned the tables and sacrificed himself for humankind.[348] He promised that this good news would be preached to every nation after which time he would return again bringing justice and establishing a perfect and eternal society in a new heaven and new earth.[349]

Critical Theory, in the end, has no answer except to try to force people to believe what they do not believe and behave in a way they are incapable of behaving to create a world that will not work. Their world will fail, but, before it does, it will leave piles of corpses in the streets and prisons filled with dissents. It will be dark, ugly, and seem like hell.

The Westminster Shorter Catechism summarizes biblical teaching on the purpose of each person's life: "To worship God and to

---

[347] Gen 3:8-11; Rom 3:10-18
[348] Rom 5:6-8
[349] Matt 24:14; Rev 20-22.

enjoy him forever." The secular atheists who formed the Critical Theory do not know the purpose of the human race because they rejected revelation and limited themselves to human reason and a good guess. They think people exist primarily for personal pleasure and enjoyment because without God there is no other sensible purpose. And if you are hindered from that pursuit of pleasure, then society must rectify the problem, even by violent means. That is the lesson of the French Revolution.[350]

The biblical answer to oppression, injustice, and suffering is repentance toward God, reconciliation with God through Jesus Christ, and then living the reality of the new nature God gives. That new nature equips and empowers us to be peacemakers in the biblical sense of the word.[351] The answer is vertical. As people make peace with God, then society really does change horizontally when those who live for him start loving their neighbors as themselves.[352]

---

[350] The French revolution was a lesson of the pursuit of freedoms granted by the society or state. The American revolution was the pursuit of freedom with the understanding that those freedoms were granted by our creator. They are divine in nature. The American experiment is about whether a people can govern themselves through representatives who work for them and who are accountable to the people.

[351] Rom 6:1-23; 2 Cor 5:20; Heb 8:10-12.

[352] Mark 12:30-31. An example of a changed society can be seen in the Waodoni people of Ecquador. Formerly known as the Auca Indians, the tribe used spears to kill the first Christian missionaries who tried to make contact with them on January 8, 1956. The widows of two of those missionaries stayed and ministered to the people who killed their husbands. Eventually, tribal leaders trusted Christ and began adhering to biblical teachings. Mincaye, the first convert, described the transformation in this way: "We lived angry, hating and killing, 'ononque' (for no reason), until they brought us God's markings. Now, those of us who walk God's trail live happily and in peace." "Remembering Mincaye," *ITEC*. https://www.itecusa.org/mincaye/.

Three Things Every Journalist in America Should Read Right Now

"You can't do political philosophy on television. Its form works against the content . . . Therein is our problem, for television is at its most trivial and, therefore, most dangerous when its aspirations are high, when it presents itself as a carrier of important cultural conversations."[353]

Neil Postman, *Amusing Ourselves to Death*

Anderson Cooper and Chris Cuomo discussing the philosophical rationale behind their decisions to abandon classic journalism for partisan politics might as well be smoke signals.[354] They only have eight minutes to debate it. Often some serious person like Shelby Steel or Victor Davis Hanson will appear on Fox News Network and they are given a mere two minutes to explain the development of America's Faustian bargain with race or the role of Greek mythology in the development of the city-state. It just does not work. Yet this is how people in a high-tech media age get their education, in fragments and in "the news"—a concept invented with the advent of the telegraph.

---

[353] Postman, *Amusing Ourselves to Death*, 125-41.
[354] Anderson Cooper hosts *Anderson Cooper 360* and Chris Cuomo hosts *Cuomo Prime Time* on Cable News Network (CNN).

Watching the news used to be a noble activity. Its purpose was to properly inform citizens in a non-partisan fashion so said citizens could elevate their lives and make wise choices regarding their vote and investments of time. Politicians could exaggerate, speak in generalities, even lie, and the press would hold them accountable and sort out truth from fiction. That is no longer the case. We will never pass that way again, but can we restore some meaningful contact with reality? Thanks to the First Amendment, the press is free—free to be corrupt, partisan, revengeful, and to make "the news" all about their moral outrage. However, because of that abuse of freedom, trust and truth are absent from the American conversation. The entire foundation of knowing the truth must be rebuilt.

I propose a required reading program for all journalists—print, television, long and short form writers, column writers, bloggers, and tweet types. Let us go back to the typographical age, the time of the printed word. There are three books or documents that I would recommend, the first being the United States Constitution because the media needs to reacquaint itself with the First Amendment. The second is *Amusing Ourselves to Death: Public Discourse in the Age of Show Business* by Neil Postman. We must understand the difference between rational thought and emotional charges shooting through our bodies. Finally, the Bible—the world's best-selling book and the foundation of Western civilization. The Bible contains truth that never changes about humans. Humans have not changed since it was written. It tells us what people are for, why we are here, what we are to do, and how it all will end.

The Constitution of the United States of America

The purpose of the Constitution is described in the first paragraph:

We the People of the United States, in Order to form a more perfect Union, establish Justice, insure domestic Tranquility, provide for the common defense, promote the general Welfare, and secure the Blessings of Liberty to ourselves and our Posterity, do ordain and establish this Constitution for the United States of America.[355]

This is followed by seven articles dealing with the establishment of the government. One marvels at the genius and forethought that went into this declaration of freedom and its practicality. Then comes with the First Amendment to the Constitution of the United States of America:

Congress shall make no law respecting an establishment of religion, or prohibiting the free exercise thereof; or abridging the freedom of speech, or of the press; or the right of people to peaceably to assemble, and to petition the Government for a redress of grievances.[356]

Such a simple statement yet there have been so many arguments and court cases trying to interpret its application. It is clear that Congress is prohibited from interfering with religion, free speech, freedom of the press and the freedom to peacefully gather and petition the government. However, right now, there is a surprising and serious assault on freedom of speech. It is even more interesting that the press has joined in. Talk about biting the hand that feeds you! Like Esau, they are selling their birthright for a pot of bad stew.[357]

---

[355] Preamble, United States Constitution, 1787.

[356] First Amendment, United States Constitution, 1791.

[357] Gen 25:29-34; Heb 12:16-17. Esau was the eldest of Issacs's sons. Esau's conniving, ambitious younger brother Jacob convinced him to sell his birthright for a simple pot of stew. Esau became bitter about this and was estranged from Jacob until many years later.

The press has now joined a syndicate of big tech, big business, big sports, big Hollywood, and the Democratic Party to censor any speech they do not agree with or that is in any way associated with Donald Trump. The irony is the grab your head and roll on the floor kind. You laugh; you cry; you scream; you lament; and, finally, you try to find something else to think about. It could be said that Republicans do not know how to lose, and Democrats do not know how to win. Missing on both sides is grace, dignity, humility, and a commitment not to seek reprisal and revenge.

It is quite clear in recent days that the government has stated they have been working with Facebook, Google, and Twitter to remove any misinformation from their sites. That means any information that the present administration deems false. This is what we have condemned in many non-democratic countries around the world such as Communist China or Soviet Russia. It clearly is a violation of the freedom of speech clause in the First Amendment. Yet, the Justice Department will not enforce our laws because their administration is made up of the same leaders who are censoring speech. Never in America's history have such dramatic steps been taken to smother free speech.

Freedom of speech must be protected, treasured, and fought for because tyranny will be the result. In fact, this action alone is tyrannical. The most heinous statements, even speech that is heinous must be tolerated. Right now, it is the power of the left who is censoring. In a few years, it could be the right with the power. It is true that big tech and big business are not Congress, and it is not illegal for them, as private enterprises, to censor speech and content on their platforms. But monopolies are illegal, and these companies will be broken up. New media will replace the present media, and old media will be powerless to stop it. Then the left will reap what they have sown. This can be avoided if wisdom is practiced by our nation's leaders. We are speaking here of political leaders, both elected and appointed, and CEOs of major corporations, sports leagues, and, of course, respected members of local communities. But right now, censorship and repression, revenge and political vendettas are on the menu. They will drive the rebellion deeper into the darkness and the monsters that emerge will be more dangerous to all of us than anything we have seen before because they will come from within. The attitude used to be, "I'm right and you're wrong." Now it has become, "I'm right and you're evil" There will not be peace until every voice can be heard again.

Amusing Ourselves to Death

A prophetic passage from Neil Postman's 1985 Introduction contrasted George Orwell's *1984* vision of the future, published in 1949, with Aldous Huxley's 1932 vision in *Brave New World*:

> Orwell warns that we will be overcome by an externally imposed oppression. But in Huxley's vision, no Big Brother is required to deprive people of their autonomy, maturity and history. As he saw it, people will come to love their oppression, to adore the technologies that undo their capacities to think. What Orwell feared were those who would ban books. What Huxley feared was that there would be no reason to ban a book, for there would be no one who wanted to read one. Orwell feared those who would deprive us of information. Huxley feared those who would give us so much that we would be reduced to passivity and egoism. Orwell feared that the truth would be concealed from us, Huxley feared the truth would be drowned in a sea of irrelevance. Orwell feared we would become a captive culture. Huxley feared we would become a trivial culture, preoccupied

with some equivalent of the feelies, the orgy porgy, and the centrifugal bumblepuppy. As Huxley remarked in Brave New World Revisited, that civil libertarians and rationalists who are ever on the alert to oppose tyranny "failed to take into account man's almost infinite appetite for distractions." In *1984* Orwell added, people are controlled by inflicting pain. In *Brave New World*, they are controlled by inflicting pleasure. In short, Orwell feared that what we hate will ruin us. Huxley feared that what we love will ruin us. This book is about the possibility that Huxley, not Orwell, was right." [358]

I think they were both right. From the 2021 vantage point, dystopian cells are multiplying like a cruel cancer into our culture. Elements that both Orwell and Huxley predicted are fully in play. Big tech is now the nation's teacher. There is much good that the tech giants Google, Facebook, and Twitter do, but their dystopian tendencies to censor and control content is lethal to democracy. The nation's ability to read important books has been greatly diminished in the last seventy-five years as we have moved from a printed-word culture to a screen-based or image-driven culture. Fewer people read books, and have, therefore, lost the skills, discipline, and thinking capacity of earlier generations. A well-educated person graduating from high school in 1950 was far superior to a 2020 high school graduate. The ability to be rational and to sustain attention to a complicated book or speech has been largely lost.

What has truly been lost is knowledge that leads to the ability to think cogently and to make good decisions about life. That is why every journalist should read Postman's book at least once and

[358] Postman, *Amusing Ourselves to Death*, 218.

perhaps annually: to remind them of what is happening to them and to all of us.[359]

The Bible

The world of journalism's level of biblical ignorance is pervasive, deep, and abiding. Ever since Dustin Hoffman and Robert Redford portrayed *Washington Post* reporters Carl Bernstein and Bob Woodward in *All the President's Men,* the ambition to become famous has dominated journalism. I loved the movie, and I was rooting for "Woodstein," as the *Washington Post* Managing Editor Ben Bradlee liked to call them, as the two worked to expose the political misconduct that resulted in President Richard Nixon's resignation in 1972. But I also have seen what journalism has become since, and it could use a refresher on what human beings are for, what human life means, and who is in charge and why. In other words, is there anything a journalist is not willing to do, even if it would cost them their fame and fortune? Would they be willing to be honest and get at least two independent sources before going to press? Ben Bradlee required the two sources. Watching the portrayal of Woodward and Bernstein hustling to meet the standard required to print a story is what made the movie (and real-life story) so compelling. That ethic has largely disappeared in today's journalistic morass.

The Bible is the world's best-selling book for a reason, and that reason has nothing to do with guilt, shame, and fear. It is the compelling story it tells, the greatest story ever told. The story makes sense. "In the beginning God created the

---

[359] Another recommended resource on this subject is Allan Bloom's masterpiece *The Closing of the American Mind: How Higher Education Has Failed Democracy and Impoverished the Souls of Today's Students,* originally published in 1987 and reissued by Simon & Schuster in 2012.

heavens and the earth" (Gen 1:1, NASB). Immediately we understand that there was a beginning and God was behind the creation. The Bible also declares that there is an end as well. It comes with violence, death for some, judgment for everyone, and justice for all.[360] But something went wrong. This is the most provable and least controversial doctrine of religion: that man sinned, made mistakes, got it all wrong, and messed things up.[361]

The second part of the story is God moving to save or redeem his world, to reclaim it. He chose to do this by becoming one of us, a human, and instead of our dying for him as a sacrifice—a very common approach offered by capricious gods throughout history—instead, he died for us. He became the God on the cross, the God who took the sin of the world upon his shoulders and into his person. He became death and sin in order to free us from it.[362] Finally, he will return to finish the job, eliminate evil, and create a new state, a new heaven and a new earth.[363] This world is not eternal. The human soul is eternal, and there will be an accounting and justice. That is all really good news for this cynical and feisty world in which we now reside.

Journalists are not any more evil than the normal person, but they, like everyone else, need moral guidance and structures to govern their vital role in our society. To my journalist friends, please heed my pastoral advice. Read the United States Constitution and remember what what we as citizens aspire to. Read *Amusing Ourselves to Death*, a serious scrutiny of our present problems,

---

[360] Rev 20-22.
[361] Rom 5:12-14.
[362] Rom 6; 2 Cor 5:21; 1 Pet 2:24.
[363] Revelation Chapters 20-22.

and, finally, read the Bible. It will sustain you when all else fails. You will find Jesus of Nazareth within those pages. He will show you what God is like.

Don't Inhale

"Don't put your confidence in powerful people; there is no help for you there. When they breathe their last, they return to the earth, and all their plans die with them"

Psalm 146:3-4

Mo Udall was a Democratic Congressman from Arizona. His autobiography *Too Funny to Be President* is delightful and filled with often side-splitting tales about his life in Congress. Once when asked what affect the rarefied air in Washington's corridors of power had on him, he answered, "There is a simple way to avoid its dangers. Don't inhale."[364]

Udall's quip never rang more true than on today, January 20, 2021, Inauguration Day for President Joseph Biden and Vice President Kamala Harris. There is some pomp and circumstance, but the typical parade, crowd, and inaugural balls are not to be found due to Covid 19.

On the back steps of the Capitol, a platform has been built and covered with red and blue carpet. American flag banners hang from the walls. It is a beautiful site, one familiar to us who live in the American democratic republic. Famous people from all walks of life descend the stairs with appropriate introductions and

---

[364] Morris K. Udall, *Too Funny to be President*, (New York: Henry Holt & Co., 1987).

music, a ritual to be treasured. The Chief Justice of the United States Supreme Court administers the oath of office to the Vice President and then President. Both will commit to defend the Constitution of the United States against all foes, foreign and domestic. The band will play "Hail to the Chief," and the new president will give a speech. Usually, that is it. By the end of the day, the new president and all of America can go to bed and rest assured that the country is safely in the hands of a person who intends to bring unity and healing to a divided populace after a tough election battle.

But there is something different about this transition of power. Washington D.C. is on a lockdown that has nothing to do with Covid 19. There are more soldiers in the nation's capital than are presently in Afghanistan and Iraq combined—more soldiers than were guarding Washington D.C. during the Civil War. The party that did not want a wall built along the U.S. border with Mexico to keep immigrants from illegally entering the country had a wall built around the ceremony to protect them from an imaginary threat that lives in their minds. Members of Congress have now identified themselves as victims when in fact their decisions and intentions are about to drive the chasm between left and right even deeper.

There is no reason to believe a word of what any of the victors say about unity and peace. They have lost credibility. Big tech is censoring free speech. Big media has shown its corruption by taking sides against anything conservative and anything that would remove the protection they built around the new president. It cannot be trusted to be a truth detector or to hold their favorite political party accountable. Big business, including the sports and entertainment industries, are full bore into punishing, canceling, banishing, reeducating, and reprogramming anyone who disagrees with them. My friends, this is untenable. There is no unity when people's disagreements are pushed further underground. Truth commissions and companies not willing to sell some guy's pillows because he had a different political view is horrifying and should frighten any person who knows anything about true tyranny and dictatorship. You may have heard it said from Lord Acton, "Power corrupts and absolute power corrupts absolutely."[365] This is it. This is a group of victors who have inhaled, and they are high on the power. Let us pray they get sober very soon or our country will explode and walls with barbed wire and the National Guard, such as are present in Washington, D.C. today, will be commonplace across the land.

There is a solution, at least for those who claim to know God and have confidence in the wisdom of Scripture: "Don't put your confidence in powerful people; there is no help for you there. When they breathe their last, they return to the earth, and all their plans die with them" (Psalm 146:3-4).

Don't wait, or, frankly, waste your time and energy expecting that anything that happened in Washington D.C. today will improve your life. Regardless of which political party is in power, they will fail and disappoint. Half of the country is in serious disagreement with the other half, and that is not likely to change very soon. We may be able to agree on some superficial things, such as roads should be passable, water clean, medical care first rate, and people should not steal, kill, lie, and so forth. (Actually, I am not sure about stealing, killing and lying because we kill the unborn with lusty approval, and stealing and lying are commonplace.) But this is a war of ideas, of worldview, of epistemology—of how we know what we know.

---

[365] Lord Acton was a British historian of the late nineteenth century and was famous for the statement.

We live in a media-driven society. We have been trained by television to think in sound bites. Television is incapable of serious discussion and thought. No one will watch serious discussion and thought—at least not enough people to make any money. Television will not show anything it cannot make money on. We are a nation educated by reading millions of fortune cookies—sayings, proverbs, quips, and tips. We are ignorant. In his brilliant book *Amusing Ourselves to Death*, the late Neil Postman pointed out that education has become entertainment. He presented three commandments of the television and electronic age:

1. Thou shalt have no prerequisites. In other words, sequence and context are not important to the presentation.
2. Thou shalt induce no perplexity. Difficult and complex argument is the superhighway to low ratings. Therefore, it is not presented.
3. Thou shalt avoid exposition like the ten plagues visited upon Egypt. In an image medium, prerequisites, perplexity, and exposition need to be entertaining, so why engage in them.[366]

This has only worsened since the days of Postman. What has changed the most is the unreliability and objectivity of those who decide what is on television and what images and messages will appear in other forms of media. Most have not thought things through and cannot define their worldview because they have not been taught how to think, do research, or communicate effectively in English or on the printed page.

However, there is hope in that Scripture is a viable option as a source of truth for our society. Presidents take their oaths on the

---

[366] Postman, *Amusing Ourselves to Death*, 147-49.

Bible. Biden brought a very big one to the inauguration to use as he took the oath of office. We all need to open the Bible and read, meditate on, and live it.

> But joyful are those who have the God of Israel as their
> helper,
> Whose hope is in the Lord their God.
> He made heaven and earth,
> The sea, and everything in them.
> He keeps every promise forever.
> He gives justice to the oppressed
> and food to the hungry.
> The Lord frees the prisoners.
> The Lord opens the eyes of the blind.
> The Lord lifts up those who are weighed down.
> The Lord loves the godly.
> The Lord protects the foreigners among us.
> He cares for the orphans and widows,
> But he frustrates the plans of the wicked.
> The Lord will reign forever.
> He will be your God, O Jerusalem,
> Throughout the generations.
> Praise the Lord!
> (Ps 146:5-10)

There is something for both the left and right in this psalm. It speaks to the wide varieties of human need. We can agree that something went wrong with the world, that there is a solution, and God as creator has better ideas than we do about how to fix it. Washington may call it public policy, but God calls it redemption or salvation.

Finally, in the end, there will be justice for all. It also is not arguable that we all return to the earth as dust and then comes the judgement.[367] If there is no prospect of judgment before an impartial and perfect judge, then what is the point of any justice at any time? It makes no sense and there is no reason to believe in it or to expect it. Justice is built into every human being. That fact alone is reason enough to believe in a personal, all-knowing, all-powerful God.

If you were born and raised in the West, everything you believe about right and wrong, what life is, and what humans are for comes from the Bible. Freedom of speech, for example, is a God-given right. Government's role is to ensure that all citizens enjoy the freedom to speak their mind without fear of retribution. Do you think that is what we have now? Do you think that is what students in high schools and universities enjoy? Of course not! They are afraid to speak, and, more so every day, are not allowed to speak.[368]

Utopian dreams always end the same way—in dystopian tyranny with reeducation camps and concentration camps where the wayward can "concentrate" on their thought crimes and be reprogrammed. Far-fetched? Not long ago I would have said yes but not today. It is real and coming soon to a business, school, or employment agency near you. So once again, "Don't put your confidence in powerful people; there is no help for you there. When they breathe their last, they return to the earth, and all their plans die with them" (Psalm 146:3-4). Don't inhale.

---

[367] Rom 12:19.

[368] Sophia Solano, "Cancel Culture Divides Students, Professors," *VOA News*, 15 April 2021. https://www.voanews.com/student-union/cancel-culture-divides-students-professors.

UNIQUENESS
OF 2020

Christianity Yesterday Suggests Tyranny Tomorrow

In *Letters to Malcolm*, C.S. Lewis wrote, "You can't think straight unless you are cool. But then neither can you think deep if you are. I suppose one must try every problem in both states. You remember that the ancient Persians debated everything twice: when they were drunk and once when they were sober."[369]

When my son called me to ask me, "Hey Dad, did you see that *Christianity Today* came out for the Impeachment of President Trump?" I was silent.[370] Then I blurted out, "Are you sure? Why would they do that?" My son asked me to read it and then get back to him. There were some "liberal Christians"— at least that is what he called them—asking him about it. They seemed to be thrilled that finally evangelicals, at least those who remain, have come around.

My first reading of Mark Galli's editorial was after two glasses of very fine red wine. I had finished my entrée and was enjoying the Chocolate gelato when my first response hit me. "It seems strange that evangelicalism's most important publication was

---

[369] C.S. Lewis, *Letters to Malcolm* (Nashville: Harper One, 1964), 61.
[370] Mark Galli, "Trump Should Be Removed from Office." *Christianity Today*, 19 December 2019. https://www.christianitytoday.com/ct/2019/december-web-only/trump-should-be-removed-from-office.html.

piling on after the feckless Democrats had violated Trump's constitutional rights for entirely political reasons. They could not name an actual crime; they had no evidence; and their case was so bad it was dead on arrival in the Senate. I heard distant voices crying out, "Crucify him! Crucify him!" This wasn't an act of courage by *Christianity Today*. It was easy and without cost. All the dirty work had been done by politicians who were no more righteous than Donald J. Trump."

This morning, like any good Persian, being of very sober mind and as prayerful as Nancy Pelosi, I am taking a second look at the problem. The headline on the editorial is "Trump Should Be Removed from Office."

"And then what happens?" might I ask.

There is no doubt that Mike Pence is clearly a Christian. That does not mean he would make a good president. If the argument is that any Democrat is more moral or more Christian than Trump, it is a losing argument. It loses with the public because clearly many Democrats are serious sinners as are Republicans, and people are hesitant to measure the sins of others. I did not vote for Donald Trump. There was much about him that repulsed me. He seemed to be suspended in perpetual adolescence. On the other hand, he is seventy-five years old and one tough hombre.

Who sent him to Washington? Some say God did—that he is anointed. Others who serve the same God propose the exact opposite. The more refined and nuanced Republican Christians like to point out that he does not repent, reflect, or apologize, and that he is rude, brutish and crosses acceptable bounds of human decorum. I think they are right about that. He has been and continues to be all those things then and now. But that does not mean that he has no good qualities. He has great hair. I would say the President's barber is earning his paycheck these days. I know he is a tough pill to swallow for many of us.

However, I must say I find myself quite pleased with the work he has done. He has stood up to the destructive leftism that threatens to destroy Western civilization and our way of life. He labeled the press as dishonest and the news they create as fake. While Fox News seems to be an exception, it is clear that *The New York Times*, *The Washington Post*, NBC, CBS, ABC, and NPR are the same thing as the Democratic Party. It does not matter if you are listening to Chuck Todd on *Meet the Press*, the evening news on CBS, or a strident Democrat senator. There is no difference. It is all the same narrative. Trump has done what no president has ever done before. He called them out. He pointed out their partisan nature, and they did not like it.

Donald Trump has stood strong for religious liberty, the right to life, and for following the rule of law on immigration. Critics point out his history on these issues and call him a hypocrite. It may be that he has changed his mind, or even is doing what is politically expedient, but I really do not care what is in his heart of hearts. I just know what he does and who he supports.

Then there is the economy. While this is great news for almost every American, it is not the most important part of his success. He has been a strong advocate for Israel, and, most importantly, he has stemmed the secular tide that threatens to destroy the family, the church, and the key institutions that keep America free, such as the military.

Donald Trump went to Washington D.C. to tell them what we think of the job they have been doing. Millions wanted him to throw a few sticks of dynamite into the swamp to see what would happen. He has done that and continues to do so. He has stopped progressivism in it tracks—a socialistic secularism that promises a dystopian world where the First Amendment gets amended, where the Second Amendment is nuanced to the point of only being able to own a squirt gun, and where sexuality is redefined to confuse children and old guys like me who still feel guilty using the ladies restroom at restaurants. Reality has its own voice, and Trump is, more often than not—when he is not distracted by Rosie O'Donnell—simply acknowledging what is real.

Progressive leftism has been eating away at the Judeo-Christian foundation of our country for sixty years. The only person standing in the way of this ideology taking us over a cliff into an abyss of spiritual darkness is Donald J. Trump. He is the enemy of my enemy. The enemy is not classic liberalism. It is leftism, and leftism always ends in tyranny. One hundred million dead bodies left in its twentieth century wake is proof enough.[371] I am so mad about the sham impeachment that if the big orange monster grows two heads, good. I will vote for him twice.

---

[371] The Marxist philosophy as practiced in Russia, China, North Korea, Cuba, and the killing fields of Cambodia left one hundred million dead victims in its wake. Included in this count are the twenty-five million victims of the Nazis. Lee Edwards, "We Must Never Forget the 100 Million Victims of Communism." *Heritage Foundation*, 12 June 2020. https://www.heritage.org/progressivism/commentary/we-must-never-forget-the-100-million-victims-communism.

The High Cost of Non-Discipleship

Hot off the press! Research from the Barna Research Group claims that the share of practicing Christians in the United States has dropped by nearly half in the last two decades. Just 25% of Americans are practicing Christians compared to 45% in 2000. [I interrupt this research to say that if 45% were practicing Christians in 2000, why did it decline nearly half in twenty-years? If half of America were practicing Christians, game, set, match, break out the party hats.] Only about half as many people go to church as did twenty years ago, except in the evangelical church where the decline is seen but is meager compared to all churches. Those who identify as non-practicing Christians have doubled.[372]

The survey confirms that lukewarm, tepid Christianity will eventually collapse in our increasingly secular culture. Active Christianity has declined in the last twenty years just as our cultural elites have managed the gradual decline of our country in the same time period.

Listen to the late philosopher Dallas Willard:

---

[372] The survey defines a practicing Christian as someone who identifies as a Christian, agrees strongly that faith is very important in their lives, and has attended church in the past month. Jesus would have rolled his eyes and walked on. Barna, "Signs of Decline & Hope." https://www.barna.com/research/changing-state-of-the-church/

Why the Christian faith has failed to transform the masses and make a more just and peaceful world is because it has failed to transform the human character. Because it most often is not accompanied by discipleship, in philosophy, program, or curriculum."[373] Another way of putting it: the high cost of non-discipleship.

Many years ago, I was sitting at a lunch counter in Indianapolis with a high school friend. We were discussing our faith, and he identified as a non-practicing Christian. I informed him that what he claimed to be did not actually exist. It exists only in a non-existent category, like a non-practicing husband or father. It does happen. It is a non-category category. That is what I think of the 20% self-reassignment from practicing Christians to the non-practicing category even though it is unlikely to be comprised of the same people throughout the twenty years that have passed. The study is not about the original group but an entirely different set of people—a people who have come behind them, a younger generation taught by a different faculty.

In 1937, Dietrich Bonhoeffer gave the world his book *The Cost of Discipleship*. Willard called it a "masterful attack on 'easy Christianity,'" or as we have discussed elsewhere "cheap grace." [374] "But the book did not succeed in setting aside—perhaps it even enforced—the view of discipleship as a costly spiritual excess, and only for those especially driven or called to it." Willard goes on to say, "But the cost of non-discipleship is far greater."[375]

---

[373] Dallas Willard, *The Spirit of the Disciplines: Understanding How God Changes Lives* (San Francisco: Harper and Row 1989), 221.
[374] Ibid., 262.
[375] Ibid.

I would contend that the American church is reaping what it has sown. God is not mocked. What we sow, we reap.[376] We are reaping the bitter harvest of decline and irrelevancy. What have we lost? We return to Willard:

> Non-discipleship costs abiding peace, a life penetrated throughout by love, faith that sees everything in the light of God's overriding governance for good, hopefulness that stands firm in the most discouraging of circumstances, power to do what is right and withstand the forces of evil. In short, non-discipleship costs you exactly that abundance of life Jesus said he came to bring.

According to John 10:10, Satan's purpose is to steal, kill, and destroy. Jesus' purpose is to give a rich and satisfying life. We have reaped what we have sown. We have the loss of peace, love, confidence in God, the power to get through the challenges of life, and a general sense of joy and satisfaction.

I am sitting at my desk typing as the sun streams through the window and warms my hands. I see my neighbors walking by with their children. Many are wearing masks; most have dogs. The parents are masked. They understand the situation. However, the children and dogs are bouncing about with great delight. The knowledge of a pandemic has stolen peace from the parents. That is what Lucifer lives for—to know that underneath those masks are frowns rather than smiles. But then again, it is Good Friday. I once again lean on my friend Dallas Willard:

"When we look at what Christ did for us on the cross and keep that at the center of our vision. There are not many things that

---

[376] Gal 6:7-19.

will bother us, or even matter at all . . . it casts transformational light on our own sufferings."

Yes, today is Good Friday and it is only good in light of Christ's resurrection. The enemy has taken some important things from us and right now it seems dark, but context matters, and Jesus did what he did not want to do in order to give us what we desperately needed. This is a momentary light affliction that will be flung away by the eternal weight of glory.[377]

---

[377] 2 Cor 4:17.

Political Cleavage Among Evangelicals

I have briefly mentioned that a political division has developed among evangelicals in recent years that wasn't known about, talked about, or cared about in the last fifty years. We evangelicals have been busy in other fights with theological liberalism and other forces and movements that looked threatening. But now, Donald Trump has surfaced these differences and of course made what once looked simple much more complex. There used to be what was called the Evangelical Vote. Trump is a divisive personality. You either hate him and refuse to see any good in him or you just dislike him and see the good.

I rarely hear that people like him, admire him, and would like to hang out with him. I think there are reasons for this. First there is the hair, and there is the Nixonian bit where he is never dressed casually even when he is dressed casually. His language is salty. His fake tan is over the top. He continues to gain weight, eat fast food, and sleeps four hours a night; but he is the picture of health. He a huge energy reserve. He does not seem normal.

This drives his political opponents crazy. He is reasonably bright, and he is gutsy. He is also suspended in some sort of perpetual adolescence. He sighs with relief and melts like butter when people say nice things to him. He calls people "mean, awful, dishonest, and disgusting" when they challenge him, and he cannot seem to stay out of Twitter spit ball fights with others who say stupid stuff. He exaggerates. His self-aggrandizement is never ending. He has an empty hole in his soul that requires praise, and it never loses its appetite. He speaks with the precision of a carnival barker, but the key to Donald Trump is not to listen to what he says, but to pay attention to what he does. He is off-putting. He offends the ruling elites because an outlier from Queens with his gaudy gold bling, buildings, and décor—the brunt of their jokes—now rules them and is successful. He seems to really enjoy rubbing their noses in it.

In 2015, when he announced he was running for president, like most people, I laughed it off and thought he had no chance. When his seventeen competitors for the nomination began to drop away and then out, people stopped laughing and started to try and figure out what was happening. I started to select my favorite new candidate. I liked Carly Fiorina, then John Kasich, then Marco Rubio, but they dropped out. When election day came, I left the presidential box unchecked. I voted but not for president. Of course, I live in California, so what difference did it make, really?

To many evangelicals Trump is just too much. I thought the Access Hollywood recording of his lewd comments about women would sink him. His campaign seemed over at that point, but like some indestructible superhero, he rose up and survived. Then, my Lord and my God, he won the election. I must admit that as I lay in a Houston hotel room that night alone, I had the best time watching the world come to an end for those in the media who had hated and mocked him so much. They could not understand what had just happened. I normally do not like to watch suffering, but in this case, it made me so happy.

What did happen? I think the general consensus is America's stealth vote shot a big middle finger into the face of the crazy liberals, anarchists, and said, "Hey, not so fast!" As I heard one pundit put it, "Americans just said, 'Let's heave some hand grenades into the swamp and see what happens.'"

I have seen what has happened. I like the results, and I plan to vote for Trump this time.[378] If I lived in Chicago, I would vote early and often, but I live in California, which means I can register as Robert William Hull, as Robert Hull, as Bill Hull, as R.W. Hull, as William Hull, and the state will send me five ballots. I can get a worker to come by and help me fill out my ballots and they will harvest them and send them in. This is so cool. As Nathan Hale probably said, "I regret that I only have five votes to give to my country."[379]

I have much more to say about the church, the actions it can take, the evangelical movement, how many are working from the wrong premise, and how prayer for a great awakening is exactly the wrong strategy for the church.

---

[378] This essay was written prior to the 2020 Presidential election.

[379] "I only regret that I have but one life to lose for my country," were the last words of Nathan Hale, a twenty-one-year-old captain in the Continental Army during the Revolutionary War. Hale spoke these words right before the British hung him in 1776. "Nathan Hale Volunteers to Spy Behind British Lines." *History.com*, https://www.history.com/this-day-in-history/nathan-hale-volunteers-to-spy-behind-british-lines.

Chaos and the Sliding Scale of Morality

Plato proposed that out of chaos comes either the rule of law or tyranny.[380] America now has chaos. We have a written rule of law, one codified in the law itself and another inscribed on the tablets of our hearts.[381] And we have tyranny waiting in the wings offering its dystopian dreams in utopian costumes. A recent poll cited that 80% of Americans think the country is out of control.[382] Hopeful leftists danced for joy on the corpses they have left in the streets as they cried out, "See! The oppressors are the problem— those in power. Let's vote them out, tear down the system, and establish a transformed society."

However, that is not what the majority, the 80% who believe things are out of control, are saying. Many among that group are people like me who believe the country is out of control in major cities because of weakness and cowardly action on the part of mayors and governors who are appeasing the mobs, destroyers, criminals, and thieves. Where are the police? Where are courageous leaders who will stand up and stand down the

---

[380] "Plato and Aristotle on Tyranny and the Rule of Law," Constitutional Rights Foundation, *Bill of Rights in Action* 6, No. 1 (Fall 2010). https://www.crf-usa.org/bill-of-rights-in-action/bria-26-1-plato-and-aristotle-on-tyranny-and-the-rule-of-law.html.

[381] Rom 2:13.

[382] Oma Seddiq, "Poll: 80 Percent of Americans Think the Country Is Out of Control." *Politico*, 7 June 2020. https://www.politico.com/news/2020/06/07/country-out-of-control-305451.

mob? Having to watch the mayor of Minneapolis be shouted off his lawn for having an opinion was disheartening and sickening.[383] That is what we mean. I would bet that more than half of the 85% who say the nation is out of control are regular citizens who want law and order established. Without that, tyranny will become our way of life.

In recent days on what is called Capitol Hill in downtown Seattle, a new land has been established—Capitol Hill Autonomous Zone or CHAZ.[384] It cries out for a poem or at least a rhyme. "Once upon a time in a land called CHAZ . . . " You take it from there. It is as though some progressive or permissive (I repeat myself) parents told their kids to have a drunken dystopian orgy at home—kind of a home alone eyes wide shut dive into the flesh pots of Seattle— and said, "Be safe. We will clean up in the morning." I have lived for over seventy-five years, and, for the first time in recent weeks, the wisdom and necessity of the Second Amendment has become crystal clear to me. I do not own a gun and have never fired one. But it is now clear to me that if any of the far left or right utopian idealists ever get power, owning a weapon to maintain our freedom and to protect our communities will be essential because I will not allow looters and thieves to attack my home or family.

I am amazed at the politicians who have a sliding scale of morality that changes at lightning speed. Ten years ago, any politician who would have called for defunding of police would have been

---

[383] "Minneapolis Mayor Heckled and Told to 'Go Home' by George Floyd Protestors," posted June 7, 2020. https://www.youtube.com/watch?v=OdT2ZR0uuu8.

[384] "Seattle Protestors Take Over City Blocks to Create Police-Free Autonomous Zone." *The Guardian*, 11 June 2020. https://www.theguardian.com/us-news/2020/jun/11/chaz-seattle-autonomous-zone-police-protest.

roundly booed, discredited, and not reelected. Because of initial pushback, those calling for "defunding" today are changing the meaning of words like "defund" to "review." Soon it may mean "never mind." Today's politicians are weak, easily wrecked by public opinion, and intellectually homeless. Unlike Archimedes or Jesus, they have no place to stand. They are without any serious argument because they are defending lawlessness. It is a feckless race to power.

Americans had been cooped up for months due to Covid 19 shutdowns and were restless and ready to get out and live normally when the George Floyd tragedy took place.[385] The people threw off all restraints. Governors, mayors, and chiefs of police who had complained of demonstrations against their draconian lockdowns now allowed crowds to overwhelm the police and gave those law enforcement officers orders to stand down. Looters burned the cities, with no idea of what would replace their cities.[386] "They are angry!" many said in their defense. Yes, they were, and they had good reason to be because they were bewildered by the chaos. They were also incited by power-hungry, partisan leaders who wanted to use their misery to advance their power. The participants were also largely young, a generation cut off from history and from knowing the reasons for this country's existence—a cut flower generation of morally confused reeds blowing in the wind.

---

[385] Jennifer Levitz, Erin Ailworth, and Tawnell D. Hobbs, "George Floyd and Derick Chauvin: The Lives of the Victim and His Killer." *The Wall Street Journal*, 21 June 2020, https://www.wsj.com/articles/george-floyd-and-derek-chauvin-the-lives-of-the-victim-and-his-killer-11592761495.

[386] Andrew Tangel, Erin Ailworth, Akane Otani, and Katie Honan, "Protests Sparked by George Floyd Death Descend into Violence Despite Curfews." *The Wall Street Journal*, 2 June 2020. https://www.wsj.com/articles/minneapolis-unrest-subsides-as-cities-rage-over-death-of-george-floyd-11591018710.

Older adults have failed this generation three times. First, they deconstructed the family unit in the lower economic communities. The fathers left. The families became fragmented, and the government treated Blacks like dependents by perpetuating economic reliance on government subsidies in a cynical crusade to control their vote and maintain power.[387] The elites or ruling class of America keep telling minorities that they are victims who cannot make it on their own. They are told to get mad, ask for stuff, and take what the rich have in the belief that it already belongs to them anyway.[388]

I am with Shelby Steele on this one. Steel is a scholar at the Hoover Institute who says he will take Jesse Jackson and Al Sharpton seriously when they and other Black leaders turn the focus on the Black community and say, "How have we been culpable in our own problems? What about our absent fathers and our music that treats women as sexual toys and objects to abuse? Why have we allowed our modern educational masters to continuously fail our children with bad schools? Why won't the government break up the teacher's unions and allow parents to fix our schools or

[387] A government report shows a great disparity in the economic status of black and white Americans and argues that fifty years of government programs have only perpetuated this disparity and actually made it worse. "Shelby Steele Interview. Race and Liberty in America: What Killed Michael Brown?" *Independent Institute*, https://www.youtube.com/watch?v=OgNYJJ3XP14 posted March 28, 2021; "The Economic State of Black America in 2020," *Joint Economic Committee*, Congressman Don Beyer, Chair, https://www.jec.senate.gov/public/_cache/files/ccf4dbe2-810a-44f8-b3e7-14f7e5143ba6/economic-state-of-black-america-2020.pdf.

[388] Jacobs, David, and Daniel Tope. "The Politics of Resentment in the Post–Civil rights Era: Minority Threat, Homicide, and Ideological Voting in Congress." *American Journal of Sociology* 112, no. 5 (2007): 1458-494. https://www.jstor.org/stable/10.1086/511804

give us better teachers, or at least provide opportunities for quality education in our own communities rather than in other communities?" Our leaders, namely politicians, mayors, school board members, and parent-teachers' organizations have failed them at the personal family level and moral development level.

Thirdly, we, the voting public have failed them at the national level by telling them they are not really Black if they do not appreciate what we have done for them when, in fact, we created, perpetuated, and interned them in a servile underclass.[389]

Then there are the white privileged oppressors under the age of thirty-five who have become by far the largest number of protestors. Among the young whites are Antifa, a militant group whose purposes in joining protests are sinister, revolutionary, and clearly mustering insurrection. They exacerbate and inflame progressive's version of injustice, which is ginned up resentment. They orchestrate looting, violence, and chaos. The vast majority of protestors have been peaceful, but it only takes a handful of agitators to inflame and use a crowd for purposes for which the crowd had no agreeable intent.[390]

Charles Malik, president of the Commission on Human Rights in the United Nations General Assembly in 1958, spoke prophetically about what is happening among the affluent young whites in America. Malik spoke to the Christians of his day about their quest to reach the world with the message of Jesus. "You may win every battle, but if you lose the war of ideas, you will have

---

[389] I focus on African Americans because even though they comprise only 14% of the U.S. population, they have a special place in our history of discrimination and have been the recent focus of urban violence.
[390] Rachael Levy, "What is Antifa?" *The Wall Street Journal*, 7 January 2021. https://www.wsj.com/articles/q-a-what-is-antifa-11598985917.

lost the war. You may lose every battle, but if you win the war of ideas, you will have won the war. My deepest fear and your greatest problem are that you may not be winning the war of ideas."[391]

People of every philosophical ilk comprise today's protestors. Various worldviews fill the night air mixed with smoke, fire, and sounds of pepper shots and tear gas. Some are there to lament, to show their friends that they mourn what has happened to George Floyd, to the African American community, and to decry the division in our country. However, what truly divides us is not always on the surface. It is not so easy to see where the cracks in the national divide begin. The divide is visible economically and racially, but its origins are about ideas, words, concepts, and ideologies held by people long gone from this earth—people whose destructive beliefs live on in the minds of academics, public and professional intellectuals, the media, in movies and on television—ideas which are reflected in the political class and perpetrated by actors who speak memorized lines and newscasters reading teleprompters.

For brevity and clarity, allow me to contrast two ways of looking at the present situation.

The Christian Worldview

1. God created every person in his image. Therefore, every person, regardless of color, creed, nation, slave or free, Jew or Gentile, male or female are of equal value. To deny this or to treat anyone differently based on these things alone is a sin against God and humanity.

---

[391] Malik,"The Two Tasks," *JETS*.

2. Humans sinned. This is called the Fall. We have all become sinners. Humans are therefore alienated from God and each other. The more tribal we are, the worse it becomes. We need repentance as individuals and, in some cases, as organizations.
3. Redemption and forgiveness are essential and available, having been provided by God in Jesus Christ.
4. Christ came, lived, died, was buried, and then raised to new life. One day he will return to bring justice to all people and to the earth.
5. Summarized as Creation, Fall, Redemption, and Restoration

Progressive Culture Worldview

1. No Creation story. Origins of existence and life cannot be known or are not important. This is the worldview of agnostics, atheists, and benign conventional religion.
2. Oppression: Society is defined not by who people are as individuals but by which groups they belong to. This is known as Identity Politics. If you are a white male, then you are identified as an oppressor using terms such as classist, patriarchal, white supremacist, and toxic masculinity.
3. Redemption comes by protest, resistance, and education
4. Restoration is defined as equality, power reversal, justice, diversity, and liberation.
5. Common statements in this worldview include:

    *   No more patriarchy
    *   White fragility
    *   Sexual orientation as identity
    *   Systematic privilege

- Hear the oppressed voices. They have a right to be heard. The patriarchy needs to be quiet and listen because whatever they say is merely an attempt to protect their privilege.
- Lived experience is truth [even if it contradicted by proven reality]

This country made a courageous decision in the 1960s. It said, "We have been wrong about a number of things. Let's make it better." That led to discrimination based on race rightly being outlawed. Now that we are attempting to live it out, it is painful. It will take humility by people on all sides, not just the "privileged" whites. The danger we face now is that a class of Americans who believe they have become morally superior to other races or classes of people have begun to shame the most understanding and forgiving country in the world.[392] My word to them and to all of us is remember who you are: one hundred percent sinners and, for those who know Christ, also one hundred percent saints, one hundred percent of the time. Our righteousness is as dirty rags to the Lord. Come humbly before your God and one another, and he will heal our land.

"Then if my people who are called by my name will humble themselves and pray and seek my face and turn from their wicked ways, I will hear from heaven and will forgive their sins and restore their land" (2 Chronicles 7:14).

---

[392] Char Adams, "Black Lives Matter Faces Backlash for Statement on Cuba Protest." *NBC News,* 16 July 2021. https://www.nbcnews.com/news/nbcblk/black-lives-matter-faces-backlash-statement-cuba-protest-rcna1438.

Should a Christian Leader Flee a Deadly Plague?

The above question was stated to Martin Luther in 1527 by the Reverend Doctor Johann Hess, pastor at Breslau, Germany. Luther answered several months later with what is now a ten-page letter in very small print.[393] The same kind of issue came up for Charles Spurgeon during the Cholera outbreak in London in 1854.

Long before either of these famous preachers faced the question, it was answered by scores of Christians during the first three centuries. Plagues that killed thousands were regular events in many of the cities mentioned in Scripture, such as Antioch.[394] Christians became known as those who would stay behind to nurse their own as well as those outside their circle of friends

---

[393] This letter was delayed because Luther had suffered a severe attack of cerebral anemia, an illness from which he suffered repeatedly. It would be followed by a deep depression. Martin Luther, "Martin Luther Whether One May Flee from A Deadly Plague." *Christianity Today,* 19 May 2020. Reprint of Luther's original letter. https://www.christianitytoday.com/ct/2020/may-web-only/martin-luther-plague-pandemic-coronavirus-covid-flee-letter.html

[394] Kenneth Berding, "How Did Early Christians Respond to Plagues? Historical Reflections as the Coronavirus Spreads." *The Good Book Blog,* Talbot School of Theology Faculty Blog, Biola University, 16 March 2020. https://www.biola.edu/blogs/good-book-blog/2020/how-did-early-christians-respond-to-plagues

and outside the church. It was this courage and great love that melted the hearts around them.[395]

The coronavirus is real and serious, but not nearly as lethal as what our ancient brothers and sisters faced. The likelihood of death was all that they knew, and they responded in that context. We must respond in ours. Very few plagues then were pandemics because they were local in nature. Because of modern day travel and communication conveniences, the coronavirus and the panic surrounding it can spread rapidly.

The general response of believers through history is that Christians should do the sensible and necessary thing without fear, in a spirit of peace, and with an extended hand to those in need. Luther's letter is nuanced and sounds quite sensible. He groups Christian leaders, such as pastors, with city officials and medical personnel into a special category. According to Luther, they must stay and minister to those in need.[396] He speaks to the responsibility of Fathers to their families, of one neighbor to another, and essentially says, "You cannot flee until all those in your sphere of influence have the care they need."[397]

Much of our modern response to Covid 19 is governed by modern hospitals, medical professionals, pharmacies, and communications—all helpful resources to society in meeting the needs caused by this deadly virus. Because it is a worldwide

---

[395] Rodney Stark, *The Rise of Christianity* (San Francisco: Harper Collins Books, 1996), 75-90.

[396] "From Martin Luther to Rev. Dr. Johann Hess, (1520). Reprinted in (bibliographic info for the source where this letter can be read). *Luther's Works Vol 43: Devotional Writings II*, (Minneapolis: Fortress Press, 1968), 117.

[397] Ibid., 117-121.

pandemic, there is no place to flee. There is your house. There are precautions, such as social distancing and frequent handwashing. But something the modern resources and communications outlets are incapable of doing is calming the inner spirit of a person.

I woke up a few days ago with a knot in my stomach and had to run it down, "Why is it there?" I asked myself. Basically, it was there because I like to control my life. I like to have a good schedule that I can keep and to be able to reach goals I have set. Now, all of that is topsy turvy. I think things through, and sometimes, I take them to their logical conclusion, which has me in an ICU on a respirator as one possibility. After all, I am officially a soft target due to age. So I go out to the pharmacy or grocery store with hand sanitizer that is homemade by my wife, who seems to be at perfect peace. As I pray for protection, I realize that virtually all my neighbors and fellow shoppers are praying the same prayer as they stand gawking at the empty shelves in the paper goods aisle—something about needing toilet paper and, "Please, God, don't let anyone sneeze on me." My wife says, "Don't watch cable news! Watch the Hallmark Channel instead. Every show is the same and there is always a happy ending." I prefer old sporting events where I already know the winner.

I recall that a few years ago my former physician, a very acerbic New Yorker, looked at me one day and said, "Reverend Hull, I've known you for several years and you always seem to be on top of your game. But today, you don't seem right. What is wrong? You have lost fifteen pounds, and you are very stressed." I confessed to him what I had told God earlier that morning. "Doctor, I've taken back control of my life. Jesus told me I shouldn't do it, but gradually I've done it. He told me to give up my life, to hold it loosely. I've been holding on tight. I've been trying to control my physical problems, and I've been racked with anxiety." My agnostic Doctor looked at me. He was seated on one of those short stools that doctors seem to like—the ones that roll. He shoved off and rolled over to where I was seated and grabbed me by the knees and said, "Reverend Hull, it's time to believe."

I was shocked. I went out to my car where I wept for several minutes, embarrassed, ashamed, and rebuked. I repented. That was a big moment for me and one which is serving me well today. I took solace then as now that God gives a peace that is unlike the world's. God's peace is supernatural, nonsensical, and beyond human comprehension[398]

I want you to know that we at the Bonhoeffer Project pray for you. We pray for the church we love, and we pray for the nation, our President, and the other leaders and health professionals that are working to help us through this crisis. For us, it is a time for peace, prayer, and proclamation through our extended hands and our supportive words to those around us.

---

[398] John 14:27, Phil 4:6-7.

Impeached but not Convicted

Today, January 21, 2020, the trial of President Donald John Trump begins in the United States Senate. When you are about to do something awful to a person, you use their full name. You don't put "the Donald" on trial. This is supposed to be serious business. As so many say, "This is a constitutional crisis." Or you may hear, "Donald J. Trump is a threat to our nation's security."

Excuse me if I laugh out loud at such disingenuous rhetoric. The trial will be over soon enough, and the Democrats will have done their best to damage Trump in order to give them a chance to win the 2020 election. The unspoken truth that no one wants to say out loud is that in order to win, the Democrats need a candidate who can win, and, as of right now, they do not have one. The crisis we face does not have to do with Democrats or Republicans or who runs for office. The underlying problem will not go away.

We have the president we deserve in this reality TV show-based culture we have created. Who rose up out of this glitzing culture we have built? Donald J. Trump. I am just thankful it was not Homer Simpson or Archie Bunker or even Howard Stern. People wanted to drain the swamp and give the middle finger to the cultural elites, so what we have witnessed in Trump is one tough dude draining a swamp. The reason he is so good at it is he is sort of a swamp creature himself. He mocks and ridicules the Democrats and the press, but I repeat myself.

The battle lines are easily drawn. There is Trump, the Republicans, Fox News, *The Daily Wire*, talk radio, and a rock-solid conservative nation versus the Democrats. The Democrats have the media and its stars, such as *The New York Times*, a former newspaper which at one time practiced real journalism, and *The Washington Post*. I never thought I would long for the latter's former managing editor, Ben Bradlee, but I do. Then there is television: CBS, NBC, ABC, NPR, CNN, MSNBC, Bloomberg Media, and others. A new player, *The Babylon Bee*, is a satirical Christian site that mocks and ridicules everyone. But CNN and the left have no sense of humor. They have mocked and ridiculed the right and the religious for decades. Now Trump and *Babylon Bee* have become adept at doing the same to them, and they do not like getting their feelings hurt.

Back to the underlying problem that will not go away.

I have just been rereading *Amusing Ourselves to Death* by the late Neil Postman—a masterpiece of the 1980s. Postman writes, "Contrary to common belief, Huxley and Orwell did not prophesy the same thing. Orwell warns that we will be overcome by an externally imposed oppression. In Huxley's vision, no Big Brother is required to deprive people of their autonomy, maturity, and history. As he saw it, people will come to love their oppression and adore the technologies that undo their capacities to think. Huxley feared that there would be no reason to ban a book, for there would be no one who wanted to read one. Orwell feared those who would deprive us of information. Huxley feared those would give us so much that we would be reduced to passivity and egoism. Orwell feared that the truth would be concealed from us. Huxley feared the truth would be drowned in a sea of irrelevance. [399]

That sea of irrelevance is before us in the impeachment of Trump and in the basic narrative being fed to us through the

---

[399] Postman, *Amusing Ourselves to Death*, vi.

media—a narrative which says Donald Trump is evil and a danger to democracy. Truth and objectivity have become a relic of the past in the fantasy world of politics, image projection, and competition for power. The general excitement in Washington D.C. concerning the Senate trial is due to the massive screen time given to Senators and lawyers. It is all political theater. The grease paint is in abundance. They want to make sure they are on in prime time. Careers will be made, fees will go up, book deals will be made, and the elite will flourish. The funny thing is that, in the meantime, the big orange swamp thing whose actual hair makes toupees look cool is making America safer, your job more secure, your health care costs less, and religious liberty to flourish. As a bonus, he protects the unborn, and periodically, when he is not thinking up new names to call his opponents, he assures you that the government will not steal your money, your freedom, or confiscate your saltshaker and handgun. Reality has its own voice, and if you turn off your TV and shut down your media feed, your head might clear. You will find yourself thinking for yourself and hearing that voice of reality which will come through loud and clear.

Bernie Sanders and Elizabeth Warren sit next to each other in the Senate. Late last night—it was well after midnight in the Senate chamber—I began to drop off. I thought I saw Bernie and Liz holding hands under their desks. What was I watching? Our government at work or a made-for-Netflix movie about political enemies who have a secret love affair and shock the world by moving to Cuba because of their swell free health care and free college tuition for their grandchildren?

Huxley was right. The truth is underwater and may have drown. I don't know about you, but I am amused. Bill Maher performs a comedy bit in which he says, "I can't prove it, but I just know that it is true." I know the entire Trump impeachment thing is phony. It is the 2020 Democratic political campaign strategy. By their own standards of impeachment, I think I can impeach them in my own court, but I will not be able to convict. I can't prove it, but I just know it is true. By the way, I did not vote for Trump in 2016.

Take the "Babble" Out of Babylon

The election is over, I think. It appears that President Donald J. Trump will now have time to drop forty pounds, lower his golf handicap, start his own television network, and prepare to run for President in 2024. You thought the chaos would end, you naïve thing you. In four years, he will be the same age as President-elect Biden will be when he enters office on January 20, 2021. Since the run for President will begin after the mid-term elections in 2022, Trump and Vice President Kamala Harris will need to start their campaigns two years from now. Okay. I'm just having a bit of fun with you, my friends. This couldn't happen, could it?

So what does this have to do with Babylon? Babylon was a real place where at minimum, the crème de crème of Jewish society was in exile for seventy years. The story is told in some detail in the book of Daniel in the Bible. If you want to know how to live in Babylon, read the book of Daniel. Many moderns only know Babylon as a metaphor for the flesh pots of society, or as a nifty satirical website, *The Babylon Bee*. There is another vivid descriptor of Babylon recorded by the Apostle John:

> The woman wore purple and scarlet clothing and beautiful jewelry made of gold and precious gems and pearls. In her hand she held a gold goblet full of obscenities and the impurities of her immorality. A mysterious name was written on her forehead, "Babylon the Great, Mother of All Prostitutes and Obscenities in the World." I could see

that she was drunk with the blood of God's holy people who were witnesses for Jesus. I stared at her in complete amazement (Rev 17:4-6).

The remainder of this passage goes very deep into the multi-layered meaning of everything Babylon. "The kings of the world have committed adultery with her, and the people who belong to this world have been made drunk by the wine of her immorality" (Rev 17:2). The bottom line is that this metaphor of Babylon, in the language of ancient imagery, ends up representing all things that are anti-Christ. It becomes clear through John's narration that God will see to it that Babylon will be destroyed.

God has put a plan into their minds [the kings of the earth]—a plan that will carry out his purposes. They will agree to give their authority to the scarlet beast and so the words of God will be fulfilled. And this woman you saw in your vision represents the great city that rules over the kings of the world (Rev 17:17).

Finally, Revelation Chapter 18 describes the cries and laments of the world's leaders at the complete destruction of all things Babylon. There is one short interlude, a parenthesis from the horror:

Rejoice over her fate, O heaven and people of God and apostles and prophets! For at last, God has judged her for your sakes. Then a mighty angel picked up a boulder the size of a millstone. He threw it into the ocean and shouted, "Just like this, the great city of Babylon will be thrown down into violence and will never be found again." (Rev 18:20-21).

Babylon is a metaphor that applies to any system that sets itself up against the plan that God has for his creation. In the end, God will personally see to it that it is crushed and eliminated. The present temptation is to listen to voices in our society that believe they know what Babylon is right now and how to get a head start on punishing the evildoers. You may have already heard about truth and reconciliation commissions or finding out who voted for Donald Trump—essentially half the country—and exposing them as enemies of the state.[400] Congresswoman Alexandria Ocasio-Cortez (D-NY) has called Trump voters, at least 70 million people and their children, sycophants.[401] A sycophant is a self-seeking, servile, fawning parasite. Synonyms include creep, toady, flunkey, doormat, lickspittle, minion, hanger-on. She has her millstone fixed in her hands ready to smash her version of Babylon.

On the other hand, some Christians think that the election was crooked. They believed victory was well in hand for Trump as the polls closed nationwide but that strange shenanigans took place in the overnight hours. As the sun rose in the east, Joe Biden had moved ahead. It is doubtful that those shenanigans were substantial enough to change the result. It just seems that for 49% of Americans, the election was not a fair fight. Big tech censored Trump; big media served as the Democrat campaign staff; the professional sports leagues and the film and television communities all aligned themselves against President Trump. Some could say that Covid 19 defeated Trump or that Trump beat Trump

---

[400] Quinta Jurecic, "Don't Move On Just Yet: Could A Truth and Reconciliation Commission Help the Country Heal?" *The Atlantic*, 23 January 2021. https://www.theatlantic.com/ideas/archive/2021/01/how-to-not-bury-the-past/617723/.

[401] "AOC Asks for Record of Trump 'Sycophants' Who Were Complicit in His Administration." *Independent*, 7 November 2020. https://www.independent.co.uk/news/world/americas/aoc-donald-trump-2020-election-b1652462.html.

with a great deal of his odious and self-defeating behavior.[402] Who can blame many for believing that Babylon is not Trump voters who need to be identified, tagged and punished but rather the radical left who supports abortion, infanticide, and champions every sordid sexual practice, including the sexualization of small children?[403] They want to rewrite the Constitution, restrict freedom of speech to what they like to hear, and keep religion indoors and sealed off from public life. Their education plan is to malform the young and cut them off from actual knowledge of the origins of the United States so that no one will ever be willing to die for it again.[404] And when that happens, good luck defending something you do not really believe in.

There is honest disagreement between evangelicals who, I believe, will argue together, will pray together, and will finally find common ground. I believe that common ground will be easier to find in a couple of years as the dust settles.

For me, this fight is not about personalities or political parties. It is a battle between what God has prescribed for his people and those who would attempt to destroy what God intends. I would suggest that a key decision now needs to be made by America's

---

[402] Kevin Liptak, "Inside Trump's Loss: A Cumulation of Self-Destructive Decisions." *CNN,* 8 November 2020. https://www.cnn.com/2020/11/08/politics/donald-trump-loss-election-2020/index.html.

[403] Emilie Kao and Andrea Jones, "We Must Fight the Sexualization of Children by Adults." *The Heritage Foundation*, 5 October 2019. https://www.heritage.org/marriage-and-family/commentary/we-must-fight-the-sexualization-children-adults.

[404] Moriah Balingit and Laura Meckler, "Trump Alleges 'Left-Wing Indoctrination in Schools, Says He Will Create National Commission to Push More 'Pro-American' History," *The Washington Post*, 17 September 2020. https://www.washingtonpost.com/education/trump-history-education/2020/09/17/f40535ec-ee2c-11ea-ab4e-581edb849379_story.html.

pastors. And by pastors, I mean people with a "bully pulpit"—not just the officially ordained, but anyone who has a following and influence: a newspaper columnist, a member of a golf foursome, a school principal, a coach, a university professor, a PTA chapter leader, or a businessperson. Anyone in these roles is shepherding flocks to some degree.

What Pastors Can Do to Help

Church pastors have a special position in that we are the custodians of knowledge. We are largely able to speak our minds weekly to millions of people who gather online or in person to hear our sermons. This all takes us back to Paul's clear charge: "We destroy arguments and every proud obstacle raised up against the knowledge of God, and we take very thought captive to obey Christ" (2 Cor 10:4-5).

It is imperative that pastors define the knowledge of God and then compare both religious and political beliefs in light of that knowledge. Our understanding will be flawed, imperfect, and there will be disagreement around the edges. But we should be able to attain unity on the essentials and accept diversity on the non-essentials. That is hard to do for those who are consumers of media. They are in a blitzkrieg of partisan argument. Let's let Dallas Willard help us hit reset:

> Jesus did not send his people out to make Christians or to start churches as we understand them today. He sent them to make disciples [students, apprentices] to him and, supported by his presence, to teach them all that he had taught by word and deed. That is a very different type of enterprise! [405]

---

[405] Dallas Willard, *Knowing Christ Today* (New York: HarperCollins, 2009), 195.

We must wear a political and cultural flak jacket with a helmet and facemask as we try to concentrate on what really matters. Knowing what really matters can be perplexing because we are told daily that what really matters is the real life we are living and the kind of country we live in. Therefore, we need to fight the good fight and right now that fight is partly political and cultural. I do not deny this is an important piece of our reality, but should pastors concentrate on the political and cultural battle and lay aside the disciple making?

I believe there are many good and articulate national leaders, media personalities, writers, bloggers, and activists who are making arguments hourly that are available on social media and through television. If someone, pastor or not, wants to join in that chorus, I am in no position to tell them what to do. But I do believe that the unique role of pastors in American right now is that we are the nation's teachers. We are the only teachers who will be able to reach people by the millions. Hardly any one of us has millions or tens of millions of ears and attention, but collectively we certainly do. "We are servants of Christ and stewards of the mysteries of God" (1 Cor 4:1). We are called to:

Preach the word of God. Be prepared, whether the time is favorable or not. Patiently correct, rebuke, and encourage your people with good teaching. For a time is coming when people will no longer listen to sound and wholesome teaching. They will follow their own desires and will look for teachers who will tell them whatever their itching ears want to hear. They will reject the truth and chase after myths (2 Tim 4:2-4).

It is somewhat counterintuitive, counter cultural, and has a passive feel to it, but the most productive action pastoral teachers can take is to teach a biblical worldview to all those who will listen. In practical terms, that begins and ends with the Great Commission.[406] Then people can determine how Babylonian society is and who leads them. There will not be unanimity on that determination, but there should be unity on the central themes.

Jesus told his followers to make disciples, teaching them to obey everything he commanded.[407] Make new disciples. Make many disciples. Make many more disciples. Make mature disciples. How do you know when they are mature? They multiply. How will you know when you are done? When the Gospel of the kingdom is preached to every nation. Then and only then will the end come.[408]

This work cannot be left to secular experts. The wisdom of the world is foolishness.[409] Apart from Christ, the world's leaders do not have the same set of knowledge that is available to every faithful pastor in America. Hopefully we can be something like C.S. Lewis was to England during World War II with his radio addresses to a nation at war. He set before them *Mere Christianity*. Allow me to close with more from Professor Willard:

Divine service is not church service, though it might include that. Divine service is life. It is in the world, in daily business of whatever level and importance, that there unfolds, in Paula Houston's wonderful phrase, "the great adventure that was once Christianity." It can be for every one of us. The most important thing that is happening in your community is what is happening there under the administration of

[406] Matt 28:18-20.
[407] Matt. 28:18-20.
[408] Matt. 24:14.
[409] 1 Cor 3:19.

true pastors for Christ. If you, as a pastor, do not believe that, then you do not understand the dignity of what you are supposed to be doing. Whatever your situation, there is nothing more important on earth than to dwell in the knowledge of Christ and to bring that knowledge to others.[410]

---

[410] Willard, *Knowing Christ Today*.

It's Thursday. It Must Be the Stockholm Syndrome

Did you notice the large number of white people kneeling before their self-appointed moral superiors taking oaths written for them during the protests? Unlike prisoners of war reading scripts written for them after days or weeks of torture, these "repentant sinners" seemed to be doing this of their own free will. It called up memories of the Stockholm Syndrome.

The term was first used by the media in 1973 when four hostages were taken during a bank robbery in Stockholm, Sweden. The hostages defended their captors after release and would not testify against them in court. Stockholm Syndrome has four components:

1. A hostage develops a positive feeling toward the captor
2. No previous relationship existed between the hostage and the captor
3. Refusal by a hostage to cooperate with police
4. A hostage's belief in the cause of the captor because they ceased to perceive the captor as a threat and the victim holds the same values as the hostage taker

What is it that causes particularly the young white protestor who has no previous relationship to a Black protester with a bullhorn to submit to the dictates of the stranger leading the rally? It could be that they agree that the murder of George Floyd was so heinous that such injustice needs to stop right now. Good! More than 90% of the United States agrees with that. In that way, we all have a bit of Swedish blood in our veins. It could be that they agree that police brutality is wrong, and it needs to be reformed. Good! A large portion of America agrees with that as well. But what got them on their knees, confessing their collective white sins, apologizing for four hundred years of slavery, and paying homage to Black Lives Matter?[411]

Before I answer that question, let me tell you whose hands are not clean even though they think they are. They have no plans to repent of any sins anytime soon.

The 1619 Project

I will refrain from calling out people by name or even political parties if I can avoid it. As many of you know, the 1619 Project is an alternative view of history that proposes America started and is largely built on the foundation of slavery. It is sponsored by *The New York Times*, and its leading spokesperson is Nikole Hannah-Jones.[412] It proposes that the country started in 1619 with the arrival of the first slaves, rather than in 1776 with the Declaration of Independence. Several states and many school districts intend to implement a curriculum presenting this false history to its students. Two things can be true at the same

---

[411] Who is guilty for what has happened in our country to our Black citizens? One approach that should be considered is Paul Vischer, *Race in America: A Holy Post Video*, June 14, 2020. https://www.facebook.com/PhilVischer/videos/2611898429058130. Video transcript with citations at: https://www.holypost.com/post/racism-video-transcript-w-citations.

[412] https://www.nytimes.com/interactive/2019/08/14/magazine/1619-america-slavery.html.

time. America was founded in 1776 as an idea that a people can govern itself, flourish in liberty, and have justice for all. It is also true that slavery came to America in 1619. America is the most free, forgiving, least racially biased country in the world. That is why so many want to live here. It is also true that America has done evil, continues to do some evil, and one of those evils is to rewrite history and lie to our children. What was our country built on, slavery or liberty? The correct answer is liberty. As a nation, we sinned, and we paid for our sins in the Civil War. The Black community has suffered, but the young white protestors were not on their knees to ask God for forgiveness of actual sins they committed. They were intimidated by bullies who told them *they* were guilty. They were trying to say, "Hey we're sorry, but we are not racist. We are innocent." But the bullies with the bullhorns had no plans to confess their own sins.

A Government that Created the Black Underclass

Fredrick Douglass, a former slave and leader in the abolitionist movement, proposed, in response to the 1863 Emancipation Proclamation, that best thing the government could do for Black Americans was nothing. Yes, nothing. Leave them alone and allow them to build their own lives. Douglass presented a speech in January of 1862 concerning what should be done with slaves once emancipated. He outlined a number of malady or tragic results for the Black person if put into positions they did not want or were unprepared for. Some of his predictions were spot on, some of them not, for he was limited by not knowing the future. He thought the best course was to allow former slaves to be able to naturally assimilate themselves into culture over several generations.

The government did not listen. Several states instituted racist policies which were later known as Jim Crow laws. These were not outlawed until 1954 when the Supreme Court of the United States rendered the *Brown v. Board of Education of Topeka* decision outlawing "separate but equal" public education. America repented and started to change. During this period, the government took a more active role in trying to fix and compensate for past mistakes. Much of that was justified. There were some things that only the government could do. The courts had to rule. Congress had to write legislation in order to outlaw discrimination based on race in the United States. Refinements had to be made. But allow me to make a larger point.

The 1964 Civil Rights bill was vital and pivotal, but what came on its heels created a Black underclass that is the source of the majority of racial injustices our nation faces today. The problem is so big and complex that it seems hopeless.

I will stipulate that racism does exist in America. It is in the air we breathe. It is present in passive forms, and sometimes in active forms. I notice it in my attitudes and responses. But it is not malicious, nor do I intend to do harm to anyone. Now many want all of us to repent again, not by rules written in Scripture but by those written in their organization's manifesto. The Bible calls for heart reflection and repentance of attitudes and actions that do harm to others. Not even God expects all thoughts to be free of any temptation or attitudes that are natural to humans. For example, to feel more comfortable with your friends rather than strangers or people of a different culture does not mean you are racist. Racism is assuming that one is inherently superior in some way to another based on race alone. By some standards, a white person is racist simply by being white. It does not matter to some that many whites are born into poverty or hardship, more so than many non-white people. The entire idea is divisive and destructive to unity and to people caring for one another.

Government leaders have wanted to help. I cannot know the motives of politicians, and I cannot say that I would have been wise enough to do any different. But they created a welfare system and culture of dependence among African Americans. The most recent culture shaping example is the War on Poverty and the Great Society program that was signed into law by President Lyndon Johnson in the 1960s.

I suspect that Fredrick Douglass would have said, "You didn't listen to me. You did way too much."

We now reward children being born out of wedlock, and today 75% of Black babies are born out of wedlock. A young woman can receive more welfare by having a baby, but not if she is married. This encourages young Black men to produce children but not care for them and live with them. This is a national crisis because these children must grow up without fathers. Until that is fixed—and this is a long-term fix—you will not be able to fix the schools, the communities, the prison problem, violence in the streets, and the educational crisis that is Black America. It is all linked together. The government has trained Black America to believe they cannot make it on their own and need the white man's help. The white man was wrong, but it will not be until Black Americans say, in the spirit of Frederick Douglass, "Stop! We can do it. We are capable. Quit treating us like wards of the state," will young Black men marry the mothers of their children, raise their families, read to them at night, pray with them, take them to church, keep them out of gangs, and teach them to work and to take care of themselves and others. It just will not happen. It must begin somewhere. Young men need mentors, good examples, and a reason *not* to follow the others around them who choose gangs or a life of crime.

The welfare state is not an answer. In fact, it is the Black man's enemy. I agree with much of what Bryan Stevenson did and wrote about in *Just Mercy*. That is the best movie I have seen in ten years. It was a powerful portrayal of injustice in the court system. Stevenson was a Harvard-trained African American attorney who moved to the South and defended many death row inmates who were wrongly imprisoned. I agree with Tim Keller's theological arguments regarding race and justice. Proximity and giving to others in concrete ways is part of our discipleship. If we do not act proactively, our discipleship is greatly diminished.[413] This could very well be the reason we have made disciples for the past fifty years and have lost the culture at the same time.

Black Lives Matter: The Organization

Black lives do not matter to *Black Lives Matter*. If they did care about Black lives, they would not support Planned Parenthood and the abortion rights movement, which is the number one killer of Black children in America.[414] They would march through

---

[413] "Grace, Justice, and Mercy: An Evening with Bryan Stevenson & Rev. Tim Keller," *Center for Faith and Work*, posted June 3, 2016. https://www.youtube.com/watch?v=MyBfOX5OHRQ.

[414] "Abortion: The Overlooked Tragedy for Black Americans." *Arizona Capitol Times*, 25 February 2020. https://azcapitoltimes.com/news/2020/02/25/abortion-the-overlooked-tragedy-for-black-americans/.

the South Side of Chicago because Black on Black crime is the biggest killer of Black men in America.[415]

As for the organization, its true name should be Black Leftist Lives Matter. If you go on the website and click the "donate button," you will be introduced to ActBlue Charities.[416] ActBlue is another way of saying Democratic Party and other related causes. Black Lives Matter is anti-Christian and seeks to exploit both white guilt and the African American community in the United States to implement its radical agenda. One of the organization's primary objectives is the undoing of the traditional family. They disparaged the "Western-prescribed nuclear family structure." The reason for this is that the family is one of the last carriers for Judeo-Christian values and its commitment to sexual moral codes. The organization Black Lives Matter came under scrutiny for their anti-family agenda, and their criticism of it was scrubbed from their website. [417]

We are all susceptible to Stockholm Syndrome, to sympathize with our captors. Our captors are the purveyors of the erroneous idea that because you are born into privilege you are an oppressor. Not only that, you are guilty and therefore must cleanse your soul through repentance, confession, and forking over the goodies. White guilt reigns supreme. Whites live under the constant threat of being stigmatized as racist. The judge and jury are

---

[415] Linda Qiu, "Juan Williams: No. 1 Cause of Death for African-American Males 15-34 Is Murder." *Politifact*, The Poynter Institute, 24 August 2014. "https://www.politifact.com/factchecks/2014/aug/24/juan-williams/juan-williams-no-1-cause-death-african-americans-1/.

[416] https://blacklivesmatter.com/about/

[417] Joshua Rhett Miller, "BLM Site Removes Page on 'Nuclear Family Structure 'Amid NFL Vet's Criticism." *New York Post*, 24 September 2020. https://nypost.com/2020/09/24/blm-removes-website-language-blasting-nuclear-family-structure/.

primarily white institutions, businesses, teachers' unions, major corporations such as Coca-Cola, Nike, Facebook, Twitter, and others, which have granted themselves moral authority. They manipulate white guilt and hold your public reputation in their hands. I entreat you to think, read, study, and listen. Figure out before God what you should do. The first thing I did was pray. Then I researched and confessed my sins before God. The sins I confessed were ones I could recount and that I had actually committed and was accountable for. I did not confess fabricated sins that people I had never met laid on me. Now I want to do what I know to do: pick up my pen and write about the primary moral issues of the day, how following Jesus interfaces with the cultural narratives of our time, and how I can be a faithful witness of Christ my Lord in the middle of it all.

That Hideous Strength

To govern means to rule or preside over a nation, state, or town. Some do so with the greatest of care to empower a free people to exercise their will. The underlying premise of such governance is that the human will has been created and granted by God. People, therefore, thrive when their governor leads with the knowledge that humans are best left alone to govern themselves through an inner strength of character.

That Hideous Strength, the third volume in C.S. Lewis' fictional space trilogy, is a work of social criticism. It challenges the totalitarian impulse of societies and leaders who try to socially engineer human nature. In that sense, it is similar in theme to more popular works such as George Orwell's *1984* and Aldous Huxley's *Brave New World*. Lewis clearly argues in the work that such an impulse and exercise of power is hideous.[418]

The present pandemic will become endemic in the next few months. Covid 19 will become common place. It will be ever present like the flu and other viral suspects that break through herd immunity and the vaccinated, on occasion. That will cause us to set aside the two extremes of wearing masks until every last case is snuffed out and never wearing masks in the belief there is no pandemic. Human behavior will adapt. Airlines and public transportation will

---

[418] C.S. Lewis, *That Hideous Strength: A Modern Fairy-Tale for Grown-Ups* (reprint), (New York: Scribner Book Company, 2003). mhttps://www.amazon.com/That-Hideous-Strength-Space-Trilogy/Scribner Reprint May 2003. Originally published in 1945.

undoubtedly require certain behaviors and restrictions that were before considered unacceptable or even unconstitutional. What I think promises to become hideous will be the lust for power by some governors that will spill over into a soft totalitarianism. Totalitarianism means to govern the total realm of citizens' everyday lives, issuing edicts based on governors' own ideologies.[419]

Many leaders deserve a lockdown dunce cap and must be the original signers of the Hypocritical Oath, saying one thing and doing another. To the hard-working scientists who have attempted to present medical facts without a political slant, we say thank you for the work and the studies. To the federally employed epidemiologists who read the data and interpreted it wrongly and who unnecessarily mischaracterized the entire problem, your science card, your logic card, and most importantly, your courage card has been hereby revoked by the American public. New York and California prove lockdowns do not work. Subsequent data proved that lockdowns did more psychological and economic harm than they did to slow down the virus. Washing your hands, social distancing, and wearing a mask work. Dining out of doors works; going to work works; keeping kids in school works; and allowing people to make their own decisions works. And leaving alone anyone under eighteen works. The death rate of people under age eighteen is less than the seasonal flu.[420]

----

[419] For further discussion on Soft Totalitarianism, see previous essay.

[420] This study shows that among those eighteen years old and younger, the flu was more dangerous than Covid 19. Prof. Lionel Piroth, MD, Jonathan Cottenet, MSc, Annie-Sophie Mariet, MD, Prof. Philippe Bonniaud, et.al, "Comparison of the Characteristics, Morbidity, and Mortality of Covid-19 and Seasonal Influenza: A Nationwide Population-Based Retrospective Cohort Study, *The Lancet: Respiratory Medicine* 9, No. 3, (March 1, 2021), 251-59. https://www.thelancet.com/article/S2213-2600(20)30527-0/fulltext.

I recall laughing the first time a good friend told me that Siri was listening to our conversation over lunch. I told him that she was programmed to respond to the sound of my voice but that did not mean anything. Then one day Siri started interrupting my conversations and asking me questions. I realized some algorithm really was listening and recording my words. Subsequently, reputable news sources have reported that China is already practicing what Orwell wrote about in *1984*. All citizens are assigned a social score. If you do not think and say the right things, you may lose your ability to travel or you could lose your job.[421]

This is being practiced in less intentional ways in the United States through big tech's benign surveillance. They are interested in monetizing the information, but they are tracking our movements and building files of our conduct and interests. It is primarily used to make shopping easier for me—everything from my clothes and films to travel interests and reading habits.[422] Technology in the wrong hands is a hideous strength that can manipulate thoughts and decisions.

Tyrants want control in order to create their dystopian paradises where they flourish and the populace obeys. Please see the former paradise called California, where 19% now live at the poverty level. This does not consider the homeless and illegal immigrant

---

[421] Alexandra Ma and Katie Canales, "China's 'Social Credit' System Ranks Citizens and Punishes Them with Throttled Internet Speeds and Flight Bans if the Communist Party Deems Them Untrustworthy." *Insider*, 9 May 2021. https://www.businessinsider.com/china-social-credit-system-punishments-and-rewards-explained-2018-4.

[422] Allen St. John, "How Facebook Tracks You, Even When You're Not on Facebook." *Consumer Reports*, 11 April 2018. https://www.consumerreports.org/privacy/how-facebook-tracks-you-even-when-youre-not-on-facebook/.

population which increases the number significantly.[423] California is the heartland ten years from now, make that five. No, on third thought, make it three years from now.

Companies desire to make our lives easier with their products and make our behavior more predictable. Big tech has already proven they have a monolithic political viewpoint that they favor and will, without apology or guilt, coach the society toward. The question that naturally comes up here is who has an interest in moving the culture away from a more biblical worldview? Who is the prime mover who keeps the glacier moving forward with slow and steady progress? To focus on politics is to miss the point, for politicians only reflect the culture and then give back to it what they think it wants so they can stay in power. The culture is composed of institutions such as universities, public education, media, technology giants, the arts, movies, music, and sports. These entities were used historically to build a great country and culture until they were highjacked by forces that have used them for more sinister purposes.

I have often wondered why all the movement in society attempts to destroy the Ten Commandments, rewrite laws, and deconstruct the Bible. These are all things that made us great. Who could be so hideous that they want all of these things destroyed to build a fool's paradise? The hideous strength is the fiery and fallen angel, Lucifer.[424] What can be done about all this can only be done by going to the source of evil. Now, here is the hard part. We will lose before we win. A biblically astute person already knows

---

[423] Sammy Caiola, "California Has One of the Nation's Highest Poverty Rates, Again." *Capradio*, 12 September 2018. https://www.capradio.org/articles/2018/09/12/california-has-one-of-the-nations-highest-poverty-rates-again/.

[424] Isa 14:13-14.

that much misery comes before the promised return of Christ in triumph, and he will not and cannot win without the spilling of blood.[425] That is how difficult it is to eliminate evil. It does not go down easily.

American evangelicals, especially at the retail level, still love the Rapture theory. It is an easy sale because it promises escape from a difficult time. That theory holds that just before the persecution and plagues mentioned in the book of Revelation come upon the earth, Jesus will return and snatch away his church. The church will reside in heaven with God and wait while God reclaims the earth and turns his fury upon the population whereby 56% of the global population will perish under a barrage of horror when seals are opened, trumpets are blown, and bowls of God's wrath are poured out upon the earth. Then the church will return to earth with the triumphant Savior who will slay the armies arrayed against him in the valley of Meddigo. The blood will fill the two-hundred-mile-long valley with blood as high as the horses' bridals.[426] How appealing for us and how convenient because we escape the time of great tribulation. I cannot say this teaching does not have exegetical merit, but it has waned, even faltered, in recent years among the best evangelical scholarship. If your strategy is to hold on until Christ pulls you out of the mess we are in, then you have my best wishes.

There is, however, a more prescriptive plan given to us by Jesus, and it should occupy our time and require out best effort. The two biggest mistakes we can make if it seems we are losing moral and political ground are fatalism, waiting for the rapture, and appeasement—trying to make peace with the spirit of the age. Appeasement in all its guises is primarily trying to overcome evil

---

[425] Matt 24:21, 29-31; Rev 14:14-20; 19:11-21.
[426] 1 Thess 4:13-5:11; Rev 6:1-16:21.

with nice. You cannot be nice enough to get skeptics to believe. You cannot find enough common ground with people who fundamentally disagree with your biblical worldview in order to start a conversation that will lead to their conversion. There is, however, a promise—one among many in Scripture that can assure you that your work and life as a Christian has meaning.

After the apostle Paul's historic dissertation on the resurrection of Christ, including the basic explanation of the Ggospel itself and the implications of having a non-resurrected Christ versus the hope of having a resurrected Christ, his simple advice is found: "So my dear brothers and sisters, be strong and immovable. Always work enthusiastically for the Lord, for you know that nothing you do for the Lord is ever useless" (1 Cor 15:58).

Focus on what makes you enthusiastic for God. More than likely, that is your calling. If you are an evangelist, preach! If you are one who shows mercy, show it. If you are a scholar, study, if a writer, write. Are you a good worker? Then show it! If you can make money, make it, and give it to what you care about. You get the idea. Behind all this, of course, is the way you can fight Lucifer. The most effective battle plan is to do God's will. That is what disarms the fiery angel who seeks to destroy us all. He is the one pushing all the lies that would dismember all that Christians have built over the centuries. Get busy living as a disciple of Christ. Jesus will return, and then he will do all the things we want done and sometimes think we can do but cannot, such as changing minds and eliminating evil.

When the thousand years comes to an end, Satan will be let out of his prison. He will go out to deceive the nations—called Gog and Magog—in every corner of the earth. He will gather them together for battle—a mighty army, as numberless as sand along the seashore. And I saw them as they went up on the broad plain of the earth and surrounded God's people and the beloved city. But fire from heaven came down on the attacking armies and consumed them. Then the devil, who had deceived them, was thrown into the fiery lake of burning sulfur, joining the beast and the false prophet. There they will be tormented day and night forever and ever (Rev 20:7-10).

CONCLUSION:
FOLLOW JESUS

Capturing Reality

"The earth is the Lord's and everything in it.
The world and all its people belong to him."

Psalm 24:1

Reality is what you run into most days and there is no lasting good in denying it. When people speak of reality, they mean things like gravity, death, aging, pain, and progress of progressive thought. I viewed a seminar last evening from Harvard Divinity School. The subject was *The End of White Christian America*, a book by Robert P. Jones. The basic premise is that white evangelicalism is in decline, but so are all forms of church—Catholic, Protestant mainline, and the church among African Americans as well. Younger generations are leaving the church before the age of twenty and very few are returning. This has a great deal to do with the left's Long March through our major institutions, particularly the universities and public schools.

The problem with the deconstruction of the Bible is when you are done, you are empty handed. The only hope you can give people to handle their reality is the harsher reality that you cannot really know anything, or be sure of anything, or rely on anything, but yourself. We know that is a dead end. But they were not happily discussing this hopeless scenario. They talked about the fall of religious orthodoxy and conducted an autopsy on it.

The juggernaut that was modern white evangelicalism, started and formed by Billy Graham in the 1940s, has now come tumbling down in the time of his son Franklin Graham. We are losing numbers. The world has out discipled us. If we think that we can pray our way out of this, we are mistaken. Christ's commands to us belie such a notion.

God is the source of reality. Getting a hold on that idea is the key to the communication of the Gospel.

Last week, I watched several of the Sunday morning church services online and on television. It was the typical fare, telling this incredible story about God and how he is triune and sent his only Son to die for me. Added to this, on some channels, Christian rock was played, and hipster type singers and pastors representing an "untucked" shirt world did their best to be relevant. One historic Presbyterian church used a high church backdrop with candles, pipe organ, and a high-brow vocabulary, while the speaker appeared with sport coat, open collar, and low riding jeans.

One service had me mesmerized with a few musicians and one male singer all robed. The vocalist was probably sixty years old, and he was singing a well-known hymn. His face was radiant, his voice soft, and he sang all six verses. Behind him were a pianist and two guitarists, all playing softly, and none were in a hurry to reach the end of the song. It seemed so disconnected to reality. It was still the 1950s to them, and they could have cared less about being relevant. I thought about how absurd this all is to people who have not been converted to Christ and what they must think about this story and its people.

While watching these dear people, this realization struck me. God cannot be this small, provincial, and religious. After all, he created the universe: "In the beginning God created the heavens and the earth. The earth was formless and empty, and darkness covered the deep waters. And the Spirit of God was hovering over the surface of the waters" (Gen 1:1-2).

"In the beginning" means God created time and started the earth project. God is the source of all that exists. He always has existed outside time and space. As Saint Augustine wrote, God invented time, and he used material in its raw form, "the heavens and the earth."[427] It is very difficult, even insulting, to reduce God to some sort of religious figure that can be captured in a painting, poem, song, religious creed, joint statement, or theological system. These are all valiant efforts that fall short.[428] Even worse is the notion that the way to know God is to follow our little subcultural formulations to say a certain prayer, follow a ritual, and get baptized by the right clergy. It all seems so trivial in comparison to the power and majesty of God.

God is so vast and so far beyond human comprehension that much of his communication with us is an accommodation on his part. He created human life; therefore, he is the only one who understands us. What we need, want, and experience is part of his original knowledge base. God always has been. He has no beginning and no end and is not a captive of space and time.[429] Therefore, he is not typically what we call human. He says he is a father that has a son, but we know whatever kind of father he is

---

[427] A helpful article on Augustine's view of time is Stephen M. Barr, "St. Augustine's Relativistic Theory of Time." *Church Life Journal: A Journal of the McGrath Institute for Church Life*, Notre Dame University, 7 February 2020. https://churchlifejournal.nd.edu/articles/augustines-push-against-the-limits-of-time/.

[428] Isa 64:6.

[429] Num 23:19; Ps 90:2; Rom 11:33-36; 2 Cor 1:19.

or son that Jesus is differs from our experience.[430] He also knows sacrifice, love, hate, and anger. He can forgive, change his mind, and keep his promises.[431]

Has God always existed in three persons, Father, Son, and Holy Spirit, or did he create an image of such in order to communicate to us and to serve us? I cannot answer that question. I can only say that I believe in the authority of Scripture and that God has used images and language to reveal himself to us. In other words, there is Jesus the Son of God, the savior of the world, but also there is the cosmic Christ. There is Christ the creator. This Christ is far above all things, including religion. He has laid claim to being the head of the body called the church.[432]

Then there is God incarnate in Christ. Jesus is the word of God. He is the expression of realty, the logos.[433] What I expect when I see Jesus is not so much a religious person, a robed saint—a person who likes church music and religious artifacts. I expect to meet someone whose capacity is beyond what I can imagine: one who is able to create the universe with its great complexity; someone with unlimited power joined to perfect integrity and wisdom. It would surprise me if a being with such capacity would limit himself to one universe. He can multitask on his level.

Think about it this way. The Gospel is God's story that he created and has told through language, people, and an awesome physical creation that speaks to humans from DNA and the microscope to the heavens and the telescope. To reduce him and the church to a religious formulation is to make small what God meant to be

---

[430] John 1:1,3; 3:16, 17:5; Col. 1:16.
[431] 1 John 1:9; 2 Cor 1:20.
[432] Col 1:15-20; John 3:31; Eph 1:21; Col. 1:18.
[433] John 1:1-5, 14:9; Heb 1:3.

big. Let me find someone who can say it better. Ah, yes. Lesslie Newbigin can always be relied on. "The Bible is unique among the sacred books of the world's religions in that it is in structure a history of the cosmos. It claims to show us the shape, structure, origin, and the goal not merely of human history but of cosmic history."[434]

It is as if God wrote a story of redemption and then made himself a character by inserting himself into human life as the hero. The only way Shakespeare could meet Hamlet is if he wrote himself into the play. God comes to the world with all its problems, pain, and death and provides a way out.[435] It is irresistible in nature until the religious get a hold on the plan and make it very resistible. Christian television is a favorite tool for our enemy. It turns the meaning of the universe and our lives into entertainment. The Gospel is the best news. It is the best story, and every human can understand God's nature and person by knowing it. God is the fundamental reality.

Let me allow Newbigin to send you off with some wonderful words:

... the ultimate reality, the ultimate secret of the eternal truth for which the Greeks gave many names, but one of them was the name logos, the word, the reason with ultimately beyond history is the logos of reliable truth. That the word has become flesh in the man Jesus Christ, whose ministry, death and resurrection is the manifestation of God's eternal being. Now that created a profound crisis, *that the ultimate reality is no longer something available to reason and to the mind of the philosopher. It is known by*

[434] https://twitter.com/LesslieNewbigin, November 15, 2020
[435] Phil 2:6-8; Heb 4:15.

accepting and following the core of Jesus. That the answer to the question what is the ultimate secret of the universe is this man Jesus.[436]

My suggestion: Jesus said, "Follow me."[437] Do not try to figure it out. Just get on your feet and get moving. You will begin life in the kingdom of God.

---

[436] Newbigin, "Nihilism," https://www.youtube.com/watch?v=5WyrC7JVd5Q.

[437] Matt 4:19; John 21:22.

Making Disciples
in Dystopia

"Men have forgotten God; that's why all this has happened." [438]

Aleksandr Solzhenitsyn

There is much written about us living in a post-Christian era. There is also a subscript aspect to this called the post-Easter period that the Sacerdotal church starts with Easter Monday, followed by a series of seven Sundays called Easter Tide until the Feast of Pentecost.[439]

Lent, that period of denial that prohibits the gathered church from crying out "Hallelujah" [Praise the Lord] from Ash Wednesday until Easter morning is followed by the call to celebrate Easter for a good long while. It seems like the church year is just picking up some momentum and all the priests go on vacation anyway.

This Easter weekend was filled with cliches that rolled off me like the proverbial water off a duck's back. First, I spent some of my weekend trying to find my celebratory button so I could

---

[438] Aleksandr Solzhenitsyn, "Men Have Forgotten God: 1983 Templeton Address." *National Review,* 11 December 2018. https://www.nationalreview.com/2018/12/aleksandr-solzhenitsyn-men-have-forgotten-god-speech/.

[439] The Sacerdotal church consists of groups whose services are organized around a planned liturgy or prayer book.

push it and feel the proper level of sadness or gladness that everyone is supposed to feel. On Good Friday, which is a day for contemplation, I tried to think about the suffering of Christ. Streaming the movie *The Passion of the Christ,* directed by Mel Gibson, usually works to tap down any residual good feeling.[440] Toward the end of the day, cliches piled up, dominated by Tony Campolo's famous sermonic phrase, "Its Friday, but Sunday is coming." That phrase has become part of Christian tradition though it cannot be found in *The Book of Common Prayer.*[441]

I was locked away most of "Good Friday" finishing up writing projects so I could enjoy some time off during the weekend and worship with my family on Sunday. On Good Friday evening, I did what any normal pastor/theologian/writer would do. I began watching *The People v. O. J. Simpson: American Crime Story*—ten hours of detailed dramatic portrayal of the ins and outs of the trial of the century. After two hours, I was hooked, but I had a number of conflicts on "Holy Saturday." The key to "Holy Saturday" is to celebrate nothing because nothing is happening. The church is closed. Jesus is dead and buried, and he has no disciples. They have quit. They are hiding and licking their wounds.

After a morning of planning, which is the key to a great next week, I was able to relax. I even knew when I would review my notes, when I would work on what and for how long. It came time for the Final Four games. For you who have not been baptized with a love of basketball, the final four teams in the NCAA tournament

---

[440] *The Passion of the Christ,* a 2004 film about the last days of Christ's life, produced and directed by Mel Gibson, grossed $612 million and received three Academy Award nominations.

[441] *The Book of Common Prayer* was first published in England and released in 1549. Later revised, it now exists in different forms and continues to guide the worldwide Anglican Church in worship.

play on a single day on CBS. It is the apex, even more than the Championship Game of March Madness, even though it is April—sort of like Christians celebrating Christ's birth in December when he was born in April.

The more I watched the O.J. story, the more I learned about many of the intriguing details. I was traveling and very busy back when the trial was actually going on in 1995, and I did not pay close attention. I do recall the day when the verdict came in. I was speaking to a group of pastors in northern Minnesota. Someone came into the room and told us the verdict was in and we if we wanted to see the result, we would all need to go down the hallway to the bar to watch it on TV. After the obligatory hesitations regarding pastors going into a bar, we voted and took the pilgrimage. [Not really.] Thirty of us who were at the luncheon walked into the bar and, of course, were shocked by the verdict. We shook our heads in despair and walked back to our meal. Thirty white pastors in northern Minnesota did not understand it. I do now, however, know how prosecutor Marsha Clark likes her coffee: black with two packets of Sweet 'N Low.

There I sat in my office, O.J. streaming on Netflix, the Final Four with the sound off on my iPad, and the book, *The Rise and Triumph of the Modern Self* by Carl R. Trueman on my lap. I was there for five hours. This is making disciples in dystopia. I am a product of my time, an elder boomer who is coming to the end of his string, in full distress about the decay and decadence around me, but at the same time swept up with the tools, networks, and narratives swirling around me and holding a book by a brilliant scholar who is attempting to explain why this has all happened. But like Trueman says, trying to explain it all simply is like saying that the Twin Towers fell on 9/11 because of gravity. True, but something is missing in that explanation.

The more I watched *O.J.*, the more I saw it as an early warning sign of the present-day blend of *Brave New World* and *1984*. Watching O.J.s defense team spin their cynical yarn about the Los Angeles Police Department's plot to frame O.J., I could identify with Marsha Clark and her fellow prosecutor Chris Darden when they rolled their eyes. As Simpson's defense attorney Robert Shapiro later stated, "Not only had Johnnie Cochran dealt the race card, but he had also dealt it from the bottom of the deck." The entire narrative was from the Theater of the Absurd. Cochran, Shapiro, F. Lee Bailey and Alan Dershowitz, the Four Horseman of Gobshite, developed a narrative they created in order to cynically influence jurors. Yes, there were elements of truth. The police have racists in their ranks. Yes, Mark Furman was an angry young officer, but that was not a major factor. The evidence was overwhelming that Simpson was guilty and, basically, everyone knew it then. Even those who pretended to believe in his innocence then do not defend him now.

O.J. Simpson is universally persona non gratia. Would you join O.J.s foursome at your golf club? It seems like the prosecutors were focused on evidence and justice whereas O.J.s legal team was motivated by fame, power, and to making a phony version of a supra-point. That supra-point was important concerning racism, but it was made in a shameful way by using the race card and blaming the Los Angeles Police Department for their prejudice.

This leads me to making disciples in a dystopia. The controlling forces in American life right now are those who control the narrative, freedom of speech, big tech, big media, big business, the universities, public schools, sports, and entertainment. This cabal is progressive, anti-Christian, and committed to ideas that have been repeatedly discredited for thousands of years. Even China, Vietnam, and Russia have rejected socialism because it never has worked. Often, white, highly-degreed Americans point to Scandinavia as successful socialist experiments. The leaders of Norway, Sweden, and Denmark deny this. They have high taxes, but they are capitalistic in their practices. They too know socialism does not work. I bring this up because only the leaders of North Korea and Cuba still hold to these false narratives, but even they know it does not work, except for the few leaders who can enjoy the limited wealth.

In America, the controlling elite, like O.J.'s late defense attorney Johnny Cochran and his team, are presenting a narrative that is cynical. They call for unity but divide the nation along group identity lines and plan to indoctrinate children to view themselves as either of the oppressed victimized class or the oppressor class. How do you know which class you are? By your race or by your gender, even though the definition of gender is no longer biologically based. Science does not matter. Reality is what you want it to be; therefore, reality is unreliable and the ground underneath you continues to shift. The elite have their own memory hole to shove history down.

Oh yes, remember that book I had in my lap, *The Rise and Triumph of the Modern Self* by Carl Trueman? Here is something relevant to our subject. This deserves its own space but pardon the abridged version. I often ponder, "Why does progress always seem to move away from the Christian narrative and common sense?" If I wrote a manual, *How to Ruin Your World*, what is happening right now would be its content. The longer humans live on earth, they gain knowledge. With that knowledge comes confidence, then arrogance, and then they flip the narrative. Humans started in a world that God ordered, and our role was to discover that order and conform to it. Now, with a hubris that combines knowledge and independence, humans claim that the earth and everything in it is the raw material and we create our own meaning from it.

In his book, Trueman summaries it through representative men. Idiotic Man, one fixed on himself; Political Man, one engaged in public life; Religious Man, one who interprets the world through God and revelation; Economic Man; Therapeutic Man; and finally Expressive Individualist Man. The last one is a bit "I think, therefore I am."[442] "I think, I feel, I declare, therefore I am."

"I am a woman trapped in a man's body." A phrase unknown to people two generations ago is now understood by everyone. A society that declares a reality which denies actual reality is doomed to failure. It will prove to not be a satisfying life to most, and they will attempt to reverse their field as they become painfully disillusioned. It is part of the hubris of expressive individualism that aspires to a utopian dream which will collapse under the weight of its own tyranny.

The Gospel and the call to follow Jesus is an entirely different reality that challenges the prevailing cultural mood and story of expressive individualism. That is the main reason the church has lost twenty points in public opinion polls in the last twenty years. Twenty years ago, 70% of the public claimed to be a member of a church or religious body. Today the figure is 50%.[443] The dystopia is upon us meaning that in order to force a utopian dream, those in opposition must be silenced, marginalized, punished, even

---

[442] Carl R. Trueman, *The Rise and Triumph of the Modern Self: Cultural Amnesia, Expressive Individualism, and the Road to Sexual Revolution* (Wheaton, IL: Crossway Books, 2020), 75-77.
[443] Barna, "Signs of Decline." https://www.barna.com/research/changing-state-of-the-church/.

eliminated. So Christians—and I mean real Christians who plan to follow Jesus in discipleship—strap in. It should be a wild ride. If the conversion of the apostle Paul means anything, God is at work behind the scenes, and he may choose to interrupt this disaster and change everything. We pray that he does.

DIETRICH
BONHOEFFER:
A CASE STUDY

No Longer A Bystander

Dietrich Bonhoeffer and Hannah Arendt were both born in Germany in 1906. Bonhoeffer was executed on April 9, 1945, by direct order of Adolf Hitler for participating in a plot to assassinate the Fuhrer. Arendt died in New York City in 1975. Bonhoeffer was born to privilege, the son of Germany's most famous psychiatrist, Karl Bonhoeffer. His mother, Paula was a descendent of German aristocracy, the granddaughter of liberal theologian Paul Von Hasse, counselor to Bismarck. Arendt was raised in a secular Jewish home. She loved books, concepts, and was an independent thinker from an early age.

Arendt studied with philosopher Martin Heidegger and wrote her Ph.D. dissertation, *Love and Saint Augustine*, under Karl Jaspers, who was a psychiatrist/philosopher at the University of Heidelberg. Bonhoeffer was awarded his Ph.D. from the University of Berlin. His work, *Sanctorum Communio,* [Holy Community], was supervised by Dr. Reinhold Seeberg. Later, theologian Karl Barth called Bonhoeffer's work a "theological miracle."

Precocious would be an apt description for both Arendt and Bonhoeffer. Arendt was exceedingly independent from an early age. That manifested itself in that she knew exactly what she wanted to study and from whom, and she went after it with all her might. Her infamous love affair with Martin Heidegger was part of that and as so was leaving him to study with Karl Jaspers. Bonhoeffer went against family tradition and chose theology as a profession at age fourteen. He loved his Plutarch and his Luther

Bible, once owned by his older brother Walter. He recognized evil early and was quick to step up and be counted against it.

Both grew up and were in school during the Great War, World War I. Germany lost that war and was humiliated through the Treaty of Versailles. Germany was not allowed to develop a full army and was under the economic thumb of the allied powers. This was Hitler's primary apologetic to return the Fatherland to its once great glory. It would be fair to say that the German population was in favor of a stronger, unified, and more pure German people. Hitler was appointed Chancellor in 1933 by President Paul von Hindenburg, head of the National Socialist German Workers Party. In February 1933, Hitler blamed a devastating Reichstag fire on the Communists and suspended individual and civil liberties, silencing his political enemies with false arrests. This, said Hannah Arendt, is what caused her to stop being a bystander and facilitated her decision to oppose Hitler and the Nazi cause. She was seventeen years old. Arendt escaped across the open boarder into France where she lived for several years before arriving in New York City in 1941.

Two years earlier, Bonhoeffer arrived in New York at Union Theological Seminary in order to sit out the Hitler regime. He was not able to speak freely in Germany. Neither was he able to teach, preach, publish, or escape being drafted into the army. He walked the streets in great distress. He was unsure if he could stay in the United States and still have credibility in the post-war rebuild of Germany. His stay lasted only twenty-seven days. He returned to Germany just a few weeks before Germany invaded Poland, which officially started World War II.

When Germany invaded France, Arendt was placed in an internment camp for Germans. It was called the Gurs Camp in the Pyrenees and housed six thousand other stateless Germans. She escaped in May of 1941 and was able, along with her husband, to get to New York City. Bonhoeffer was back in Germany. Arendt found "paradise" in New York.

From their respective perches, they lived, wrote, spoke, and were no longer bystanders. It was easier for Bonhoeffer and Arendt to recognize the line between good and evil than it is for people to do so now, two generations later. Most theologians in the theological world, and philosophers in the philosophical world, are bystanders. Either by disposition, training, fear, or ignorance, they simply watched. They only become alarmed when it was too late to stop it. The question for an American Christian is how to know good from evil and when to get involved.

I have found this question something between an internal struggle and a mental conundrum. Because my way of life has not been officially challenged, I have the luxury of mulling it all over and over in my prayers, mind, and in self conversation. On the other hand, as a follower of Christ, what does my discipleship to him call for? After all, discipleship is learning to live my life as though Jesus were living it. This means that if Jesus were an aged seventy plus writer, teacher, leader in 2021, what would that look like? I suppose I could think and have thought that this is not an important question because no large group of people really cares what I think about or do. But for me, regardless of audience or influence, it is a matter of conscience. Lesslie Newbigin helps me here: "A preaching of the Gospel that calls men and women to accept Jesus as Savior but does not make it clear that discipleship means commitment to a vision of society radically different from that which controls our public life today must be condemned as false."[444]

---

[444] Twitter Lesslie Newbigin Tweets. November 2, 2020.

The Gospel we preach determines the disciple we make. I do not want to make more disciples who stand by, watch, wonder, and then ask, "What happened?" when a godless society rolls over their lives and crushes them. The first impulse of so many followers of Christ is to be a peacemaker. This is because they misunderstand peace and want to avoid the discomfort and anxiety they feel when conflict and disagreement enter their lives. I'm sure many a leader wanted Stalin to go away, or Hitler, or Mao, or their next-door neighbor. But before you get peace, usually there is a fight. Is this not the way the Bible ends? God himself uses violence to end evil.[445] The most immoral act for a Christ follower is to abdicate—to step back, to pat the tyrant on the back and say you will pray for him or her. Maybe kindness will do the trick.[446]

The pacificist argument is disconnected both from the reality of Scripture and human experience. Bonhoeffer did his best to live out the Sermon on the Mount. He was attracted to the pacifist movement. But when the chips were down, he chose counterintelligence, planting bombs on Hitler's airplane, blowing him up at a conference, and various other assassination attempts. Bonhoeffer even volunteered to kill Hitler with his own hands if necessary. This is why it troubles me that many Christian leaders find and look for ways to theologize their way out of action that would threaten their power or position. It very well could be and probably is that since today's American pastors have not previously encountered a world such as the one we now live in, we are learning fast and are making mistakes as we move forward. I just know that I no longer can be a bystander. I cannot ignore what is going on around me.

---

[445] Matt 10:34; Rev 17-22.
[446] Jas 4:17.

Bonhoeffer ended up at the end of a rope, but with his dignity and integrity intact. Hannah Arendt went to Jerusalem to cover the trial of Adolf Eichmann, the Nazi colonel who had been the primary implementer of the Final Solution—the extermination of the Jews during the Second World War. Israel decided to violate international law and kidnap Eichmann from near his home outside of Buenos Aires, Argentina in 1960. Arendt covered the trial and wrote the controversial *Eichmann in Jerusalem* series of articles for *The New Yorker* magazine. Eichmann was found guilty and was hanged within two hours of the verdict. His ashes were scattered in the Mediterranean Sea outside of Israeli waters.[447]

Arendt did not take the typical view concerning Eichmann. She did not see the extermination of millions of Jews as banal, which by definition means obvious and boring. She saw Eichmann as banal. This created a firestorm because she did not see Eichmann as more evil than most people. She claimed that Eichmann's crime was that he refused to think, to stop, and to reflect morally on what he was engaged in. He was not antisemitic. He was part of a system in which he broke no law. He did exactly what the authorities duly elected told him to do.

Israel in fact broke laws, not only international law in kidnapping Eichmann but also in denying Eichmann rights normally afforded to accused Israeli citizens under their own legal system. It was a show trial. They prosecuted him for crimes against humanity. It was not only a trial for the ages; it was for all Jews for all time. It was for history and the good of humanity. Israel appealed to a higher law that superseded the mere legalities of sovereign nations.

---

[447] Further information about the life and works of Hannah Arendt can be found in her biography. Elisabeth Young-Bruehl, *For the Love of the World*, (New Haven & London: Yale University Press, 1982).

Later, Arendt accused Israel of the same hubris in their treatment of the Palestinian people. With the formation of Israel as a state, this formerly stateless and rightless people became a nation. The people of Palestine were left out of the decision and even now are stateless. For all this and more, Arendt was attacked unmercifully by the New York academic and leftist elites. Arendt stood strong.

Where did Bonhoeffer and Arendt get the courage to take a stand? Bonhoeffer said it was God. For Hannah Arendt, God does not seem to be a major force in her life in any formal way. The closest one gets to an answer is this statement: "People go about. No one is lost. Earth, Heaven, light and forests play in the play of the Almighty." [448]

Ambiguous at best, but Arendt did write her doctoral dissertation on *Love and Saint Augustine*. She did not seem to be antagonistic toward the divine, mostly reflective and general in her acknowledgment of some personage greater or different than humans. Being made in the image of God, and in God's good common grace, Arendt apparently found a resource to stay committed to the truth. She believed what she saw and what she heard—her instincts. This takes great courage when others around you are being cowered by convention.

Here is my plan. Like Bonhoeffer, I will take opportunity to freely speak, and, like Arendt, I will write what I think is true. And like both, I will live with the consequences. I doubt that I will encounter what they did. My purpose is to help build and move forward the kingdom of God through the tools God has given

---

[448] Bernauer S.J.J. (1987) The Faith of Hannah Arendt: *Amor Mundi* and its Critique — Assimilation of Religious Experience. In: Bernauer S.J.J.W. (eds) Amor Mundi. Boston College Studies in Philosophy, vol 26. Springer, Dordrecht. https://doi.org/10.1007/978-94-009-3565-5_1.

me. I will strive to talk about the issues under the issues, always reminding myself that God is over all things. His word is my guide, his calling my assignment. I will also take special care to work with the church first, the culture second, and the political world third. Because as I do believe, have written, and spoken about on *The Bonhoeffer Show* podcast, religion is upstream, culture is mid-stream, and politics are downstream. If we plan to engage in our world, then all of these are important because they do affect our lives. But I will always remember what drives it all, the living God who loves us, calls us, and disciples us every day.

The Forming of Dietrich Bonhoeffer

Let's begin with a boy in lederhosen and blonde hair sitting under a tree in his back garden reading from his Luther Bible. He is precocious, but so were his three brothers and four sisters. After all, his father Karl was the most famous neurologist in Germany, and his mother, Paula, was an informal member of German royalty. They lived in the most prestigious neighborhood in Berlin. Their home, a three-story mini mansion at 7 Birkenwaldchen with gabled roofs, numerous chimneys, a screened porch, and a large balcony overlooking the spacious garden, was idyllic. The governess could watch over Dietrich as he read his brother's Luther Bible that had been given to him after his older brother Walter had been killed in battle in the first days of his entry into The Great War. Walter's death cast a dark pallor over the family. Dietrich's mother was bedridden with grief. It was time for reflection as Dietrich would read *Uncle Tom's Cabin*, *Pinocchio*, and many literary classics.

The family was very competitive. They possessed a dominant secular mind set even though Paula made sure the children were taught the Bible. Dietrich's brother Klaus was to become a lawyer and middle brother Karl would work with Einstein. Dietrich aspired to be a concert pianist until he learned that his fingers were too short. At fourteen, he announced that he would become a theologian. His family was both surprised, alarmed, and scoffed at him for making such a useless spectacle of his life. However, a family friend, Adolf Von Harnack was the most famous church historian in Europe, so the family reconciled it to be a respectable profession.

Many have asked the question, "How did such a young man, Dietrich Bonhoeffer, make such a big impact in such a short period?" The answer is status, brilliance, confidence, and courage.

Status. Dietrich was a member of the German elite—informal royalty, if you will. He always had money, was the best dressed, and traveled first class. In fact, some would say Dietrich was spoiled. His parents made life easy with a generous allowance, nice clothes, opera tickets, special foods sent to him when he lived in less refined settings and a new Mercedes convertible. That status included the family lineage, open doors to the right schools, and friendship with the culture's decision makers. When it was discovered in Tegal prison that his uncle was in charge of the department that provided oversight of prisons, he was given better treatment.

Brilliance. Dietrich was awarded his Ph.D. at age 21, earlier than most. His dissertation, which normally would be stowed in a university library never to be read again, was called a "theological miracle" by the esteemed theologian Karl Barth. When Bonehoeffer spent nine months in New York at Union Theological Seminary, he was more than the faculty bargained for. He stood toe to toe with them, even challenging the famous Reinhold Niebuhr as to whether Union was producing politicians or theologians. Bonhoeffer believed the school to be weak in theology and shamed them by using ad hominem attacks to deal with conservative theologians. He complained that even though he had attended many hours of lecture and had heard scores of sermons in New York churches, the one thing he had not heard was the Gospel.

Confidence. Dietrich's confidence came from a combination of the cultural status that he enjoyed joined to his brilliance, which included insight with incisive thought patterns. This was seen in his contrarian nature, even with what normally would be his intimidating teachers at the University of Berlin. He somehow remained more moderate and even conservative than his mentors. He stood his ground because he honestly saw life and truth differently. This is why in his early life, Martin Luther was his model, and, in his twenties, Karl Barth, the most important theologian in Europe, became a role model. But still, when spending time with Karl Barth, a theological demigod to many, Bonhoeffer found himself arguing with Barth.

Bonhoeffer also met two people and had two experiences in New York that shaped much of his thinking. The first meeting was with Jean Lasserre, a fellow student. Through discussions with Lasserre and seeing the German-made film, *All Quiet on the Western Front*, an anti-war film banned in Germany, Bonhoeffer began to seek a way to be a pacifist. The second experience was in the Abyssinian Baptist Church in Harlem with fourteen thousand members where he heard the Gospel and later claimed to have become a Christian because of it. When he returned to Germany, he began to read the Bible, pray, go to church, and take communion.

Courage. During his twenties Bonhoeffer, even though young and considered a novice pastor/theologian, pushed his elders and church officials very hard. He was able to get an invitation to a world peace conference in Fano, Sweden, that no one wanted to extend to him. He was a member of the Confessing Church which stood against the National Socialist's doctrine and their encroachment on the German Evangelical Church.

There are many documented examples of Bonhoeffer taking a stand even when it cost him, and this, of course, extended throughout his life until his execution. The most famous or best publicized was his leaving New York the second time in June of 1939. If he would have stayed in New York, he would have lived a long life, written more books, given more lectures, got fat, been married, had children, and died of lung cancer because of his beloved cigarettes.

However, a long life is not the most important value in this life if you believe this life is simply a prelude to eternal life. If you believe that eternal life begins when you step into discipleship to Christ and continues after physical death, then there is no hurry to cram everything into this life. There is no angst that you did not finish your work and that the work of God will continue without your participation. The kind of perspective that Bonhoeffer had frees us of these humanly flawed ideas. Bonhoeffer is reported to have said either at his execution or the day before when taken to Flossenburg Prison, "This is the end, but for me it is the beginning of life." What was formed in this young man's life was that living as Christ's disciple is living fully in this world while receiving direction from another more permanent world, the kingdom of God.

Seeds of Greatness: The Character of Dietrich Bonhoeffer

"...it is not unusual to hear people ask whether the church still has relevance, whether they still need God. But the question is wrongly put, Bonhoeffer said, the paramount concern is "whether we are willing to offer our lives to the church and the world, for this is what God desires."

Dietrich Bonhoeffer's First Lecture at
University of Berlin 1932

Twenty-five-year-old Dietrich Bonhoeffer was no lightweight. He combined his social status as a scion of the Berlin intellectual elite with his two doctoral degrees and a contrarian personality to position himself for influence. He had challenged Reinhold Niebuhr and the Union Theological faculty during his nine-month stay in New York City. Bonhoeffer said that in America, Christians fashioned their theology like a man orders his car from a factory. All ideas were on the table if they could serve a useful end. Now, he would do the same with the theologian he most admired, Karl Barth.

Forty-nine-year-old Barth was just starting his *Church Dogmatics*, his attempt to rebuild the crumbling edifice of Christian orthodoxy. Almost single handily, Barth moved all of theological Europe from the far left into the middle of the theological spectrum, to a new place called neo-orthodoxy. Barth believed that theology bore no responsibility for changing society. He believed that theology makes nothing happen. Bonhoeffer argued that theology is of no use if it is not rooted in reality. Barth's students worshipped him. Bonhoeffer admired him, benefitted from him, and then challenged him.

That was Dietrich Bonhoeffer at twenty-five. At that age, he was eligible for ordination and took two part-time jobs: chaplain at Technical University in Berlin and unpaid lecturer in the theology department at the University of Berlin. But before he could begin his unpaid job, he would need to complete a full slate of comprehensive examinations. Neither job came with an office.

Just before he began his new duties, he attended a World Alliance conference in Cambridge, England. He created quite a stir with his belief that there could be harmony among nations. His views were rejected by the German delegation as both naïve and unpatriotic. Upon his return to the yellow brick train station on the corner of Wilhelmstrasse, his father's chauffeur waited in the black Mercedes to pick up Dietrich. He may not have had a paying job, but he still had his creature comforts. This is an important feature of Bonhoeffer's life. He slept on silk sheets.

He began his new assignment at Berlin Technical University, and it proved frustrating. He offered to lead discussion groups on stimulating theological subjects but found zero interest. He confessed that he felt like a housewife who prepared great meals, but no one was hungry. Students would tear down the fliers he posted of his meetings. He came up with new programs, but again, no interest, only opposition. He offered lectures, prayer services, and study groups. All were rejected by the students. He did have one student show up once. Morning devotions were cancelled because of a lack of interest. He posted his office hours and would sit for hours. No one came. Finally, there was some interest shown if he would hold his discussion at a beer hall and would pay for the beer. Bonhoeffer was not discouraged as much as he was insulted. This goes back to his confidence and his sense of rightness. He just knew better than the less noble, the under-educated.

He now turned to the job at the University of Berlin. For years, his rise had been impressive: the schooling, the special friendships, academic praise, and being taken seriously. Now he had arrived at the Great University of Berlin joining a faculty whose political orientation he no longer shared, a church that was corrupt and dull. He would sit in his office and grade papers alone.

Finally, on November 15, 1931, Bonhoeffer was ordained to ministry at Saint Matthias Church in Berlin near his home. He was now eligible to preach and administer the sacraments. He, like Barth, would now stand in strange new land of the Bible and let its "wild and crooked tree grow freely, without constraint."

He began his work as a pastoral assistant at Zionskirche, a church located in the worst part of Berlin. Fifty boys fell under his supervision—the youth group. This is what is so great about the church. It is a great leveler and even better teacher. He discovered the only way he could bring the boys under control was through dramatic Bible stories like David & Goliath, Samson, Israel crossing the Red Sea, and the plagues. He threw himself into the privation and unemployment that beset the boys' families. He visited their homes, counseling and praying with them—quite a change for this son of privilege. He would play Negro spirituals. He taught them to play chess, read Scripture, tell stories, and a bit of catechizing to boot. His work in the inner-city of Berlin made Bonhoeffer aware of the limits of his training.

It made him recall that theologians and theology are the servants of the church. Indeed, they are. In fact, when asked to describe his work in Zionskirche, he said, "What a liberation!"

He loved the retreats. The boys would sit with him as they discussed the joys of the devotional life, of prayer, and of contemplation of the beauty of the Harz Mountains. It was during this time that Bonhoeffer was struck with the simplicity and directness of Jesus' teaching as well as the concreteness of their demands. These were the roots for his most famous work, *The Cost of Discipleship.* It led to the young Bonhoeffer that stepped to the lectern at his debut as a teacher.

"A young scholar stepped to the rostrum with a light, quick step, a man with very fair, rather thin hair, a broad face, rimless glasses with a golden bridge. After a few words of welcome, he explained the meaning and structure of the lecture, in a firm slightly throaty way of speaking. Then he opened his manuscript and began."

His first words have now traveled through the decades. He said that it is not unusual to hear people ask whether the church still has relevance, whether they still need God. But the question is wrongly put, he said. The paramount concern is "whether we are willing to offer our lives to the church and the world, for this is what God desires." With that, young Bonhoeffer was on his way.

The Cost of Discipleship: Nachfolge, The Book

It was circa May 1971, and I was flying across the Andes Mountains looking out of the airplane window contemplating what I had just been reading. As beautiful as the snow-capped Andes were, it was the majesty of the words I had just read that caused my soul to rise in admiration.

Cheap Grace is the mortal enemy of our church. Our struggle today is for costly grace. The church that teaches this doctrine of grace thereby confers such grace upon itself. The world finds in this church a cheap cover-up for its sins, for which it shows no remorse and from which it has even less desire to be set free. Cheap grace is, thus, denial of God's living word, denial of the incarnation of the word of God.[449]

These words reset the course of my life. They opened my theological eyes and helped me see clearly that grace was an active force that created action. I wanted to explode out of my seat and run up and down the skinny airplane aisle to burn off the excitement I felt.

These were the words of a young pastor/theologian Dietrich Bonhoeffer. He spoke them to a group of twenty-three ministerial students in a small town of Finkenwalde in Northern Germany,

---

[449] Dietrich Bonhoeffer, *Discipleship*, Dietrich Bonhoeffer Works Vol. I. (Fortress Press, Minneapolis 2003), 43.

the site of the illegal Confessing Church Seminary. In fact, the first two hours of daily instruction were from this work simply titled *Discipleship* or **Nachfolge**—literally, *Following.* The English is *Succession.*

The faith or allegiance that Bonhoeffer spoke of is a faith that only becomes real in following. In other words, if your faith does not result in discipleship, it is not faith, not belief, and has nothing to do with grace. This new monasticism, nothing like the old as Bonhoeffer described to his brother Klaus in a letter, was his grand experiment. Twenty-three young men living in community learning a new and radical way to live as they prepared for ordained ministry in a church that had been stripped of national recognition. Its clergy would no longer be paid—no retirement, no medical care, and no prospects other than the Eastern Front once the Gestapo would close the school after two years.

The group was quite interesting. German theology was very academic, intellectual, and not very practical by today's standards. These men lived largely in their heads, so when Bonhoeffer asked them to practice the daily office—to spend thirty minutes in the morning in silence—they did not want to do it. They could not do it and rebelled against it. When he asked for volunteers to help in the kitchen, and no one offered, Bonhoeffer locked himself in the kitchen and cleaned up after all twenty-three students by himself. They soon learned that following would entail more than just passing a theology test. This was the context in which he wrote the book we know as the *Cost of Discipleship.* The men he taught it to were people like you and me—people who would rather let someone else do the dishes and who would rather smoke their pipes or cigarettes, take a walk, or get a few more winks in before a long and demanding day of class was to begin.

Karl Barth, Europe's most important theologian of the twentieth century wrote about the book some twenty years later regarding Bonhoeffer's treatment of the unity of justification and sanctification, "Easily the best that has been written on this subject . . . In these the matter is handled with such depth and precision that I am almost tempted to simply reproduce them in an extended quotation. For I cannot hope to say anything better on the subject than what is said here."[450]

We cannot understand Bonhoeffer's book unless we know that it was written in the middle of the church struggle—a struggle for the church's faithfulness to the gospel that begins with the defining the gospel and what it means to be a faithful disciple. (It is interesting that Bonhoeffer did not require his students to take political sides. He never condemned them for joining the Army or supporting the Fatherland. This was a matter of conscience.) The German Reich Church had capitulated its thinking that you could blend the kingdom of God and the kingdom of Man—that you could appease evil and possibly reach them for Christ if you befriended or joined in with them. The only problem was that much of the church was so liberal, they had lost not only their souls but also their message. Jesus said, "You cannot serve two masters."[451] Bonhoeffer was determined to break the church out of its standard mode of compromise and accommodation to political power for the sake of their own survival.

Hitler took over the church and appointed Ludwig Muller its Bishop. He was installed as Bishop after much turmoil at the Cathedral in Wittenberg where Martin Luther attached his 95 theses on the church door in 1517. Such news would have put

---

[450] Eberhard Bethge, *Dietrich Bonhoeffer: A Biography*, (Minneapolis: Fortress Press, 2000), 54.
[451] Matt 6:24

Luther in a foul mood. Not that much was required to get Luther upset.

In *The Cost of Discipleship*, Bonhoeffer proclaimed that Luther's principle of "faith alone" needed to be restored because the German Lutheran Church had retooled it to justify inaction and indifference in its pietistic evasions to the very meaning of faith. Bonhoeffer did not like pietism, emotionalism, altar calls, or easy decisions for Christ. He wanted to unify justification and sanctification under the single rubric of discipleship. As Bonhoeffer so graphically stated, "We Lutherans have gathered like eagles round the carcass of cheap grace, and there we have drunk of the poison which has killed the life of following Jesus."[452]

We are not faced with as stark and immediate crisis as the German Church in the 1930s. Our government has not yet attempted to take over the church and ask for an oath of allegiance to our nation and our leader. Our president is not talking about a one-thousand-year reign for the Reich and trains loaded with undesirables. Troublesome dissidents, writers, artists, and clergy are not headed to reeducation or extermination camps.

However, what we face are the remnants of the Reformation that shifted salvation from a community or societal focus on the holiness of God to an individualistic focus on the transaction of "getting saved" and escaping hell. Our culture has worked to eat the heart out of the church. Every television show, talk show, late night show, and live event is permeated with a multicultural narrative that champions a permissive lifestyle, a "do whatever you want, follow your heart" sentimental nonsense that is

---

[452] Dietrich Bonhoeffer, *The Cost of Discipleship*, (New York: Macmillan, 1949), 57-58; Bill Hull, *Choose The Life*, (Grand Rapids: Baker Books, 2004), 10.

destroying the family, creating a culture of murder of the unborn, and confusing the troops. Across the board, this philosophy denies or rejects virtually every New Testament norm of human sexuality, treatment of other human beings, and the good life as defined by Jesus.[453] Indeed, it is a culture war.

---

[453] Jesus defines the good person living the good life in Matthew chapters 5-7. That person is one who lives a blessed life and whose righteousness or spirituality is better than the external performance of behavior modification modeled by the Pharisees. It is a person who builds their life on the rock that is Christ and who does what Jesus asks them to do.

Is Contemporary Discipleship a Myth or Can It Actually Take on Crisis and Suffering?

The Battle of Bull Run was at the start of the Civil War. The Union was expected to win and to win easily. Union sympathizers came out to the battlefield with blankets and picnic baskets. They found grassy hills to sit on to watch the proceedings while lounging in the shade, drinking tea as the battle raged in the distance. Soon, however, they were grabbing their blankets and baskets and running for their lives.

Christianity in American is much the same. We know there is a spiritual battle raging. We know we have an enemy, and we know that Christian persecution around the world has never been worse. Over one million Christians have been killed via persecution in the last ten years.[454] As Author Matthew Walsh states in his book *A Church of Cowards*, "We are like the apostles in Gethsemane, but that would be giving us too much credit. Their spirit was willing while their flesh was weak. Our spirit is weak and our flesh even weaker." [455] He goes on to say:

---

[454] "Nearly 1 Million Christians Reportedly Martyred for Their Faith in Last Decade." *Fox News¸* 6 July 2017. https://www.foxnews.com/world/nearly-1-million-christians-reportedly-martyred-for-their-faith-in-last-decade.
[455] Matthew Walsh, *A Church of Cowards*, (Washington D.C.: Regnery Gateway, 2020), 187.

I do not believe that I exaggerate when I say that the average American Christian has never given up one single thing for Christ. I survey my own life and I write these words and I see myself in a constant state of flight. Fleeing from sacrifice. Fleeing from suffering. Jesus says, give up everything, embrace your suffering, carry your cross, go hungry for me, bleed for me, die for me.[456]

Dietrich Bonhoeffer said, "Christianity without discipleship is always Christianity without Christ."[457] Bishop Bell quoted him in his introduction to *The Cost of Discipleship*: "When Christ calls a person, he calls them to come and die."[458] It is an idea, a myth.

How does crisis and suffering define discipleship? Bonhoeffer was German. You cannot discuss German spirituality without a nod to Martin Luther. The gold standard biography on Luther is *Here I Stand*, written in 1955 by Roland Bainton, history professor at Yale Divinity School. I have read it cover to cover and made plenty of notes. Luther defined Christianity for the German people.

Luther's sermons were read to congregations. His liturgy was sung; his catechism was rehearsed by the father of a household, and his Bible cheered the fainthearted and consoled the dying. No Englishman had anything like Luther's range. The Bible translation in England was the work of Tyndale, the prayer book of Cranmer, and the catechism of the Westminster divines. The sermon style stemmed from Latimer; the hymnbook came from Watts. [I might add, the dictionary by Samuel Johnson]. Not all of them lived in the same century. Luther did the work of

---

[456] Ibid.

[457] Dr. Roland Chia, "Bonhoeffer and Discipleship," *Ethos Institute*, 20 November 2017. https://ethosinstitute.sg/bonhoeffer/

[458] Bishop Bell, "Introduction," in *The Cost of Discipleship*, Dietrich Bonhoeffer, (Minneapolis: Fortress Press, 2000), 44.

more than five men. And for sheer richness and exuberance of vocabulary and mastery of style, he is to be compared only to Shakespeare."[459]

Luther was a towering figure in Bonhoeffer's life. He also had a naughty sense of humor and an explosive temper. He was a big man with many physical maladies. He suffered greatly. These sufferings contributed to his outbursts and sometimes offensive and combative statements. He was stubborn and, in some cases, unforgiving, especially against what he considered to be an ungrateful Jewish population. Luther was anti-Jewish for theological reasons, but in later years he slipped into anti-semetic statements.

Luther was looked to for his attitude concerning deadly plagues. I must be careful here, but plagues in the 1500s were deadly for up to half of the population—something more severe than we are facing right now in over 150 countries of the world with Covid 19. It is deadly for the 1% of the population who get the virus. We dare not discount the damage that will do. We must not underestimate the financial ruin that may visit the world or the long-term emotional trauma that may ensue. Globalization has changed the game. The anxiety level is a great threat because worldwide news can multiply the fear, panic, and difficulty. But what can we learn from Luther, Bonhoeffer and others? I have read and have sent out an article summarizing a letter Luther wrote on the subject, "Whether One May Flee From A Deadly Plague."[460]

---

[459] Roland H. Bainton, *Here I Stand: A Life of Martin Luther* (Meridian Books, 1955), 301.
[460] Martin Luther, *Luther's Works*, Vol. 43: Devotional Writings II, ed. Jaroslav Jan Pelikan, Hilton C. Oswald, and Helmut T. Lehmann, vol. 43 (Philadelphia: Fortress Press, 1999), 119–38.

This twelve-page letter blends together bedrock theological truth and practical advice. I would summarize it to read, "Local officials, including clergy, may not flee as long as there are people in need. Normal citizens can flee once they know their families and neighbors have what they need. One's confidence is to be found in the familiar refrain, "For me to live is Christ, but to die is gain" (Phil. 1:21). This of course is little comfort to those who don't believe it or who are so gripped by fear of death that they don't long for what lay beyond death, namely, eternal life with God. This is what I mean by crisis and suffering defining our discipleship for what it is. Luther and Bonhoeffer were together on Luther's justification by faith. Eberhard Bethge, Bonhoeffer's best friend put it this way.

> He then tried to grasp the Reformed articles of faith, justification, and sanctification with the single concept of discipleship. He did so with a key formula, "only the believer is obedient and only those who are obedient believe. He did not mean to question the complete validity of Luther's sola fide and sola gratia, but to reassert their validity by restoring to them their concreteness here on earth. He defended justification by faith; indeed he wanted to restore Luther's teaching to its full robust place. He spoke of how justification by faith had been corrupted. "Only a small, hardly noticeable distortion of the emphasis was needed, and that most dangerous and ruinous deed was done.

Bonhoeffer takes justification by faith and explains it. Faith only exists in obedience and is never without obedience. Faith's primary property is to act in obedience (James 2:14-20).

How does this apply now to the knot in your stomach, the two-year supply of toilet paper and six-month supply of paper towels in your garage? How about the eggs, and the water, the guns, the facemasks, the night vision goggles? What takes that knot out of your stomach? The realization that spiritual knowledge is as real as any other knowledge and that faith is applying it to one's thought life.

Bonhoeffer on Obedience

Rationalization is a convenient way to slip the tightening noose of obedience. It is human nature to present one's case for tithing three percent of your income. Who hasn't bargained with God about partial obedience or delayed obedience? This is why Bonhoeffer wrote, "Only the obedient believe and only those who believe are obedient."[461] In 1939, Bonhoeffer found himself once again on a ship to New York City. His first trip nine years earlier to Union Theological Seminary lasted nine months.

Since his return to Germany the situation had heated up. Bonhoeffer had pastored in London, become the leader of an illegal seminary, started as a lecturer at The University of Berlin, and participated in the creation of the Confessing Church. He had openly opposed the policies of Adolf Hitler and delivered a national radio broadcast that proclaimed Christ alone as his Fuhrer.

He had been banned from teaching, writing, preaching, publishing, and he refused to go into the Army if drafted. In other words, Bonhoeffer was persona non gratia. He was shut down and in danger. His closest friends counseled him to go to New York City and to stay there until things cooled down and then he could return to help rebuild what would be left of Germany. Best case scenario, Hitler would be overthrown, war avoided, and life would

---

[461] Bonhoeffer, *Discipleship*, 59.

return to normal. But both his brother Klaus and brother-in-law Hans told him that war was indeed imminent. None other than Reinhold Niebuhr arranged a speaking tour for Bonhoeffer plus other gainful work and employment. On a warm morning in June 1939, Bonhoeffer left Germany on his second trip to New York City.

He found the city greatly changed. The new Empire State Building had transformed the skyline. The World's Fair opened in Queens. Lou Gehrig was playing his last season of baseball for the New York Yankees. The movie *Wizard of Oz* premiered on August 17, and John Steinbeck's *The Grapes of Wrath* had won the Pulitzer Prize. Hitler's *Mein Kampf* ("My Struggle") appeared for the first time in English though it won no awards.

Bonhoeffer arrived at Union Theological Seminary during summer vacation and on the first day of a heat wave. He unpacked his bags in the "prophet's chamber," a room for visiting scholars. Because of the heat he could not close the windows. The temperatures were in the high nineties. On one side he had the inner courtyard and on the other, Broadway. The street noise persisted until late at night. For a German, this was pretty much intolerable.

No one was around. He passed the time by smoking cigarettes, reading, and taking walks. He visited the Metropolitan Museum. He read articles in *The Nation* and *Christian Century*. He bought and read Niebuhr's newest book, *Interpretation of Christian Ethics*, which he found filled with wrong and superficial statements. He did like H. Richard Niebuhr's, Reinhold's younger brother, summation of American Christianity.[462]

---

[462] Edwin H. Robertson, ed. "Protestantism without Reformation" in *No Rusty Swords: Letters, Lectures, and Notes, 1928-1936*, from the *Collected Works of Dietrich Bonhoeffer*, Vol. I (New York: Harper & Row, 1965), 117-18.

After socializing for a few days with the Manhattan elite, Bonhoeffer began to think that he made a mistake in coming to America. "All I need is Germany, the brethren," he lamented. "I do not understand why I am here."[463] Bonhoeffer had already reached the conclusion that a year in America would be far too long. He spent hours in the Scriptures, wrote thoughtful prayers, and took long walks. He kept asking the same question over and over, the only relevant question, "What is the will of God for me here and now?"

Part of Bonhoeffer's combination of homesickness and depression was his analysis of American Christianity, New York style. "The American churches had surely produced thrifty churchmen, earnest theologians, and revivalist preachers, but they had failed to reckon seriously with the 'scandal of the Cross.'"[464] He asserted that American Christians had not learned to trust God fully and did not know what it meant to stand under the judgment of the Word. American Christians, he believed, preferred to forgo suffering and "live out their faith in freedom without a struggle." Between fight and flight, flight has been the American experience, at least in matters spiritual. Of course, World War II proved otherwise.

Finally, Bonhoeffer wrote, "I no longer know where I am . . . I cannot make out why I am here. I cannot believe it is God's will that I should stay on here, in the event of war, without any particular assignment."[465] In the end he wrote to Reinhold Niebuhr that he would be leaving New York City for Germany. He had arrived in New York on June 12. He was to depart on July 27, 1939. After six weeks of feverish prayer and self-examination, he had come to know his own heart. He wrote, "Manhattan at night, the moon

---

[463] Marsh, *Strange Glory*.

[464] Ibid.

[465] Ibid.

stands above the skyscrapers. It is very hot. The journey is over. I am glad that I was there, and glad that I am on my way home again."

Bonhoeffer made the decision that would cost him his life. He would plot to overthrow his government. He would spy. He would pray. He would write. He would follow Jesus and take up his cross.[466] It all reminds me of these words by C.S. Lewis:

> I would rather say that every time you make a choice you are turning the central part of you, in the part of you that chooses, into something a little different from what it was before. And taking your life as a whole, with all your innumerable choices, all your life long you are slowly turning this central thing either into a heavenly creature or into a hellish creature.[467]

---

[466] Much of the information regarding Bonhoeffer's time in NYC was gleaned from a Marsh, *Strange Glory*, 275-86.
[467] Lewis, *Mere Christianity*, 92.

Bonhoeffer: Pastor? Spy? Traitor? Coward?

Back from New York and in Germany meant that Bonhoeffer and his colleague Eberhard Bethge were together again. On June 19, 1940, they were sitting in a café on the Baltic seaside when news arrived that France had surrendered. Everyone rose, hopped up on chairs, and gave the infamous Nazi salute. They began to sing "Die Fahne Hoch"—"The Flag Held High," also known as the "Horst Wessel Song."

Bonhoeffer joined in shouting a triumphant "Heil Hitler" Bethge objected. Dietrich said, "Are you crazy? Raise your arm!" Later he explained to Bethge, "We will suffer far greater things. Let's not get arrested over a song." Bonhoeffer was back walking the razor's edge.

He applied for a military chaplaincy—a good way to avoid being arrested, yet not having to kill for the Reich. His application was rejected, so he accepted a position in the Abwehr, the German equivalent of the FBI—a position arranged by his brother-in-law, Hans Von Dohnanyi. Because of his friendship with Hans Oster, a general and deputy chief of the Abwehr, Bonhoeffer would have a dual role as Abwehr officer and a spy for the resistance—a double agent. He also expressed an interest in a military coup, just for emphasis. At the same time, he was summoned for a medical examination and passed. It would now only be a matter of time until he would be drafted. He was fit for military service.

Dietrich was banned from public speaking and could not live in Berlin. Even a small gathering of students he led had been reported to the Gestapo. One person who was baffled by Bonhoeffer's clandestine life was Karl Barth. He could not figure what a pacifistic evangelical monk was up to. How was it that a professed anti-Nazi, beset with various bans and restrictions, and the most persistent voice of the Confessing Church would have been given a position in military intelligence?

The answer was very much Bonhoeffer. He had connections, and, because he was clergy, he could walk both sides of the street. His motives were to escape war but that would be impossible. He would get his hands dirty no matter what. The question he was really facing was, "Who do I kill? I must kill someone. Will it be Hitler, Himmler, and his henchmen, or will it be a Russian soldier?"

Bonhoeffer had come to believe something quite compromising to a pacifist, but so true, "It is better to do evil, than to be evil." Killing Hitler would be evil. This is pacifistic doctrine. But Hitler was evil, evil incarnate. Some, even Barth, saw the cowardly side of Bonhoeffer's position. It goes something like this. A pacifist will not act against evil in a violent way, but they will pray for everyone else to strike down evil and die to keep them free to be a pacifist. This, to some, is highly immoral and not at all what the Bible teaches. How God managed the Israeli Army in taking the Promised Land does present a major problem for the pacifistic position. At some point the question becomes, "Should we allow the strong evil leader with the best army to destroy other nations, take away their freedom, subject their people to tyranny of every kind that the twentieth century displayed?" Even the idealist Bonhoeffer saw a limit to this kind of thinking.

Suddenly, Bonhoeffer was thrown into a secular existence with a non-clergy role. He was no longer writing sermons, preparing lectures, coaching pastors. The desire to build a spiritual nobility, an elite class of theologians who could be retrofitted to any and every national emergency faded into the background. Ironically, Bonhoeffer had to establish his Aryan descent for final clearance with the Abwehr. His mother Paula did the paperwork, and periodically, Bonhoeffer would ship his laundry home to be cleaned. He was a pastor without a church, a professor without a class. He was a double agent without an assignment, a single man without a home. While he waited, he read, he prayed, and he worked on his magnum opus, *Ethics*.

He spent evenings at the opera and during down moments wrote about his life and even his body:

> Bodily life is meant for joy. Eating and drinking not only sustains bodily health, but also the natural joy of bodily life. Clothing is not only necessary covering for the body, but an adornment as well. Relaxation and leisure not only facilitate the capacity for work, but also grace the body with the measure of rest and joy that is its due. In its essential distance from all purposefulness, play is the clearest expression that bodily life is an end in itself."[468]

Bonhoeffer was concerned about the separateness of his body from his spirit. In October, the waiting was over. The Abwehr granted the so-called UK status "indispensable" to state security and, thereby, he was exempt from military service. His role would be as a courier, assigned to engage in covert talks with foreign church leaders who would communicate with Allied leaders. This was the work the resistance really wanted him to do. The

---

[468] Marsh, *Strange Glory*, 306.

official instructions were to represent the Third Reich to churches around Europe.

Bonhoeffer began to travel widely from late October 1940 until 1943. His mind now went to more secular issues. He thought and wrote about wide cultural issues in *Ethics*, and he realized his future was in the secular world. He spoke of a religionless spirituality, meaning a rebirth of spiritual health through a new monasticism, nothing like the church-based old.

> My recent activity, which has been predominately in the worldly sphere, it gives me plenty to think about. I am amazed that I live and can live for days without the Bible. I should feel it to be auto-suggestion, not obedience. If I were to force myself to read it. I understand that such auto-suggestion might be, and is, a great help, but I would be afraid in this way of falsifying a genuine experience and ultimately not getting genuine help. When I open the Bible again, it is new and wonderful as never before, and I should like just to preach. I know that I only need to open my books to hear what can be said against all this. I have had much richer times. But I feel how my resistance against everything religious grows. Often it amounts to an instinctive revulsion, which is certainly not good. I am not religious by nature. But I think continually about God and Christ, authenticity, life, freedom, and compassion.

I can identify with Bonhoeffer. I recall the late William F. Buckley confessing, "I am conservative in doctrine, but I am not of the breed."

A human cannot command emotion. One can only discipline them to a degree. Like preschoolers in church, if the meeting is too long, eventually they will start crawling beneath the pews.

Bonhoeffer's life was about to change and his faith tested like never before. What would erupt from him would be some of the greatest devotional literature ever written along with radical thinking that still shakes those who read it.

Bonhoeffer: Prison

By early April 1943, the Gestapo had gathered enough evidence to arrest Dietrich Bonhoeffer. On April 5th, Bonhoeffer was at home. Around noon, he called the home of his sister and brother-in-law, the Von Dohananyis. Their phone was answered by an unfamiliar man's voice. Bonhoeffer hung up. He knew that the Gestapo had made their move. He informed his sister Ursula and told her he would be next. He returned to his room, put his papers in order, and had a meal with his father. Around 4:00 p.m., his father came over and told him that there were two men upstairs and they wanted to talk to him. He went to see them. He took his Bible and a copy of Plutarch. He was escorted in handcuffs to their black Mercedes. He was thirty-seven years old. He would never return.

That night, April 5,1943, even though his uncle had been the Commandant of Berlin, Bonhoeffer shivered from the cold in his reception cell. The blankets were soiled and the wooden bed hard. He could not stand the stench. For a young man of privilege who had slept on the best linen and always was German clean, it was very unclean. Someone wept loudly in the next cell. The next morning dry bread was tossed through a crack in the door. The staff had been instructed not to speak to the new arrival. The warden called him a scoundrel. It would be four months before he was shown the warrant for his arrest.

He was in solitary confinement, shackled hand and foot, for his first twelve days. Nights carried the sobs of his fellow prisoners broken by confinement—his new congregation.

Once he was released from solitary, given pen and paper, he would write prayers and blessings for his fellow prisoners. He would mail them to his parents who in turn would mail them directly to prisoners. The prayers were not spontaneous. They were carefully composed after hours of prayer and meditation. Charles Marsh wrote these revealing words about Bonhoeffer:

> But God would not bring down the walls of the prison like those of Jericho. Nor would a violent earthquake shake the foundations, freeing him as Paul and Silas were freed in Acts. Bonhoeffer knew this. And so in the first weeks he fell into a deep despair. Over the years of the Kirchenkampf, he had observed holy silence and practiced the contemplative disciplines, but in solitary confinement, when silence was imposed, he did not feel the consoling presence of his beloved in Christ, only the cold surroundings of concrete and iron. It was overwhelming loss, to which no prayer or blessing seemed equal.[469]

In a letter written to his best friend, Eberhard Bethge, after he had settled in, he described his daily routine:

> I've again been doing a good deal of writing lately and for the work that I have set for myself, the day is often too short. Sometimes, comically enough, I feel that I have "no time" here for this or that. After breakfast I read some theology and then write until midday; in the afternoon I read, then comes a chapter in Delbruck's World History, some English grammar about which I can still learn all kinds of things and finally, as the mood take me, I write or read again. Then in the evening I am tired enough to be glad

---

[469] Marsh, *Strange Glory*, 349.

to lie down, though that does not mean going to sleep at once. Confinement produces opportunity.[470]

He told his parents that prison was not all that bad. It was a "steam bath" for the soul. This was only partly true. He was being interrogated. He fought serious bouts of depression. He missed his friends and family terribly and lived with a continued sense of dread. He finally made it to cell block 25 where he would spend the next eighteen months. After talking about the freedom of not smoking, he took it up again once permitted. He was allowed thirty minutes a day outside for exercise. He told his parents, "Here in the prison yard a song thrush sings most wonderfully in the morning and now also at nightfall."[471]

The simple pleasures took on a new power in his life. His family was suffering. His brother-in-law Hans von Dohnanyi and brother Klaus were also in prison along with his sister Christine. His parents were grief stricken, and his mother Paula was as distressed as when she lost her eldest son Walter in the Great War.

During the two years between his arrest and death, Bonhoeffer never stopped writing: letters; poems; prayers; drafts of novels, plays, stories; outlines of future books and essays; aphorisms and exegeses of Scripture; and sketches on various themes. Collectively, his letters and prison papers document a great unburdening of an active and varied mind who would have influenced the world in so many ways—but never as much as his ultimate death would.

Confinement and punishment squeeze the best and the worst from a person. This is the reason that we call our work The

---

[470] Ibid.
[471] Ibid.

Bonhoeffer Project, not only for his writing, but also for his living, and not only his living, but his dying. Circumstances do not create our spirit. They reveal it!

I must interject that once it became known who Bonhoeffer was, he was given special favors. At first it was not known that he was a Protestant theologian and pastor; nor did they recognize him as the son of the famous psychiatrist, Dr. Karl Bonhoeffer, who, as a state employee, had received a dispensation form the Nazi Party to continue his directorship of Berlin's Charity Hospital. Nor did they know that this Pastor Bonhoeffer was the nephew of General Paul von Hase, former city commandant of Berlin. Once this all came to light, the warden provided Bonhoeffer with more food, better food, hot coffee, and cigarettes. He was even served meals on the same China as the guards a few times a week. He was treated with exceptional kindness and some guards even came to apologize. Sometimes the commandant of Tegal would take walks with Bonhoeffer. His parents were given special visitation privileges. His uncle, a German general, visited once, and they sat and drank champagne for five hours.

For Bonhoeffer, the rickety scaffolding of Protestantism had tumbled finally to the ground in the wake of the German church's complicity with the Nazis. A reckoning had come for the church. "If religion is the only garb in which Christianity is clothed—and this garb has looked very different in different ages—what then is religionless Christianity?"[472] How could one be a disciple, clothed not in the garb of tradition, but having, as Paul tells the Galatians, "Put on Christ. Clothe yourselves with Christ?"[473]

---

[472] Ibid.

[473] Rom 13:14.

Bonhoeffer in Crisis

"I am still discovering, right up to this moment, that it is only by living completely in this world that one learns to have faith. I mean living unreservedly in life's duties, problems, successes and failures, experiences and perplexities. In so doing, we throw ourselves completely into the arms of God."[474]

On July 18, 1944, in a letter from prison to his best friend Eberhard Bethge, Bonhoeffer commented on his life and its purpose. He reflected on what it means to choose a life of discipleship to Christ. He believed a true disciple was never engaged in partial or "merely religious" acts. Faith is something whole, involving all of one's life.

He had already spent one year in prison. He had not lost all hope that he would be freed but had settled into a "this is what I have for now" kind of resignation. His life had been a series of crises, interrupted by periods of exciting travel, significant teaching and writing, attending operas, the theater, playing the piano, and defeating most of his opponents in tennis matches, and, of course, plotting the death of Adolf Hitler. But now he spent the last year in a small cell, furnished with a simple table, a bed, a bucket, a light with books, pencil and paper in order to write his friends and work on his planned magnum opus, *Ethics*. Many of his former students in Finkenwalde were now soldiers on the dreaded Eastern

---

[474] Dietrich Bonhoeffer, *The Cost of Discipleship: The Scholars Edition* (Minneapolis: Fortress Press, 2003), 307.

Front or in their grave. Around eighty former students from a total of 150 had been killed.

On July 20, 1944, an attempt on the life of Adolf Hitler had failed. Hitler survived an explosion and proclaimed his survival as the hand of God. This proved, said Hitler, that providence had anointed him. With the failed assassination, Bonhoeffer's story of innocence presented to his interrogators begin to unravel. In the letter to Bethge, he recalled a conversation he had in 1931 with his pacifist friend at Union Theological Seminary in New York:

> We were asking ourselves quite simply what we wanted to do with our lives. He said he would like to become a saint [and I think it's quite likely that he did become one]. But I disagreed with him and said I would like to learn to have faith. For a long time, I didn't realize the depth of the contrast. I thought I could acquire faith by trying to live a holy life, or something like that. I suppose I wrote *Discipleship* as the end of that path. I can see the dangers of that book, though I still stand by what I wrote.[475]

God does some of his best work in caves and prison cells. History is replete with powerful writing from men and women who have been held captive against their will. Usually, they are jailed or in hiding for something good. Not always, but often the best words have come from the best prisoners or fugitives. Now you have the context for Bonhoeffer's famous statement that stands at the head of this article. Let's look at it again.

> I am still discovering, right up to this moment, that it is only by living completely in this world that one learns

---

[475] "Bonhoeffer's Words of Praise - 1944," *Christian History Institute*, https://christianhistoryinstitute.org/dailyquote/7/21/.

to have faith. I mean living unreservedly in life's duties, problems, successes and failures, experiences and perplexities. In so doing, we throw ourselves completely into the arms of God, taking seriously, not our own sufferings, but those of God in the world-watching with Christ in Gethsemane. That I think, is faith; that is metanoia and that is how one becomes a human being, a Christian.[476]

Bonhoeffer is saying that only through tension, trouble, and challenge can a person actually learn to have faith. The means to get there is what he called the penultimate, but faith is the ultimate. Another way of saying it is the Great Commission is penultimate. It is a mission; it is a method. It is the way God has given us to experience the ultimate of faith in God and the abundant life he promised. The ultimate is being with God, and part of that is learning to obey him and to engage in the mission to help others find him. This is life with dirt on it, the grit and grime of trouble. It also means ascending to the heights of surrender to God and his agenda. This is why Bonhoeffer mentions Jesus in Gethsemane, God watching his Son suffer in the Garden and telling him, "No. I won't let you out of this."

Bonhoeffer prayed daily to get out, to escape. The answer was always no. An escape was even planned with his family and a friendly prison guard. An electrician's coveralls had been provided for Dietrich, smuggled into the prison by one of his sisters. It would have been easy to do, but again the answer was no. He couldn't go. His family would have been arrested, imprisoned, tortured and possibly executed. He could not allow that to happen to his elderly parents, two brothers, and four sisters.

---

[476] Ibid.

Why do we call what we do the Bonhoeffer Project? Not because he was a great scholar, a highly talented pianist, or swell tennis player with a Mercedes Convertible. It is because when it really counted, this child of privilege and member of the aristocracy displayed the ultimate faith in the living God.

The Last Days

And though this world with devils filled,
Should threaten to undo us;
We will not fear, for God hath willed
His truth to triumph through us.

"A Mighty Fortress Is Our God"

Martin Luther

Berlin now lay in ruins. Whole streets disappeared under piles of cascading rubble. Smoke filled the air, and broken water lines created vast sheets of black ice. In his prison cell at night, as he lay in the dark, Bonhoeffer would sing quietly to himself "St. Matthew's Passion," which he thought was Johnann Sebastian Bach's most beautiful work. He would inscribe from memory the musical notations of sacred songs. He prayed, wrote poetry, and spoke about an array of emotions. He lamented that he would die a celibate. The fears of oblivion weighed heavily on him. The worst times were those when the past felt lost forever. "I wanted my life" he had whispered in the dark in the summer of 1944. "I demand my own life back." In his last letter to Marie Wedemeyer he wrote, "My past life is brim-full of God's goodness, and my sins are covered by the forgiving love of Christ crucified. I'm most thankful for the people I have met, and I only hope they will never have to grieve for me, but that they too, will always be certain of, and thankful for, God's mercy and forgiveness."

The war was almost over, defeat was imminent, But the Gestapo's work continued. On the afternoon of February 7, 1945, Bonhoeffer was taken from Berlin and transported to an unknown location. On April 4, 1945, the diaries of Admiral Wilhelm Canaris, head of the Abwehr were discovered in a deserted safe at the Supreme Command headquarters. Furious at what he read in them, the next day Hitler ordered the execution of all the imprisoned Abwehr conspirators.

Himmler relayed the order directly to the Gestapo. By this time Bonhoeffer had been at Buchenwald concentration camp for a few weeks. He had recently celebrated his thiry-ninth birthday. He had stopped denying any involvement in the conspiracy but was also hopeful that soon the German soldiers would run for their lives, and they would be released. Buchenwald was one of the extermination camps where death was celebrated and worshipped. It was the embodiment of the satantic worldview of the SS where weakness was preyed upon and crushed.

The prisoners were to be kept well enough to be interrogated: soup and bread for lunch; bread, fat and marmalade for dinner. On Easter Sunday, the thunder of Allied guns could be heard in the distance. Soon it would all be over. Just hang in there. That was the hope of each inmate. But that same day they were told, "Get ready. We are leaving." Sixteen prisoners were crammed into a van along with their luggage. It was one of those airport vans that hotels send to pick up customers, except this bus was designed for gassing prisoners. The exhaust would be piped back into the van in order to kill all passengers. This made it easy for unloading when it backed up to the crematorium ovens.

Bonhoeffer's Last Day

On April 8, the first Sunday after Easter, Bonhoeffer was asked to lead a service. It was held in a bright school room which served as their cell. He prayed and read the verses from the prayer book and expounded on Isaiah 53:5, "With his stripes we are healed." When he finished, two men came for him, and he went with them. They all knew what it meant. He was to be executed. A Mr. Best wrote, "He was, without exception, the finest and most loveable man I have ever met."

Bonhoeffer took a blunt pencil and wrote his name and address in the front, middle, and back of the volume of Plutarch—the one the family had given him. He left it behind. It was given to his family years later. As he jumped into the van to go to Flossenburg, he had his volume of Goethe with him.[477] Later that day, all five conspirators were tried and convicted of the crime of treason.

Early on April 9,1945, camp doctor H. Fischer-Hullstrung recorded his impression.

> On the morning of that day between five and six o'clock the prisoners, among them Admiral Canaris, General Oster, General Thomas and Drs. Sack were taken from their cells, and the verdicts of the court martial read out to them. Through the half-open door in one room of the huts, I saw Pastor Bonhoeffer before taking off his prison garb, kneeling on the floor praying fervently to his God. I was most deeply moved by the way this loveable man prayed,

[477] Johann Wolfgang von Goethe (1742-1832) was a German poet whose works included plays, novels, general literature, and treatises. He is considered Germany's greatest literary figure and is best known for *Faust*, published in 1790.

so devout and so certain that God hear his prayer. At the place of execution, he again said a short prayer and then climbed the steps to the gallows, brave and composed. His death ensured after a few seconds. In the almost fifty years that I worked as a doctor, I have hardly ever seen a man die so entirely submissive to the will of God.[478]

The men's bodies were burned in a pile and thus they joined the millions of other victims of the Third Reich. There may not be any better way to explain the man, the martyr, the pastor, the scholar, and human being than the words he spoke at just before his death. He had hardly finished his last prayer when the door opened and two evil-looking men in civilian clothes came in and said, "Prisoner Bonhoeffer, Get ready. Come with us." These words "Come with us" for all prisoners had come to mean only one thing—the scaffold. Bonhoeffer at this point was reported to say, "This is the end. For me the beginning of life." [479]

---

[478] Eric Metaxas, *Bonhoeffer, Pastor, Martyr, Prophet, Spy* (Nashville: Thomas Nelson, 2010), 532.
[479] Ibid, 528.

Bonhoeffer Wanted More and So Do We

Devotional guides are plentiful. I expect that with the present coronavirus crisis, Christians will produce many more. I see them as nice but not necessary. Actually, they indicate that somewhere below the surface of devotional Christianity is a hallowed out spirituality.

This was generally true of Bonhoeffer who disliked emotionalism, Pietism, altar calls, and sentimentalism. Feeling good, while quite popular in the human race, has a poor record in actually changing people. This is not easy to say when people in general are acting so Christian. Even those who are clearly not Christians know how to act Christian in a pinch. I recently told a neighbor who went to the store for us that he might as well become a Christian because he was acting like one reaching out with love to his neighbors.

While I hope and pray that things will not get worse, if they do, we will go to the next level. Each new level into inconvenience and lack of resources will produce more pressure on the system and our personal systems. Pressure produces. Pressure on coal produces diamonds. Too much pressure on systems breaks them. Pressure on people pushes them into fear, panic, anger, and survival of the fittest. Gun sales are on the rise because someone may come for your food, your money, or even for your toilet paper.

I hope and pray that I am surprised and that we all hold up better than expected and will rue the day that we thought less of who we are than should have been thought. But I cannot get out of my mind that Dietrich Bonhoeffer linked the failure of his own German Lutheran Church to the rise of Adolf Hitler. I do not believe he drew a straight line. It was more about how liberal theology had hallowed out the heart of the German State Church. They then failed to stand up to Hitler when he began to oppress the Jews. Our particular crisis is nothing like the rise of National Socialism in post-World War I Germany. But our nation is under siege. The future is uncertain. The great security we once felt in a strong economy is threatened by governmental overspending which leads to inflation which reduces buying power. The savings and investments of millions are at risk. What can we do?

We can hold on tight and get through this pandemic. That is certainly part of it. I expect that Americans, in fact much of the world will do that. Survival is a very high human value. Bonhoeffer wanted more for his country, and, long-term, we want more for ours. Possibly the best-known passage from Bonhoeffer's *The Cost of Discipleship* says it well: "Cheap grace is the mortal enemy of the church"[480]

Bonhoeffer believed cheap grace is what caused the German Church to fail. Their hallowed-out heart had nothing to give when it was required. They did not have what it would take to stand up rather than shut up. I think the American church is stronger than that, much stronger. We are especially great when we face something we can see and feel, like a virus, a hurricane, or some natural disaster. However, we are pretty clueless when it comes to the hidden world. Paul says we wrestle not against flesh and blood, but against the principalities and powers in the

---

[480] Bonhoeffer, *The Cost of Discipleship*, 46.

unseen world.[481] Even at that, when confronted with demonic manifestation, more Christians than we think know what to do. I learned this as a pastor. Many brave and strong believers took on the dark forces of evil as manifested in their fellow human beings. Here, however, is what is at work that is unseen and hidden: a gospel that saves but does not call; a gospel that forgives but does not catapult a person forward; a gospel that only deals with forgiveness of sin without expecting, even requiring a life of discipleship.

What harm can an easy gospel create? It warms our hearts to see hundreds or even thousands streaming forward at large meetings around the world. The problem is that we are consigning them to a cheap imitation gospel that is a vaccine against the real thing. This cheap gospel dominates the church around the world, and it is reaping a bitter harvest of new disciples who do not believe in discipleship. Discipleship to Christ, engagement in his mission, and replication of themselves in others is considered optional.

The United States is not only one of the most difficult mission fields; it is large and resistant. The major urban centers of the United States from Washington D.C. to New York City, from Seattle, Washington to San Diego, California basically ignore the cheap gospel. They rightly refuse to believe it. They do not chew it up and spit it out. They lean back and laugh you out of town. Even these undiscerning souls recognize a stupid idea when they hear it—namely, pray this prayer and you get to go to heaven no matter what you do, and anyone who does not do this will spend eternity in hell. I must stop for now, but I leave you with a suggested antidote from the great writer of the nineteenth century, George MacDonald.

---

[481] Eph 6:12-13.

Instead of asking yourself whether you believe or not, ask yourself whether you have this day done one thing because he said, 'Do it' or once abstained because he said, 'Do not do it.' It is simply absurd to say you believe or even want to believe in him if you do not do anything he tells you.[482]

---

[482] George MacDonald, "The Truth In Jesus," www.online-literature. com/george-macdonald/3672/; georgemacdonald.info/the_truth_in_ jesus.pdf.

Other Books by Bill Hull

Conversion & Discipleship
You Can't Have One Without The Other

The Cost of Cheap Grace
Reclaiming the Value of Discipleship

The Discipleship Gospel
What Jesus Preacher - We Must Follow

The Disciple-Making Pastor
Leading Others on the Journey of Faith

The Disciple-Making Church
Leading a Body of Believers on the Journey of Faith

Choose the Life
Exploring a Faith that Embraces Discipleship

A Disciples Guide to Choose the Life
Exploring a Faith that Embraces Discipleship

Revival That Reforms
Making It Last

the BONHOEFFER project

[GOSPEL]

change your mind

[MAKE DISCIPLES]

change your heart

[THE PLAN]

change your behavior

You can't make a Christ-like disciple from a non-discipleship gospel because **the gospel you believe in determines the disciple you make.**

thebonhoefferproject.com

About The Author

Bill Hull is an author who has written several classic books on disciple making, Jesus Christ Disciple Maker, The Disciple Making Pastor, and more recently, Conversion & Discipleship. Bill has devoted his adult life to pastoring, teaching, and writing about Christ's command to make disciples. Bill's primary means for pursuing his mission as a discipleship evangelist has been pastoring for twenty years, teaching in more than fifty countries of the world, and authoring more than thirty books. Bill is co-founder of The Bonhoeffer Project, which is devoted to the creation of disciple-making leaders. He and his wife, Jane, continue to serve as teachers, writers, and learning guides to those who seek their counsel. You can learn more about Bill's work at *TheBonhoefferProject.com* and *BillHull.com*.

You can reach Bill at bill@billhull.com

the BONHOEFFER project

BECOME A DISCIPLE-MAKING LEADER

Our cohort model is a year-long leadership development community

RECLAIM THE DISCIPLESHIP-FIRST GOSPEL • CRAFT YOUR DISCIPLE-MAKING PLAN • CHANGE THE WORLD

TRADITIONAL

The original cohort model where participants gather in person on a monthly basis. This experience allows you to learn from each other in real time and make lasting connections.

HYBRID

Having participants around the world we needed to adapt - enter our hybrid cohort model. Some participants will meet in person and some will join online via Zoom technology for monthly gatherings.

VIRTUAL

Get the full Bonhoeffer Project experience in a virtual cohort setting. You can learn at your own pace & connect with participants from all over the globe.

SEE OUR UPCOMING COHORTS
& REGISTER ONLINE

thebonhoefferproject.com/upcomingcohorts